THE VOICES OF FRANCE

A Survey of Contemporary Theology in France

A Survey of
Contemporary Theology
in France

THE
VOICES OF
FRANCE

❁

James M. Connolly

New York
The Macmillan Company
1961

nihil obstat:	James F. Rigney, S.T.D.
	Censor Librorum
imprimatur:	✠ Francis Cardinal Spellman
	Archbishop of New York

December 20, 1960

First Printing

The Macmillan Company, New York
Brett-Macmillan Ltd., Galt, Ontario

Printed in the United States of America

Library of Congress catalog card number: 61–6686

The author wishes to thank the following for permission to reproduce copyrighted material: Bruce Publishing Co., for *Père Lagrange and the Scriptures*, ed. Richard T. Murphy, copyright, 1946, by Richard T. Murphy; Doubleday and Co., for *The Catholic Church in the Modern World*, by E. E. Hales, copyright © 1958, by Doubleday and Company, Inc.; Duquesne University Press, for *Contemporary European Thought and Christian Faith*, by Albert Dondeyne, copyright, 1958, by Duquesne University Press; Editions du Cerf, Paris, for *Chrétiens désunis*, by Yves Congar, copyright, 1939, Editions du Cerf; Farrar, Straus and Cudahy, Inc., for *The Meaning and Matter of History*, by M. C. D'Arcy, S.J., copyright, 1959, by Martin Cyril D'Arcy; Grail Publications, for permission to use translations of Papal Documents in *Rome and the Study of Scripture*, copyright, 1946, by Grail Publications; Harper & Brothers, for *The Phenomenon of Man*, by Teilhard de Chardin, copyright © 1959, by Wm. Collins & Co. Ltd., London, and Harper & Brothers, New York (Originally published in French as *Le Phénomène Humain*, copyright, 1955, by Editions du Seuil, Paris); Hawthorn Books, for *Why We Believe*, by Leon Cristiani, copyright, 1959, by Hawthorn Books; Helicon Press, for *The Mystery of the Church*, by Yves Congar, copyright, 1960, by Chapman and Helicon Press; *The Dead Sea Scrolls*, by Jean Danielou, copyright, 1958, by Helicon Press; *Holy Pagans of the Old Testament*, by Jean Danielou, copyright, 1957, by Editions de Seuil; B. Herder Book Co., for *The Theology of the Mystical Body*, by Emile Mersch, copyright, 1946, by B. Herder Book Company; P. J. Kenedy & Sons, for *God, Man and the Universe*, ed. Jacques Bivoort de Saudée, copyright, 1954, by P. J. Kenedy & Sons; Longmans, Green & Co. Ltd, London, for *Catholicism and the Ecumenical Movement*, by John M. Todd, copyright, 1956, by Longmans, Green & Co., Ltd; National Catholic Welfare Conference, for translations of Papal Encyclicals; Thomas Nelson & Sons, for *A Catholic Commentary on Holy Scripture*, copyright, 1953, by Thomas Nelson & Sons, New York; The Newman Press, for *Christ, Our Lady and the Church*, by Yves Congar, copyright, 1957, by The Newman Press; *The Angels and Their Mission*, by Jean Danielou, copyright, 1957, by The Newman Press; *Contemporary Moral Theology*, by John Ford and Gerald Kelly, copyright, 1958, by The Newman Press; Henry Regnery Company, for *Lord of History*, by Jean Danielou, © Longmans, Green & Co. Ltd, 1958; Saint Anthony's Guild Press, for *The Old Testament and the Critics*, by Joseph Coppens, copyright, 1942, by E. A. Ryan; Sheed & Ward, for *Origen*, by Jean Danielou, copyright, 1955, by Sheed & Ward, Inc., New York; *Advent*, by Jean Danielou, copyright, 1950, by Sheed & Ward, Inc., New York; *The Salvation of the Nations*, by Jean Danielou, copyright, 1949, by Sheed & Ward, Inc., New York; *Catholicism*, by Henri de Lubac, S.J., copyright, 1958, by Sheed & Ward, Inc., New York; *Splendour of the Church*, by Henri de Lubac, S.J., copyright, 1956, by Sheed & Ward, Inc., New York; *The UnMarxian Socialist*, by Henri de Lubac, S.J., copyright, 1948, by Sheed & Ward, Inc., New York; University of Notre Dame Press, for *The Bible and the Liturgy*, by Jean Danielou, copyright, 1956, by the University of Notre Dame Press; *Liturgical Piety*, by Louis Bouyer, copyright, 1955, by the University of Notre Dame Press.

The author also wishes to thank the following periodicals for permission to quote copyrighted material: *The Catholic Biblical Quarterly*, for "Anointings in Galilee and Bethany," by André Legault, Vol. XVI; *Catholic World* for "France Catholic" by D. P. O'Connell, October 1958; "The Marxist Influence in Catholic France" by Borisz de Balla, March 1953; *Commonweal* for "The Worker Priests" by H. A. Reinhold, March 1, 1956; "Contrasts in Catholicism" by Walter Ong, December 2, 1955; *Crosscurrents* for "Attitudes Toward Reform in the Church" by Yves Congar, Summer 1951; "Christianity and Evolution" by Bruno de Solages, Summer 1951; *Lumen Vitae* for "The Bible and Modern Man" by Charles Moeller, January 1950; "Religious Education in the Modern World," by Albert Dondeyne, January 1952; *The Tablet*, London, for translations of letters and statements appearing in the issue of September 26, October 3, and October 10, 1959; *Theological Studies* for "Introduction à la Bible—A Review" by John MacKenzie, March 1959; "A Christian Philosophy of History" by Paul Henry, September 1952; *Thought* for "The Evolution of the French Church" by Robert Rouquette, Spring 1953; "French Catholicism Confronts Communism" by Robert Rouquette, Autumn 1953.

And Saint Joseph College, West Hartford, Connecticut, for "Towards a Biblical Theology of the New Testament" by David Stanley, in The McCauley Lectures of 1958.

FOR MY MOTHER

ACKNOWLEDGMENTS

The author wishes to acknowledge his appreciation to the many people who rendered valuable help in the preparation of this manuscript, especially the Reverend Maurice Carroll, Reverend Donald Hendricks, and Reverend William Murnion; and also to the Reverend Francis Boyle and Miss Margaret Connolly for their long hours of typing. Most especially is the author grateful for the patience, assistance and continual encouragement of the Reverend Myles Bourke, Professor of Sacred Scripture at St. Joseph's Seminary, Yonkers, New York.

INTRODUCTION

When the history of the twentieth century is written and the place of the Church in the modern world is evaluated, then as now the French will exercise a fascination for the historian as well as the theologian. This fascination is rooted in that singular intellectual quality of the French which characterizes their scrutiny, investigation and careful exploration of reality, and which reaches out to scrutinize even the Revelation of God Himself.

The Church today is witnessing an enormous intellectual revival. Throughout the world there is an upsurge of writing, research and contemplation of her theological truth overwhelming the observer with a swelling tide of books, pamphlets and periodicals. The growth of the sciences of language, history and archeology have turned the theologian back to the sources of Christian Revelation—the Bible, the Word of God entrusted to His Church. Philosophy and the physical sciences, psychology and sociology, every facet of man's intellectual horizon has widened, and in turn brought to the theologian not only new problems but also new possibilities for the settlement of old ones. No small part of this world-wide revival and upheaval in theology has been centered in France; in fact, since the turn of the century the French have spearheaded this theological movement.

The path trod by the French to this preeminence in the theological sciences has not, however, been an easy one. The names of theologians, such as de Lubac, Danielou and Congar, have become for the modern man the symbols of controversy as well as of leadership. The application in the practical order of the implications of Christian theology have led to numerous "apostolic experiments" in France itself. Not a few of these have become internationally famous because of melodramatic circumstances rather than for the theology-in-practice which they represented.

The worker-priest experiment, conclusively terminated in 1959, the catechism affair, in which modern French catechetical approaches were criticized by some Church authorities, and other projects of the French Church are chiefly known to Americans through newspaper and magazine accounts of their demise at the hands of Church officials. These accounts have frequently been surrounded by an air of sensationalism, so that the picture many Americans have formed of theological and apostolic activity in the Church in France may be epitomized by a news magazine headline of one such affair: "France—Rebellious Eldest Daughter."

Misconceptions of the depth and content of the theological revival in France are prevalent not only in the American journals of current affairs, but unfortunately exist as well in many clerical circles. Her theologians are represented as "radical," "modernists," and their work dismissed as unworthy of study, or even perusal, because of their alleged heretical content.

Is this an inaccurate and erroneous picture, perhaps founded upon the unsympathetic treatment that the French have received in some clerical journals? Is it possible that their work has been presented in a rather jaundiced way by conservative theologians, whose moderate and cautious approach to theology has been dictated by their training and by their memories of the modernist period?

The principal aim of this book is not strictly theological, nor is it controversial. It is not my intention to enter into theological debates better left to more skilled and competent experts. My point of view is primarily historical: to survey rapidly the growth of the theological movement that has produced the contemporary work in French theological circles, and to examine the work being done today by French theologians. It is also my intention to survey the historical causes and forces that have determined the French ecclesiastical tradition, that have evoked from the theologians certain themes for treatment, and also to survey the relationships of these men with the Teaching Authority of the Church.

It is upon this latter point, their relationships with the Church, that the French have suffered most in distortion, erroneous reporting and unfair critical judgments. It is my contention that in the cold light of contemporary history, the Church—absolute authority for every Catholic—is not, as many suppose, the antagonist in the story of the French Church, but rather the focal point of its thought and activity; that the theological revival and its apostolic implications in modern France are unfathomable without grasping the fact that it is the Church that makes the entire scene of the French revival intelligible. To take the Church from the picture of French theology, or worse still to make it the nemesis of France's contemporary theologians, is to warp and even destroy historical fact.

A few more words of introduction remain. First, in this study of the theological revival in France today this nomenclature "French" will apply in a broad sense to the Franco-Belgian complex, and to certain other theologians such as those who write in French at the University of Fribourg in Switzerland, and those French theologians now in residence outside her borders in Jerusalem and Rome. Although historical traditions differ in Belgium and France, there is the common use of French language, geographical proximity, similar intellectual traditions, and a likeness in spirit, temper and approach to theology.

Finally, of necessity, many works referred to and cited in the text will be French; however, because this book is intended as an introduction and historical survey for the English-speaking reader, works in translation will be cited where possible with necessary bibliographical details. A word of apology is directed to the professional theologian for what may seem to be an arbitrary designation of works. Of necessity, such a survey as this cannot cite every work in the field of theology, but, where possible, those representative of the work of certain theologians or important as indicative of a trend will be cited. In a short work such as this, the treatment of the forces that shape contemporary theology must perforce be shortened as well. Many volumes could be written upon the singular influences of Existentialism, science and Marxism upon contemporary theology. We have tried only to highlight and sketch the difficulties these influences create for theologians, and the response of the French to them.

It is my hope that this little work will prompt many not only to respect the work of theologians in France and Belgium, but also to read their works, at least in translation.

CONTENTS

THE VOICES OF FRANCE

A Survey of Contemporary Theology in France

I

✿

THE HISTORICAL TRADITIONS OF
FRENCH THEOLOGY

It would be misleading in any study of the present state of theology in France to forget the past, for the intellectual contributions of the French are not limited to our century. Nor may we say that the contributions of this century are entirely unrelated to the past. To state that one intends to survey the state of theology today among the French does not justify isolating this phenomenon, emptying it of meaning and ignoring its causes. To isolate the theological phenomenon of modern France, to cut it off from the historical forces and causes that give it meaning and location in the flow of human events, to pursue any such policy of deliberate or affected historical ignorance is to make such a survey historically meaningless, theologically insignificant and to strip it of all value.

The appreciation of contemporary theological development among the French demands not only the knowledge of the singular contributions of capable individuals, but also the understanding of those historical lines that have converged in the present situation in which the French Church finds itself. Those movements in intellectual history that weigh heavily upon the theologian and his contribution serve to place in perspective what is being done today.

In short, the historian cannot approach his subject with the purposes or methods of the surgeon, skillfully extracting the object of study from its surroundings, for this would be to change, to tamper with, to alter appreciably the event as it is found in history.

The French theologian today inherits a tradition of writing, scholarship and controversy extending back to the age of the Fathers. He inherits an intellectual tradition to which Gallicanism and Cartesianism are intimately linked; a tradition which looks to Pascal and Newman for its spirit; a tradition influenced in modern times by the figures of Lamennais and Lacordaire, Loisy and Lagrange.

Through the first Bishop of Lyon, St. Irenaeus, disciple of St. Polycarp, the French can trace at least a contact with the Apostolic age. During the age of the Fathers, the first of her native theologians emerged in the person of St. Hilary of Poitiers and his substantial theological treatise against the Semi-Pelagians. In this he was joined a century later by St. Prosper of Aquitaine. During the transitional period of the fourth and fifth centuries, we have the first rumblings of controversy and theological debate, for if St. Hilary championed the faith against the Semi-Pelagians, St. Vincent of Lerins and the school of John Cassian at Marseilles were—in good faith be it noted —most firmly in the school of Semi-Pelagianism in their opposition to the teachings of St. Augustine.

The sixth century continued the traditions of monasticism under St. Caesarius of Arles, himself no mean theologian. In scholarship he was joined by St. Gregory, the Bishop of Tours. The French Church, from the tenth to the twelfth centuries, was dominated by the growth of monasticism. Cluny was founded in 910, Citeaux in 1098 and Clairvaux in 1115. Still other monastic orders were founded in France: The Carthusians in 1084 and the Premonstratensians in 1120.

The Scholastics and the Gallican Tradition

The twelfth and thirteenth centuries marked the great period of intellectual renewal in the Church—a period dominated by the French. Scholasticism was making the enormous contribution of systematizing philosophy and theology. Toward the end of the twelfth century the school connected to the Cathedral of Notre-Dame became the University of Paris. Throughout the intellectual tumult of the thirteenth century this school set the pace for all of

Europe. The list of those who taught here throughout the thirteenth century included every major theologian of the period: St. Thomas Aquinas, St. Albert, St. Bonaventure, Alexander of Hales, Henry of Ghent, William of St. Amour, Duns Scotus and Raymond Lull. In 1277, three years after the death of Aquinas, the Bishop of Paris, Stephen Tempier, published a list of "errors" including not only those patently Averroistic but also propositions drawn from Aquinas. St. Albert made an arduous trip to Paris to defend the works of Aquinas at the university. Thomism's early struggle for intellectual vindication was fought in the halls of the University of Paris. It is an amusing sidelight, in the light of historical development, to recall that in its infancy Thomism was looked upon in Paris as "suspect," radical, too modern and completely unpalatable to conventional thought patterns.

Through the fourteenth century the University of Paris continued to dominate the intellectual life of Europe and became the center of an antipapal intellectualism. We find the teachers, John of Paris, Marsilius of Padua, and William of Occam, and later, Peter d'Ailly, teaching there. With them came the corruption of scholasticism in the philosophy of nominalism. Upon the broad philosophical base of nominalism they constructed conciliarism—a theology of the Church investing General Councils with the authority they felt was being encroached upon by the papacy. Upon these men and their theories of nominalism and conciliarism was founded the tradition of Gallicanism that plagued the Church for centuries. Their Gallicanism, however, was more antipapal than pro-French. John Gerson, Chancellor of the University, completed their work and Gallicanism became the dominant force in the French Church until the nineteenth century.

The Gallicanism that had hardened by the fourteenth century is so extremely important that the observer of the contemporary scene cannot truly understand the French phenomenon without appreciating the Gallican spirit, its tradition and heritage in French history. The contemporary American is the product of a radically different tradition, molded by a different series of events. If he is to understand the many facets of that Church today, it is imperative to grasp these Gallican traditions of the French.

France was a country, a nation, long before many of the nations of Europe. There was a national tradition and consciousness predating the Middle Ages. In addition, the Church herself in France developed singular traditions, symbolized by the Gallican liturgy, a liturgy that in the eighth century was suppressed by men who looked back to the time of the Fathers for more ancient traditions. This "nationalism" of the French Church was accentuated in the Middle Ages under the Crown. In fact, the University of Paris was established within the shadow of the castle, and the theologians gathered there never dared display a "Romanism" that would displease the king. By the fifteenth century the liturgy in France had adopted many singular elements, its theology was centered in the University of Paris, and the Church in France was, simply speaking, the Gallican Church.

A major contribution to the intellectual development of the French-speaking peoples was made during the fifteenth century when a university was established at Louvain, one that would in time rival and eventually surpass that of Paris in its influence.

Dominated by the Gallican spirit, the Church in France came through the Reformation with substantially few inroads, while Spaniards and Italians rose to the fore in the intellectual life of the Church during this period of upheaval. During the Reformation the Gallican Church steered a middle course. The king was the dominating power in the Church, not the Pope. Faced with the widespread threat of the Protestant revolt, the Pope was unwilling to challenge the French king and assert Roman dominance. The king in turn had no desire to follow the example of Henry VIII in England, for the French king had acquired what Henry wanted: control over the Church. He had no need to leave the Catholic community.

This separation from Roman traditions created among French theologians an abiding interest in patristics. Because of the Gallican tradition the theologians felt the need for a theological continuum, which they found in the Fathers of the Church. It is interesting to note that during the years that followed the Anglican break in England there was a revival in patristic studies by the English, expressing the same desire for ecclesiastical continuum.

So strong was the Gallicanism of the French Church during the era of the Reformation that many of the reforms of the Council of

Trent did not go into effect in France. The seminary system of clerical education, among the most important of these reforms, never really became a significant influence until the seventeenth and eighteenth centuries under St. Vincent de Paul and the Sulpicians. Even then, this seminary system was founded by Frenchmen and became an entirely French institution.

A further effect of the Gallican spirit was that upon the religious orders. These, despite their international flavor, were so dominated that they were never really able to expound a Roman influence, and any influence they did exercise was orientated by the nationalism of the Church.

However, in consideration of all these influences of the Gallican spirit, one effect that has outlived them all is the establishment of a strong patristic tendency among the French. Patristic studies have become for the French theologian the abiding heritage of the Gallican tradition.

The Seventeenth Century and the Cartesian Tradition

With the dawn of the seventeenth century we have once again the upsurge of French intellectual activity. If France had displayed a lackluster intellectual mediocrity during the Reformation, the seventeenth century was most certainly hers. In almost every field of ecclesiastical activity the French dominated the times. For good or for ill it was the century of d'Achery, Mabillon, Ruinart, de Montfaucon, Fleury, Bossuet, Descartes, Petavius, Simon, Arnauld, Jansénius and Blaise Pascal.

The philosophical revolution initiated by Descartes now gave the French a national philosophy, a philosophical approach and system which they have never completely lost. Cartesianism is best characterized by its dualistic nature, its insistence upon dichotomy, and this has left its scar upon every feature of French life. It would, of course, be ill considered to attempt to reduce the history of France to a simple root principle, such as the Cartesian dichotomy, but it can be stated that the insistent divisiveness of Descartes and the constant dualism of his philosophy have become a psychological mark of the French temperament. Never again would French thinkers, philosophers and theologians shake off the necessary dualism of Descartes and it is this inclination toward dualism that has characterized French intellectual tradition. For example, in the years that followed the Revolution, churchmen would say that one could be only for the Revolution or against it; there was no middle ground. And in the years that followed Descartes, two theological traditions grew up among the French, and always, as we shall see, with the same demand: one or the other—you cannot have the best of both.

The seventeenth and eighteenth centuries bore witness to the patristic tradition of Gallicanism. The insistent demands for reform in the Gallican liturgy were based upon a return to the more ancient traditions of the Church in the age of the Fathers. Quesnel, the Maurists and even the Jansenists were marked by a tone and appeal that was basically patristic. In addition, as the French carried into the modern world the Gallican, Cartesian and patristic traditions, they also bore to it the enduring influence of Blaise Pascal.

Pascal

Born in 1623, Pascal lived his life in the midst of controversy. He was sympathetic to the Jansenist cause and left in his *Provincial Letters* a literary masterpiece recording his determined opposition to the Jesuits of his time. In many ways Pascal, the mathematician and philosopher, surpassed himself in his religious genius. A convinced Augustinian, preoccupied with the real condition of man as a finite creature and a sinner, Pascal in unrivaled literary style and with rare psychological perceptiveness displayed in the *Pensées* the limits of man, and yet the power, the force and the meaningful strength of human thought. For Pascal, each man, each individual, possessed an incalculable dignity arising as much from his status as God's creature as from the possession of reason.

The towering stature of Pascal continues even until today to overshadow French thought. For many scholars and theologians in present-day France, Pascal has assumed the eminence of a patron saint because of his approach to the mind of his age. Today he is admired for his attempts to win over to the Gospel of Christ those of his contemporaries for whom that Gospel had become lost in what they considered an outmoded philosophical system. In a discussion of the relationship of faith and knowledge, Professor Dondeyne of Louvain gives us a glimpse of this "approach" of Pascal:

. . . Have we not all met sincere and intelligent unbelievers who, in spite of their honesty and their hunger for the truth, remain unconvinced by even the best proofs for the existence of God? The latest studies on the psychology of conversion are very revealing in this regard. They are unanimous in telling us that conversions following purely rational demonstration are rather rare, and that the living witness of a sincere and radiant faith has a power of persuasion beyond the best treatises of philosophy and apologetics. Not that the convert looks upon his faith as a blind urge or as an arbitrary choice which cannot be objectively justified. In most cases what actually seems to happen is that before conversion the rational proofs have no "bite" to them, whereas, when they are taken up again in the light of faith, they acquire at once an unquestioned probative force. Pascal saw this long ago and made it, as we have said, the central idea of his work. . . .[1]

Following Jansenism and the era of Pascal, we meet the high tide of French rationalism in the movement called the "Enlightenment." At the same time as this rationalist rise to power, we have significant theological contributions in the field of scripture of Calmet and Houbigant, and to a lesser degree by Lamy. Earlier in the sixteenth century Richard Simon had published the first critical history of the Old Testament, and Jean Astruc continued in the seventeenth century the new tradition of critical scholarship with the publication of a short work on the Pentateuch, in which he tentatively suggested a many-document hypothesis for the origin of the Biblical text.

Revolution and Restoration: Lamennais and Lacordaire

When one speaks of the making of modern France, he begins quite obviously with 1789, the year of the French Revolution. In no less a manner the traditions of the French Church were radically influenced and affected by the Revolution. With the Revolution the Church was, as it were, seized up by the roots: and the Church was so utterly shaken up (the orders expelled, property seized, persecution inflicted) that in the nineteenth century the Church in France had to begin again, with an almost completely new slate. The Concordat of 1801 destroyed Gallicanism as a political factor; that is, insofar as state control was concerned, this facet of Gallicanism

[1] Albert Dondeyne, *Contemporary European Thought and Christian Faith* (Pittsburgh: Duquesne University Press, 1958), pp. 74–75.

began to fade from the picture. But the *emigré* clergy, the exiled bishops who came back with the restoration brought back to the Church their traditions, and the Gallicanism of these men was a spirit of independence from Rome and a dependence upon the support of the state to keep it that way.

In the restoration of the religious orders, the newer orders were reflective of French spirit, and the older ones, brought back by men like Lacordaire and Guéranger, were without what might be termed their "house traditions." All of the elements of the French Church were starting again, building anew, and the spirit of these men would be derived from Lacordaire, Guéranger, and through them from this master, Lamennais.

The momentous events of the nineteenth century are the immediate forebears of the present state of the French Church. The traditions and pressures, Gallican and Roman, that had come to restoration France boiled in ferment awaiting the event or person that would serve as the catalyst for the establishment of concrete lines of action. The catalyst was found in the work and life of the Abbé de Lamennais. His influence extended from the circle of followers about him at La Chesnaie, followers who would influence and shape theological thought in France: Lacordaire, Montalembert, Guéranger and others. The basic problem of the age in the eyes of Lamennais was the reconciliation of the Church with the principles of the French Revolution. The Church must accept and live in an age she had not made, and from La Chesnaie came the concept of the separation of Church and State—a *sine qua non* of the theological and political orders. This solution provided, however, a corollary equally important, namely, a concentrated attack upon Gallicanism. Gallicanism was, for Lamennais, the condition of the Church's servitude. She, who had been master of the house, had in time become a political prop for the discredited *ancien régime*.

Thus, with Lamennais was revived the ancient French concept of Church and State going back to John of Paris and the fourteenth century. However, it is significant to note, this revival of a fourteenth-century theory is absolutely devoid of antipapalism; in fact, Lamennais, while reviving the concept of Church-State separation, links to it—because of historical, political and theological reasons—

an unswerving fidelity to Rome. It is Lamennais who sounds the strident tones of a growing ultramontanism.

The principles of Lamennais met with instant opposition from the Gallicans and from the traditionalists. The bishops of France began a program of implacable opposition. At Rome the implications of the principle of separation, namely, the destruction of the concordat system of maintaining a *modus vivendi* for the Church in many lands, forewarned its eventual condemnation. The tradition of union of Church and State, which had survived from the Middle Ages when both were united in the person of the prince, had achieved in the eyes of many traditional theologians a status of certain teaching. Suppressed by the bishops, hemmed in on all sides, Lamennais, with the impracticality of an idealist, accompanied by Lacordaire and Montalembert, journeyed to Rome for vindication. The significance of his proposed separation of Church and State for the existent concordat system guaranteed the failure that followed. The suppression of the ultramontanist *Avenir* and the propositions of *Mirari Vos* were the logical outcome of the venture, for Lamennais, instead of adopting a policy of watchful waiting, had forced the issue upon the Pope. The decision could not be postponed and the decision was inevitable. Experience had taught the Church that separation, the idea of a lay State, could never lead to a free Church in a free State but a "despoiled Church in a despoiling State." The dissent of Lamennais and his consequent defection, and the loyalty of Lacordaire conclude one of the most fascinating periods in the history of the French Church.

Although the work of the *Avenir* collapsed, and in time the Abbé Lamennais withdrew from the Church, a constant factor was established and provided for the French Church, that of ultramontanism. It was this pro-Roman spirit of the French intellectuals that provided in time for the complete eclipse of Gallicanism. No doubt for many ultramontanism was no more than an affectionate spirit toward Rome, yet in time its influence and meaning deepened. One may see today its ultimate flowering in the present full-blown theology of the Church, in no small way indebted to the example of Lacordaire. Within all the wide fields in which French theological writers today labor, one thought overshadows them: that no true, lasting or worth-while work may be accomplished unless it is accomplished within the Church. So, Yves Congar has written of Lacordaire:

The life of Père Lacordaire was punctuated by acts of docility, often of a very meritorious nature, whose profound secret was his will to be in harmony—he who was at the very center of the religious movement of the century—with the ordinary life of the Church.[2]

This compelling conviction of concrete unity with Christ in his Church is Lacordaire's lasting contribution. This contribution is well expressed, again by Congar:

When these practical rules of action which had been for him [Lacordaire] a sort of conclusion drawn from the history of Lamennais: moderation in polemics; charity in action, the avoidance of forming a faction, of separating oneself from the others; the pursuit of nothing outside the jurisdiction of the episcopacy.[3]

Cardinal Newman: His Influence

During the nineteenth century in England the figure of John Henry Newman emerged as the most capable intellectual of the Church. Today, within France, he is looked upon as an intellectual patron. Newman's greatness, in the eyes of the French Catholic intellectuals, lies in his implacable opposition to rationalism, in his careful thinking through of the problems that face theologians, his approach to noting the "senses" of Scripture and by his willingness to grapple with contemporary approaches to the Christian faith.[4]

The themes of Newman so suitable to the contemporary intellectual scene in France are expressed by Abbé Dondeyne:

Most of the themes that we have encountered in Marcel were touched upon by Newman too, sometimes in the very same words. There is the

---

[2] Yves Congar O.P., *Vraie et fausse réforme dans l'Eglise* (Paris: Ed. du Cerf, 1950). A substantial amount of the book has been translated into English and made available in the periodical *Cross Currents*, I, 4 (Summer, 1951), pp. 80–102; III, 4 (Summer, 1953), pp. 358–365.

[3] *Ibid.*

[4] A brief treatment of Cardinal Newman, highlighting those qualities most admired by the modern French Church may be found in Frank O'Malley, "The Thinker in the Church: The Spirit of Newman," *The Review of Politics*, XXI, 1 (January, 1959), pp. 5–23.

same tendency towards "objective and systematic knowledge," with the same tendency to identify conceptual knowledge in general with its rationalist interpretation. There is the same preoccupation with the existential concrete, betraying itself in the priority given to "personal thought" and "concrete reasoning" in opposition to "notional" dialectic. The same way, too, of getting beyond rationalism by a philosophy centered around subjectivity, personality and community, being in history and mystery. Finally, there is the same conception of formal philosophical or apologetic thought, understood not so much as a rational demonstration of the truth than as an invitation to render oneself receptive to the same experiences and to enter personally into the truth.[5]

Newman's influence upon modern French Catholic thought is constantly reflected in the vast number of works devoted to him. Many of the major theologians of twentieth-century France have appealed to his work and example, and no small number of them have published some book or article devoted to him. Thus, in modern times any bibliography on Newman must contain reference to the work of men such as Bremond, Guitton, Nédoncelle, Thureau-Dangen, Granmaison, Seynaeve, Walgrave and Bouyer. At the present time, with the cooperation and assistance of the Fathers of the Oratory, two eminent French scholars, Maurice Nédoncelle and Louis Bouyer, are publishing a French translation of the entire corpus of Newman's work.

In speaking of Newman it is interesting to note the strong affection of the French for the Anglican Church. In many ways the English have been idealized by the French because of common traditions, historical similarities and geographical proximity. Cardinal Newman has been idolized as the theologian of the modern age; the twentieth century scriptural studies of the Anglicans have influenced the researches of the French, the primary interest and initial steps of ecumenicism by the French have always been directed toward the Anglican communion.

A fascinating historical comparison may help to demonstrate the close affinity of the Anglican and French churches during the nineteenth and twentieth centuries. Both churches have been considerably nationalistic, developing away from the Roman influence, and both consequently have had strong patristic movements. During

---

[5] Dondeyne, *op. cit.*, p. 101.

the nineteenth century both churches experienced great ferment vis-à-vis their relationship with the state and each attempted to bring new life to their theological traditions. Lamennais and Newman found themselves in the same position with regard to their bishops. Each had reached the point of rejecting the "national" spirit that lay like a dead hand upon the Church, and sought a return to the Roman See. And yet for each, orthodoxy, if it was to be maintained, demanded disobedience to their bishops. In both France and England the secular universities demanded from the Christian Church immediate answers to pressing problems, and both countries witnessed liturgical reform and renewal, though to an unimportant degree at Oxford as compared to Solesmes. Toward the end of the century both French and English theologians were profoundly affected by the modernist crisis.

It would be extremely cavalier to dismiss the Anglo-French relationships of the nineteenth century, or to find in their comparative development the simple strain of coincidence. The French interest in, and affection for the Anglican Church continues until today. A wistful desire for some form of "corporate reunion" has always characterized the French theological approach to ecumenicism. In the twentieth century Anglican Biblical critics have maintained cordial intellectual relationships with the French. The French proclivity for the English, so noticeable in the nineteenth century, remains as a very real influence in the theological tradition of the French.

Restoration and Rebellion

During the pontificates of Leo XIII and Pius X, the Church in France experienced a number of significant events: the revival of Scholastic philosophy in 1891, the work of the Institut Catholique in Paris and the beginnings of the modern theological revival in the Church. In 1893 Leo XIII issued his encyclical on Sacred Scriptures: *Providentissimus Deus.* During these pontificates we have two great controversies in Catholic theology, one minor and one major: Americanism and Modernism.

"Americanism" in its French aspect may be considered not so much a heresy as an indication of the willingness of some in France to try a fresh approach, even, one might say, an "imported" one toward the world in which the Church found herself. The *Testem Benevolentiae* of Leo XIII put a speedy end to any tendency of minimizing doctrine that this approach might imply. The Mennasian doctrine of Church and State, the alleged superiority of the active virtues over the contemplative, and an ecumenicism that tended toward indifferentism were the particular forms of "Americanism" that the Pope wished to challenge and reject. That the American Church as such ever held such positions is historically doubtful, so that one may conclude that the storm raised by the "Americanism" issue did serve to provide an occasion for the Pope explicitly to reject these same tendencies and currents where they existed.

The initial attack upon this "heresy," allegedly propounded by the Abbé Klein in his translation of Eliot's *Life of Isaac Hecker*, was led by the French Vincentian, Maignan. Although most of Maignan's censures carried the day against this "new Catholicism," and although, as a result, there were some defections from the Church (as, for example, that of Père Charbonnel), nevertheless, it does seem in the light of fifty years that Americanism was for the most part what the Abbé Klein labeled it in his memoirs: "Americanism—A Phantom Heresy." [6]

If the tragic figure of Lammenais stands in the early nineteenth century as the dominant figure of French theological thought—and of rebellion as well—so at the turn of the twentieth century stands the figure of Loisy. The Abbé Loisy has assumed in the eyes of many a stature far beyond his actual influence. He is for many not only a historical personage but also in some strange way the symbol of French Modernism: an adequate representation of the French Church during the modernist crisis. While this remains at best questionable, at least this can be said, that it was with the rise in prestige of Loisy, the intellectual, that we have signaled for us the era we call Modernism.

Modernism, that heresy so sweeping and inclusive as to be vague in its full dimensions, was not a purely French phenomenon. Its basic

[6] A brief account of Americanism but one open to serious criticism may be found in E. E. Hales, *The Catholic Church in the Modern World* (Garden City: Hanover House, 1958), pp. 167–176. However, a longer and far more objective account may be found in McAvoy, *The Great Crisis in American Church History* (Chicago: Regnery, 1957).

causes may be found in the intellectual achievements of the nineteenth century. The progress of science, archeology and the historical method were inevitably brought to bear upon Sacred Scripture. The inroads of modern philosophies, particularly of immanentism, took their toll in the areas of dogmatic, moral and ascetical theology. Nor was the movement, as we have said, a purely French one, nor even predominantly French. The enigmatic Von Hugel and the mystic Tyrrell in England, Murri and Fogazzaro in Italy were major voices in the modernist camp.

Although history has divested Modernism of its "French" label, there still exist those who profess to find that heresy, or at least its "vestiges" in contemporary French Catholic thought. Their facile identification of Modernism with the French ignores the historical facts of the immense and incalculable service rendered to the Church at this period by Duchesne, Lagrange, Battifol, Grandmaison, Vigoroux and others. It was Lagrange who, as the saying goes, "blew the whistle" on Loisy. These were the men who made the Catholic world aware of Modernism, and it is these men who are the true intellectual forebears and founders of the modern revival in France and Belgium.

The exodus of thinkers from the Church that followed St. Pius X's *Pascendi* was not as great as generally supposed. There were those who were sincerely and truly modernist and yet willingly submitted to the Teaching Church and abandoned their errors. There were few either of the stature or the pride of Loisy who willingly left the Church: many minor figures, now forgotten or relegated to dated bibliographies defected, but few major ones.[7]

Despite the initial havoc wrought by the modernists one may, however, speak of a certain "contribution" that Modernism itself made to the Church. We may speak of this contribution as a reaction within the Church itself. Because of the intellectual attacks of the modernists in those vital areas of conflict—philosophy, theology, scripture and history—there was produced in the Church a new

[7] A detailed account of the Modernist period may be found in Jean Rivière, *Le modernisme dans l'église* (Paris, 1929). Few accounts exist in English. Among the best are Hales's chapter on Modernism, *op. cit.*, and a longer and more personal account in Ward, *Insurrection versus Resurrection* (London: Sheed & Ward, 1937).

and lasting intellectual movement. The contemporary theological revival in France has for its immediate roots the modernist crisis. One might rightly speak of the modern French theologians as "owing" much to the modernists, not in their attitudes and teaching, but simply as a historical reaction. The initial fear displayed in the Church when faced by such an enormous attack upon her very theological foundations has disappeared in our time. However, the work begun in reaction has continued. Theological thought and a serious approach to the problems of the Church in the world today still continue with unabated force among modern French intellectuals.[8]

The Predatory State and Plundered Church

Not only did there exist in France an intellectual attack upon the Church but at the turn of the century there was also an attack upon her material resources. The struggle between the Church and the Third Republic was marked by the educational laws of Ferry, the suppression of the teaching orders and the confiscation of all Church property by the *Associations Cultuelles*. The Church was left completely despoiled of the physical necessities of existence. Yet, as E. E. Hales remarks:

Pius X, with the support of the majority of the French bishops, refused any arrangement by which the Church would be deprived of every voluntary association's right to dispose of its own funds in its own way. Seeking only, as he put it, the good of the Church in France and not her goods, by a gesture which astonished and edified public opinion in France and throughout the world, he renounced her buildings to the state so that she entered upon a new life untied by any secular contacts. Henceforth her priests would say Mass in the great cathedrals and churches as tenants, on sufferance, in those edifices which are the glory of Western civilization, but which soon fell into a shocking state of disrepair. . . .[9]

Hesitatingly at first, the attitude adopted by the French Church under the leadership of the Pope was one of freedom and emancipa-

---

[8] Robert Rouquette, S.J., "Bilan du modernisme" *Etudes*, CCLXXXIX (1956), pp. 321–343.
[9] Hales, *op. cit.*, p. 234.

tion. Although in time the position of the Pope was borne out, the French bishops were not as enthusiastic as Hales suggests. The dream of separation, although not so envisioned by the medievalists, was an accomplished fact. In the framework envisioned by Lamennais and Lacordaire the French Church was to grow and wax strong, and her first intellectual stumblings after the trial of Modernism were to become gigantic strides. For, as Hales continues:

From the ashes of this conflagration was reborn the Catholic Church in France. The internecine strife within the Church herself between seculars and religious, between ultramontanes and liberals, between monarchists and republicans—conflicts which had gravely weakened the French clergy throughout the previous century—disappeared now in the face of the need for a common effort to maintain her mission. And the link with the State being broken, the link with Rome was strengthened.[10]

The great themes of France's intellectual tradition now converge as the Church of France revives. As we survey the work and progress of her scholars, philosophers and theologians, many of the trends that are France's heritage stand forth in a new splendor. The emergence of modern French Catholicism is aptly sketched for us by the editor of *Etudes*, Père Robert Rouquette:

The republican parties, believing that democratic institutions are threatened by Catholicism, execute a clearly antireligious political program. . . . The Church is delivered over to heroic poverty; it is deprived of the state support that was also an alienation of its freedom. Precisely at this moment it recovers an extraordinary vitality. It abandons every attitude of political opposition and adjusts itself easily to the regime, no longer dreaming of the past. At the same time a twofold movement of creative youthfulness gives it new life. First of all a great intellectual renewal. The Modernist crisis is only an accident, soon reabsorbed, of a renovation of Catholic thought. A critical nonapologetic history of Christianity takes effect with Duchesne and his school, an increasingly objective and serious Biblical science with Lagrange and Grandmaison, a renaissance of positive theology with Lebreton, of speculative theology thanks to the upsurge of Thomism; a Christian philosophy, which had been so cruelly lacking to us, makes its appearance. This philosophy seeks knowl-

[10] *Ibid.*

edge of itself in two directions: on one hand, in a neo-Thomism adapted to contemporary thought, thanks to Maritain (whose influence, it may be said in passing, had been much less strong in France than abroad) and especially thanks to Sertillanges; on the other hand, psychological analysis rediscovers both the essential religious needs of man and the presence of the transcendent in his inner experience. This is an old French tradition that begins with Pascal, continues with Maine de Biran, with Bergson, who is one of the incontestable sources of the return of intellectuals to the faith, with Blondel, and finally leads to the contemporary Christian Existentialists, of whom Gabriel Marcel is the best known. Add to this the fact that, at one of those moments when our language attains truly classical perfection, some of the greatest French writers are converted to Catholicism and place in the center of their work and of their influence the problem of religion. Thus Catholic thought has acquired full rights of citizenship; it is no longer a poor relative. Of course, the intelligentsia is far from having been won over to the whole of Christianity, but the Catholic synthesis is no longer despised—it is considered with respect and sympathy. . . . This intellectual renewal has delivered Catholicism from a certain inferiority complex and has permitted growth in all fields. A well organized and thoughtful Social Catholicism has become conscious of the urgent problems posed by the massive irreligion of the proletariat, and an irreligion nourished by social injustice. A whole generation of young Catholics grown to maturity between the two wars can no longer conceive of Christianity except as radiating and apostolic. From them springs Catholic Action, that is, the assumption of responsibility on the part of the laity in a work of social transformation inspired and animated by the demands of the Gospel and the Faith.[11]

[11] Robert Rouquette, S.J., "The Evolution of the French Church," *The Catholic Mind*, LI (August, 1953), pp. 473-474.

II

THE INTELLECTUAL AND HISTORI-
CAL LOCATION OF CONTEMPO-
RARY FRENCH THEOLOGY

Philosophy, it seems, is second nature to the French mind. It is the philosophical background of modern France, and allied to it the immediate theological traditions, which we will examine now, and from this survey attempt to locate the theological work of modern France in that vague matrix of evolving philosophical movements.

As we have remarked, it is the philosophy of René Descartes that dominated the French scene for centuries, excluding from serious consideration the scholastics and Thomism in favor at Rome. The lack of a serious and scholarly Thomistic tradition until its revival by Leo XIII in 1879 also contributed to the perpetuation of Cartesian philosophy. To this Cartesian tradition was joined the effects of the Gallican domination of the Church. Cartesianism was perpetuated because the seminary system never really achieved a foothold at the time of the Council of Trent. The *philosophia perennis* of the scholastics had no sounding board among the French.

The nineteenth century witnessed the control of the universities, of higher education by the State. The schools of higher learning were not the Church's, they coexisted with the seminaries as the source of education for many of the French clergy in the nineteenth century. It is because of these two systems utilized by the Church for the training of her clergy that, imperceptibly at first, two distinct traditions were established among the theologians. The seminaries were self-enclosed, and in them traditionalist conservative theology achieved its foothold. The seminaries would harbor, in the years to come, the theologians and their manuals and become the foundation and support for the traditionally Thomist philosophy.

At the universities things were different. The Church did not possess them, or determine the content of their courses. Modern problems, scientific, economic, social, were forced upon the men who attended them, pressing them for urgent answers. Archeology, historical criticism, the scientific approach to "religious phenomena" demanded from Catholics the response of the faith. There was no avoiding the issues raised by the modern world. Catholics in the universities could not, as the old story goes, wait a hundred years until everybody involved in a given dispute was dead, and then settle it upon its merits. Answers were demanded of the Church's representatives in these halls of learning, and they were demanded immediately. Consequently, another theological tradition began to grow in France, a modern spirit, open to the world, caring little for the venerable disputes among the manualists. The men in the universities were Catholics faced with theology-in-the-world, and they realized the urgency in the demand for answers that faced the Church. As the century wore on, during the modernist controversy, and into the twentieth century the two theological traditions coexisted among the French. Plagued by their Cartesian heritage and without root in a traditionally Thomist framework, many moderns tried to adapt the Christian Revelation to every current philosophical trend, to what seemed the latest unalterable scientific or historical fact, and in these attempts discovered somewhere along the line a difficulty with traditional Christian teaching. Many of them were unable to accept the Thomist synthesis of the conservatives and work within it; and the dichotomy was perpetuated by conservatives unwilling to admit any progress in thought through modern approaches.

Thomism

In 1879 Pope Leo XIII set in motion the movement that has more than any other had the major influence upon philosophers and theologians of Christian France and Belgium, namely, the Thomist revival. In his encyclical on Thomism, *Aeterni Patris*, issued in that year, the Holy Father set the pace for what has become in our time a period of immense theological activity. The Pope rekindled interest in Thomism, the perennial philosophy of the Church, a new interest whose work it would be "to extend and perfect the old by new truths."

Cardinal Mercier (1851–1926) of Belgium became the first great figure in the Thomist revival. Within a year after the encyclical was issued he had founded a higher Philosophical Institute at the University of Louvain. In time, he personally contributed works on logic, psychology and epistemology. It is to him that credit is due for implementing the desires of the Pope for a renewal of Thomism in the schools.

The initial work of Mercier in placing Thomism upon respectable intellectual footing was outstripped. Today there are many Thomists, for example, who would reject his work and that of his influential disciple, Léon Noël. Mercier and Noël, they say, conceded in the first place too much to the Cartesian and Kantian statements of the epistemological problem. Nor was this weakness of Thomism limited to Mercier, for on the whole the first stages of the movement were marked by a poor, weakened and emasculated Thomism. This criticism is that of today, but honesty demands that the scholar recognize the vastness of the work undertaken by Mercier, and in that light may easily excuse his first faltering steps.

Thomism today has come to full bloom in the work of Jacques Maritain and Etienne Gilson, as well as numberless other scholars. In the years between, from Mercier's initial attempts to the present, Thomism owes its continuity to the figure of Père Antonin-Gilbert Sertillanges.

Sertillanges was born at Clermont-Ferrand in 1863. He entered the Dominican Order in 1883, and studied at Corbara in Spain. At the turn of the century he was Professor of Philosophy at the Institut Catholique in Paris, and editor of the *Revue thomiste*. Many of his works are regarded as steppingstones in the Thomist revival, among the more important, *La Philosophie thomiste* (1916), and *Les grandes thèses de la philosophie thomiste* (1928). It would be difficult to overestimate the importance of Sertillanges and his influence on the French scene. There are some who in the mid-twentieth century would regard his work as lackluster and dated, yet his historical position as one of the most fiery and influential men in the early twentieth century revival of Thomism can never be questioned. The personal conviction and enormous mastery that he exercised over his friends and students, and his persuasiveness with those outside the Thomist camp served to keep Thomism alive and reputable. It is to Père Sertillanges' influence that the era between *Aeterni Patris* and the neo-Thomism of today belongs.

The acknowledged master of neo-Thomism, Jacques Maritain, presently is associated with the Institute for Higher Studies at Princeton, New Jersey.[1] He was born in Paris in 1882, and studied at the Sorbonne and the Collège de France. He was in his earlier days a friend, disciple and student of the great figures of French thought: Péguy, Bloy and Bergson. It is through Maritain that much of value in Bergson has come into the main stream of Thomistic thought.

Maritain's Catholicism dates back to 1906, and soon after this he went to study at Heidelberg and Versailles. In 1913 he published his rejection of the Bergsonian system in *La Philosophie bergsonienne*, but his friendship with the great man remained firm. His *Introduction to Philosophy* was undertaken originally at the request of the French hierarchy, and was well received in Rome.[2] Among the greatest of his works is *The Degrees of Knowledge*.[3] Maritain, never completely losing the influence which Bergson had on him, has since turned frequently to artistic and esthetic studies. Today, as the leading neo-Thomist, he is not always looked upon favorably in the extremely conservative circle established by some Thomists. He is only too anxious to take modern work of value, as for example, Bergson, and translate them into a place in the Thomist synthesis, a process which has earned him the enmity of the most conservative of the Thomists. The range of his influence, however, has not diminished, and although he is not looked upon in France with the

[1] A fine introduction to Maritain's thought and approach may be found in Charles Fecher, *The Philosophy of Jacques Maritain* (Westminster, Md.: Newman, 1953).

[2] Jacques Maritain, *Introduction to Philosophy* (New York: Sheed & Ward, 1933).

[3] Jacques Maritain, *The Degrees of Knowledge* (New York: Scribner, 1938).

invested air of leadership he receives in the English-speaking world, he is, nevertheless, appreciated particularly for his work in relating the democratic ideal to a Christian outlook upon the world. The vitality of his mind has not diminished either, as his recent work on the philosophy of history testifies.[4]

Born in 1884, Etienne Gilson, now resident in Canada, is a native Parisian and a graduate of that city's most illustrious schools, the University of Paris and the Sorbonne. He has taught at Lille, Strasbourg, Paris, Harvard, and is now associated with the Institute of Medieval Studies at the University of Toronto in Canada. M. Gilson is an expert in the content and meaning of medieval philosophy, and the author of the incisive *Spirit of Medieval Philosophy* and the equally brilliant *Unity of Philosophical Experience*.[5] In 1954 he surpassed his previous work in a complete and capable study of philosophy in the Middle Ages.[6] A neo-Thomist, he has contributed much to the traditional Thomist system, and although Maritain's contemporary, has disagreed with him on more than one occasion.

The Thomist revival in philosophy also led to enormous strides in restoring the traditional Thomist theological system to a place of pre-eminence. The theological schools that adopted the Thomism of Mercier, Sertillanges, *et al.*, were the seminaries, and the conservative theological tradition latched on to Thomism as its own. The Thomists of the twentieth century, immediately following the modernist controversy, became extremely conservative. The period following the modernists was one of retrenchment, and this theological tradition looked with some suspicion upon the Catholics in the secular universities. This second school of theology, those "open" to the modern world, won few admiring glances from Thomists, especially when they showed a tendency to flirt with every novel current in the intellectual world. Battifol exemplified the two traditions in a story in which he compared the theologians to men building the wall of the Church. They didn't worry about what the men inside

---

[4] Jacques Maritain, *On the Philosophy of History* (New York: Scribner, 1957). He is at present working on the question of ethics according to his integral humanism.

[5] Etienne Gilson, *The Spirit of Medieval Philosophy* (New York: Scribner, 1934); *The Unity of Philosophical Experience* (New York: Scribner, 1937).

[6] Etienne Gilson, *History of Christian Philosophy in the Middle Ages* (New York: Random House, 1954).

the walls were doing, but the men outside the walls were out of sight, and couldn't be trusted. And so the two theological traditions grew with the French, the Thomists, traditionalists, for the most part the theology of the seminaries, and on the other hand, the moderns, students at the universities, men who looked upon Bergson, Blondel, the existentialists with considerable sympathy, if not outright commitment.

As we have said, theology as it developed after the modernist era was a conservative Thomism; however, it was one of no mean ability as the names of Billot, de la Taille and Garrigou-Lagrange can well testify. The renewed interest in Thomism in theology extended to a continuing study of Scripture, the Fathers and the Church. The French continued their strong patristic heritage within the Thomist synthesis, and both d'Ales and Lebreton manifested an extremely competent control of patristics. Pegues established a reputation as a theologian of value, and Gardeil led the Thomists to new considerations of the apologetic question.[7] The Dominican Henri Petitot became one of the most eminent ascetical theologians of the 1920's. Thomists faced the findings of the critics and scientific historians on the question of the evolution of dogma with the lasting work of Lebreton, Grandmaison and Marin-Sola. For breadth of scope, few Frenchmen were the equal of the tragic Cardinal Billot, the last of the "commentators on Saint Thomas." Billot's eclipse was political rather than theological, for he resigned the cardinalate over the *Action Française* affair. Among the other French theologians of the period after the modernists were Rivière, Lepin, and the imposing figure of the brilliant young Jesuit, Père de la Taille.

In 1872 at Semblancay in France, Maurice de la Taille was born, and eighteen years later he entered the Society of Jesus. Among the greatest of the Jesuit theologians in the early twentieth century, he was certainly the most inventive; he studied during the first decades of the twentieth century at the University of Paris, the Sorbonne and Lyons. In 1919 he went to Rome to teach speculative theology at the Gregorianum. His great technical masterpiece, the

[7] Gardeil's work is surveyed by his nephew, Ambroise Gardeil, *L'Oeuvre théologique du Père Ambroise Gardeil* (Le Saulchoir: Etiolles par Soisy-sur-Seine, 1956).

most original contribution to theology and Thomism in the twentieth century, the *Mysterium Fidei,* was published in 1921.[8] It is hard, even today, to estimate the influence his theory of created actuation has had in theological circles, and certainly the rich vein of thought opened up by his original intuition is yet to be fully explored by the theologians who have succeeded him.

The conservative force of the Thomist revival has continued even until today, and among the most powerful voices in this tradition is that of the French Dominican Reginald Marie Garrigou-Lagrange. Père Garrigou-Lagrange was born in 1877 at Auch Gerst in France, the nephew of the celebrated Scripture scholar, Père Lagrange. He entered the Dominicans in 1897 and studied at Rome. By 1904 he was home in France teaching and returned to Rome in 1909 to teach at the Angelicum. His first book was published in that year, and among the numerous products of his prolific pen have been the exceptionally fine *Dieu: son existence et son nature* in 1916, *La Prédestination* and *Providence.* Today, Garrigou-Lagrange is a member of the Holy Office, and although a conservative theologian, perhaps it would be more accurate to call him "traditional" in the best sense of that word. Although he is frequently impatient with the "moderns," nevertheless he bases this on his belief that the Thomism they reject is the object of their scorn but never of their study. He has used enormously and well his great natural abilities to temper at times the excessive zeal for the "new," and the overhasty conclusions of some theologians.

The Modern Tradition

In examining the philosophical and theological location of contemporary French theology it would be seriously erroneous to by-pass the "modern" tradition, based upon "openness" to the modern world; and it would be no less erroneous to regard the modern school of "openness" as entirely representative of what is sometimes called the "French mind."

At the turn of the twentieth century, Cartesianism and rationalism, so traditionally strong among the French, began to give way

---

[8] De la Taille, *The Mystery of Faith* (New York: Sheed & Ward, 1950), 2 vols. Also *The Hypostatic Union. Created Actuation by Uncreated Act* (West Baden, Ind.: West Baden College, 1952).

to the new philosophies that seemed so in accord with the scientific and psychological progress of the time. From 1890 on the stature of Henri Bergson looms larger upon the French scene. Bergson's evolutionary and vitalistic theories influenced a host of his contemporaries, and he prepared the way for the current popularity of Existentialism.

During Bergson's evolution as the dominant figure of French thought he moved at first slowly, and later more perceptively toward the Church. It is true to say that at the end of his life only the fact that he was a Jew kept him back from entrance into the Church. The Nazi persecution of his fellow Jews did not seem to Bergson to be an ideal time for proclaiming his public commitment to Christianity. Previous to this many of his disciples had taken the step into the Church, the most notable being Jacques Maritain.

Closely paralleling Bergson's maturing growth, the work of the immanentist Henri Blondel within the Church was meeting with acceptance and, later, controversy. He evolved a philosophy of action, as he termed it, and during the modernist era was roundly denounced as "suspect" of that heresy. He became involved in a theological controversy over the question of miracles. Blondel drew to himself a school of followers, the most famous of whom was Eduard Le Roy, a scientist who had been influenced strongly by Blondel, and who tried to construct what he termed a critical theology. Le Roy himself was severely criticized and denounced, and also became suspect of Modernism.

However, the years have been kind to Blondel, and as the modernist crisis subsided, his critics diminished their denunciations both in frequency and intensity. Today his work is no longer suspect, save in the most extremely conservative circles, and although no wide acceptance has been given to it, it has retained a popularity with some, and for others has provided a fruitful point of departure for discussion.[9]

The trend among the Catholic "moderns" was to construct philosophies in accord with the modern world, and few in the

[9] Blondel's most accurate commentator and devoted disciple has been Professor Henri Dumery, who has published an exposition and history of Blondel's thought in *Blondel et la religion* (Paris: Presses Universitaires de France, 1954). Dumery's works have been withdrawn and placed on the Index.

twentieth century have ever attained the prominence of Blondel. A philosophy of the spirit was attempted by two eminent Catholics, René Le Senne and Louis Lavelle.[10] Le Senne taught at the Sorbonne, and Lavelle, at the Collège de France. Their effort never met with much success, but is an interesting example of the approach of the "moderns" toward philosophical problems. A more serious work was achieved by Emmanuel Mounier during the 1930's. He evolved a "personalist" philosophy, and founded the review *Esprit* to advance his views. For Mounier the universe was basically a society of persons and "other selves": a position with wide social, economic and practical implications. A fervent Catholic, Mounier's work strongly influenced Jacques Maritain, through whom it was translated into a practical system of political democracy. It is in the work of Maritain that the lasting elements of Mounier's "personalism" have been brought into the main stream of Thomistic tradition, and the influences and intuitions of Bergson and the modern existentialists as well.

Existentialism

Contemporary French thought is for the most part today characterized by Existentialism. It is unfortunate that the word "Existentialism" is not used to delineate sharply a specific school of philosophy, but has been found wide enough to embrace the variations of thought ranging from the atheist Sartre to the theism of the neo-Thomist Maritain.

When we speak of Existentialism, we are, broadly speaking, discussing a philosophy based upon the personal confrontation of existence. The traditional philosophies have been for the most part "essentialist," concerned with essences and nature, with the "quiddity" of things. Here we meet a philosophy rooted upon the very question of existence itself, the "beingness"—as it were—of being itself. Existence, for the existentialist, is indefinable. It may have for the existentialist many predicates, none of which will really exhaust the full meaning denoted by that word.

For the existentialist, existence is met, is confronted by crisis.

[10] See the account of James Collins, "Louis Lavelle on Human Participation," *Philosophical Review*, Vol. 56 (1947), pp. 56–183.

The crisis by which one comes to grapple with existence itself is the "extraordinary life event." This event, this crisis, involves the individual thinking man with a personal and real problem, that of being itself.

Existentialism owes its immediate derivation to the nineteenth century Danish theologian Soren Kierkegaard, and has retained its theological character in many theological writings.[11] Today it is the primary factor in the syntheses of the German theologian, Karl Barth, and the American, Paul Tillich. In the main line of its development Existentialism has been joined to the important Kantian tradition by the work of Karl Jaspers, and to the phenomenological movement of Husserl by Martin Heidegger. A still more radical form of Existentialism is to be found in the work of Jean-Paul Sartre, who, upon emptying man of nature or essence, made the only thing that matters the existent human self. Existentialism has achieved predominance and popularity among the French intellectuals and writers outside the Church.

As early as the 1920's, however, we have the work of a Catholic existentialist: Gabriel Marcel.[12] Marcel, in his early days, was a friend and disciple of Bergson, and in his later days has tried to unite both the disparate elements of Bergsonianism and Existentialism into a "social Existentialism" and rejoin this end product with the main stream of Christian tradition. *"Etre et Avoir"* in 1935, and *"Homo Viator"* in 1945 were still further attempts by Marcel toward the construction of a "Christian Existentialism." [13]

For Marcel the problem of Theism is central to any philosophical synthesis. He maintains, however, an averseness to the traditional concepts of natural theology, to the Theism arrived at by natural unaided human reason. Although he does not explicitly deny the validity of such rational process he disregards it for two reasons: first, the "demonstration of God's existence" seems meaningless to the unbeliever; and, secondly, such demonstrations seem unnecessary to the believer. Furthermore, God, for Marcel, belongs to the

[11] See Regis Jolivet, *Aux Sources de l'existentialisme chrétien: Kierkegaard* (Paris: Fayard, 1958).

[12] On Marcel and the existentialists see Père Rideau, S.J., *Etude sur l'athéisme moderne* (Paris: Casterman, 1953).

[13] A synthesis of Marcel's work may be found in Roger Troisfontaines, S.J., *De l'Existence à l'être* (Paris: Vrin, 1953), 2 vols.

sphere of mystery rather than that of reason alone. In the confrontation of existence every man is aware of his dependence upon others
and upon the world itself. In this vital act of acknowledging his dependence, man perceives experienced existence as finite. Therefore,
he continues, one cannot deny the existence of an Infinite Being
through whose generosity one shares in the experience of finite
being. Because it is admittedly difficult to confine the thought of
Marcel precisely, we cannot say that his perception of God is,
strictly speaking, irreducible to the traditional conceptual demonstration of God's existence.

These then represent the modern and conservative traditions as
we find them in France today. It is interesting to observe some
definite approaches to the problem of reconciling them. Maritain
and Gilson have brought the basic impetus of Existentialism into
the Thomist tradition itself. For the neo-Thomists who follow
them the recovery of the basic Thomist intuition into the problem
of being, of existence itself, of being as the first object of the mind,
this is for them what constitutes Thomism, not only as a realist
philosophy but also as the only true form of Existentialism.

The University of Louvain at which Mercier set the revival of
Thomism in motion has also contributed through the years to a
philosophical and theological renewal with the work of Dignant,
De Smet, Waffelaert, Janssens and Van Hové; and with the work
in Scripture of Van der Heeven and Van Hoonacker. Today the
philosophical school at Louvain is distinguished by the contributions
of Abbé Fernand Van Steenberghen and the Abbé Albert Dondeyne. Van Steenberghen's scholarly researches in medieval philosophy, especially his work on Siger de Brabant, have established
him as a leading philosopher and historian of philosophy. He collaborated with Forest and de Gandillac in 1951 on the volume
Le Mouvement doctrinal du IXe au XIVe siècle for the Fliche-Martin
series. He has also published studies on epistemology and ontology.
Van Steenberghen's work on medieval philosophy has also been
supplemented by the scholarly works of the capable Abbé Glorieux,
the Rector of the Catholic University of Lille in France. Dondeyne
has long tried to work with the problem of the existentialist movement and the Christian tradition, which we shall discuss in the next
chapter. Both Van Steenberghen and Dondeyne have been most

anxious to avoid falling into any philosophical rut, and have declared their intention to rethink the Thomist synthesis in the light of modern problems.

It is in this light of the twofold tradition among French theologians and philosophers, and of the evolving modern philosophies, particularly Existentialism, that the work of contemporary French theological thinking must be examined. In this framework these men labor; and, as we shall see, this is not a taxative listing of all the forces which evoke, shape and influence the speculation of theologians today. But these particular philosophical and theological traditions are the matrix in which the labors of contemporary French theology are set.

III

❧

THEOLOGY OF THE SOURCES

The most distinguishing feature of the theological revival in France as well as throughout the world has been the preoccupation of the theologians with the sources of theology. The initial movement of the Teaching Church has driven the scholars back to a renewed study of the Word of God in the Bible, to studies of the worship or liturgy of the Christian people, and to the study of the teaching of the Fathers of the Church. This threefold movement, Biblical-liturgical-patristic, has received enormous encouragement and approval from the Popes since Leo XIII.

This dominant element in modern theology is an extremely complex and interconnected one. The desire to contact the sources of theology cannot terminate in a purely Biblical revival but continues of its nature into liturgical renewal, into the field of worship where the people of God are formed and nourished and where they receive the Word in a living Church. The writings of the Fathers from an era of Christian history in immediate contact with the Apostolic Age cannot be divorced from the consideration of Scripture or liturgy. Thus each movement as it develops tends to influence, strengthen and confirm the other. Each and all develop within the Church and by the approval and direction of her Teaching Authority.

In addition we have the growth of the secular sciences, of historical method and ancient language, as well as the vast body of scholarly researches accomplished by those outside the Church, and these intellectual achievements cannot but directly bear upon this three-fold burgeoning movement within the Church. Thus it would be rash indeed to attempt to ascribe the growth of theology-of-the-sources to any one factor. But if some orderly arrangement of the influences and causes of this movement be demanded it would not be inaccurate to catalogue them in the following manner: first, the interrelated influence of the Biblical-liturgical-patristic movements themselves; second, the encouragement, direction and approval of the Church; third, the scholarship and research of the various sciences and of those outside the Church.

Let us now turn to this threefold movement, and its various influences as they have evolved in modern France.

1. THE BIBLICAL REVIVAL

The Growth of Biblical Criticism

Critical exegesis of the Bible made its modern historical appearance at the turn of the nineteenth century in the work of the German Biblical critic, Johann Eichorn. He published a three-volume *Introduction to the Old Testament,* the most important point of which was his reintroduction for modern scholars of Astruc's two-document theory for the composition of the first five books of the Old Testament. Eichorn was soon followed in critical exegesis of the Old Testament by others: Ilgen, Ewald, Hupfeld, Reuss and Graf.

These men did not confine their critical examination to the Old Testament alone; some now turned to the New Testament. Paulus, Strauss, F. C. Baur and Bruno Bauer followed the tradition of the earlier German rationalists subjecting the phenomenon of Jesus and early Christianity to their critical approach. The early and middle nineteenth century witnessed an able and powerful, and, for the most part, Germanic attack on the Scriptures. The Christian suddenly was forced to ponder the meaning and the power in the rise of the critical movement. Whence had it arisen, and why did it mount in intensity with such undeniable force? Canon Coppens of Louvain tells us where the earlier traditional and literal Biblicism had failed: ". . . traditional exegesis looked upon the Sacred Books much as upon documents fallen from Heaven. It failed, accordingly, to take into account the part that man played in their composition, and it virtually denied any process of development in Judaeo-Christian revelation . . . nor did they endeavour to reconstruct the historical setting, the 'situation in life,' of the happenings recorded in the Bible." [1]

The crushing weight of German Biblical criticism did not derive only from the negative weakness of traditional Biblical approaches, but received its critical tools from science, the historical method, language progress, and the theory of evolution. Impetus was given by the current rationalist philosophies, so that much of their criticism arose from *a priori* principles, as, for example, the denial of the supernatural, or of miracles.

The great product of German criticism that dominated the latter part of the nineteenth century was the work of Julius Wellhausen. His most celebrated study, the *Prolegomena to the History of Israel*, was published in 1878, again in 1883, and in English in 1886. This work became the great document of the new scholarship, the ultimate triumph of the rationalist and critical approach, and swept the conservatives before it in shameful retreat. Wellhausen brought to Biblical criticism a skeptical attitude toward the historical documents of the Jews, an evolutionary hypothesis, and a firm disbelief in the supernatural. From these principles, and from his followers came the "Wellhausen school." Although in time both Wellhausen and his postulates were to a degree discredited by scientific, literary and Biblical critics, it is difficult for us to form an accurate notion of the intellectual state of nineteenth century Europe without fully appreciating the enormous inroads such criticism as Wellhausen's had made on the traditional stronghold of Christianity, the Bible.

Biblical criticism came to France in the work of Ernest Renan. Renan published his *Life of Christ* in 1863, and through this winning and stylish presentation the fundamental meaning of what the German critics had done was brought before the masses of the people. The Jesus Christ known through the Gospels, a Son of man displaying untold strength through suffering, the Son of God displaying gentleness and appreciation of human weakness, that Jesus Christ was stripped of His power, His glory and even His divinity.

[1] Joseph Coppens, *The Old Testament and the Critics* (Paterson: St. Anthony Guild, 1942), pp. 3–4.

What emerged from Renan's *Life of Christ* was the rationalist conception of Jesus as a "good and kind man."

Renan, relying on his personal knowledge of the Holy Land, had in his description re-created the life of Jesus and its events with colorful detail. An ex-seminarian, he had lost the traditional faith in Christ and presented only what would be left to a half-hearted follower of Teutonic idealism. He was dependent for the most part upon the findings of the German critic Ewald, and Renan himself did little to place the work on any scholarly basis, critical or otherwise. And yet to acknowledge this and then to dismiss any serious consideration of Renan is to miss the point of his work. While deficient in scholarship, he nevertheless displayed the meaning that lay behind German Biblical criticism; he made obvious and accessible the ultimate conclusion and end product of Biblical criticism—the destruction of traditional faith in Christianity.

The triumph of the Biblical critics, and their inevitable popularization in the work of such authors as Renan occasioned a defensive reaction in the Church. A Biblical revival at first begun in defense and timidity, was now heralded and directed by Pope Leo XIII in his encyclical on Sacred Scripture *Providentissimus Deus*.[2]

The Biblical critics by the turn of the nineteenth century began to divide into two general camps. The first of these may be called the "liberal school," and was spearheaded by the German historian and Biblical critic, Adolf von Harnack. At the turn of the century Harnack published his *Essence of Christianity*, presenting a Jesus stripped of miracles, without the "dogma" which allegedly came from a later era of Hellenistic philosophy. But while Harnack continued the traditions of Wellhausen and the earlier German critics, a new school began to develop.

For want of a better name the second group of critics that began to develop at that time may be called the "eschatologists." John Weiss published his *Jesus Preaching on the Kingdom of God* in 1892, and by 1900 his ideas of eschatology had cleaved the Biblical critics into two camps. The eschatologists took up the study of the Jews at the time of Jesus who carried on the Jewish tradition of

[2] Papal encyclicals and Church documents on Scripture have been collected and published in English as: *Rome and the Study of Scripture* (St. Meinrad, Ind.: Grail Press, 1946).

the imminence of the coming of the Kingdom of God, and the Christ of their studies became the man who heralded the Kingdom he believed about to come, rather than a Christ who believed that He would found it. Albert Schweitzer raised the eschatological principle to the position of being the entire meaning behind the life and teaching of Jesus. For Schweitzer Jesus possessed a fanatical belief in His own Messiahship, and that His death would be salvific; salvific since He visioned His death as a testimony, upon the occasion of which God would establish His Kingdom. Thus with eschatology the "riddle of Jesus," the problem of Christ was solved for the liberal critics, and the historical significance of Christ became apparent. For the liberals, the miracles, the divine names and the claims of Jesus were the accretions of a Hellenistic age and they must be stripped away. For the eschatologists the process was reversed, and for both liberals and eschatologists theory frequently dictated their method of approach to the critique of the Bible. Soon objective literary criticism proved that the eschatologists like the liberals had assumed too much, simplified too greatly and generalized in an unwarranted manner.

The Beginning of the Catholic Biblical Revival: Pope Leo XIII

The work and influence of the non-Catholic Biblical critics provoked strong reaction within France and the Church at large. The scientific advancements and telling criticism of non-Catholics, coupled with the confusion of disparate works within the Church (that is, the conservatives vainly trying to fight the critics on their own field without the scientific tools of the latter; and the few Biblical critics within the Church considered radical and ahead of their time) left the field of Biblical studies in a state of confusion and uncertainty at the end of the nineteenth century. For the growing Biblical movement the Church now decided to provide leadership and direction.

In attacking the problem in its initial stages the Church took these approaches: first, Leo XIII's encyclical on Biblical studies, *Providentissimus Deus* in 1893; second, the promotion and direction given to the talented genius, Père Marie-Joseph Lagrange, who in 1890 founded the Ecole Biblique at Jerusalem, and two years later its

publication, the *Révue biblique;* third, the establishment by the
Pope in 1902 of a Biblical Commission in order to provide guidance
and regulation on specialized or disputed points of Biblical studies.[3]
Four Frenchmen of great gifts and abilities, Lagrange, Vigouroux,
Prat and Durand provided leadership for Catholic Biblical scholarship and provided yeoman service for the Church in what had
developed into a twofold struggle against the Biblical critics outside
the Church and the modernists within.

The touchstone of the work of these devoted men lay in the
official teaching of the authoritative Church. Leo XIII in his encyclical set out before them the task to be accomplished and the
tools to be used. The consideration of the Bible as the revelation by
God of His marvelous and mysterious works, the Pope stated,
leads to the conclusion that this work of Biblical study, that this
branch of "sacred theology which is concerned with the defense
and elucidation of these divine books must be excellent and useful
in the highest degree." [4]

The Pope was well aware that the rationalists "have rejected even
the scraps and remnants of Christian belief which have been handed
down to them. They deny that there is any such thing as revelation
or inspiration . . . they see only forgeries and falsehoods . . .
stupid fables and lying stories." [5] The Pope shrewdly observed of
the alleged science of Biblical criticism, then in its halcyon days, that
it was a "science, however, which is so far from final that they are
perpetually modifying and supplementing it." [6]

The Pope went on to propose to scholars in the Church the use
of the Vulgate edition of Scripture as their official text, but at the
same time not to neglect the other versions, "more especially the
more ancient manuscripts." [7] Two guides in interpretation were
given: the common teaching of the Fathers and the official teaching
of the Church. Finally, Leo turned to the problem of defense, and
proposed the immediate use by Catholic scholars of the tools science

[3] The Decree "Vigilantiae," *Rome and the Study of Scripture, op cit.,* pp.
30–35.
[4] *Providentissimus Deus, ibid.,* p. 2.
[5] *Ibid.,* p. 10.
[6] *Ibid.,* p. 11.
[7] *Ibid.,* p. 13.

had placed at hand: a new knowledge of oriental languages, the art of criticism, historical method, and an awareness of the accurate boundaries of the natural sciences.

The Holy Father had thus presented to the Church an awareness of the problem created by the critics, and called for a solidly based Biblical revival along certain definite paths. Toward these goals Catholic scholars set themselves, the French preeminently, so that in the words of the Pope scriptural studies might "flourish in completeness and happy success . . . widened and extended as the interests and glory of truth might require." [8]

Modernism and the Emergence of Lagrange

Biblical criticism had not only set a scientific norm to be reached by Catholic Biblical scholars, it also produced within the Church the first stirrings toward its attainment. Abbé Alfred Loisy was appointed to the Institut Catholique in Paris in 1881, nine years after his ordination, to teach Sacred Scripture.[9] He was considered by many to be the most important Catholic working in the field and wielded enormous influence among Catholic scholars. By 1890 he had received his doctorate in theology, and yet, as he relates in his *Mémoires*, by this time he was secretly convinced that the unanimous consent of the Fathers could not accurately interpret Scripture.

In 1893, the year of Leo's encyclical on Scripture, his professorship was withdrawn, and within a year he had lost his faith—a fact he hid from everyone. He lived for years within the Church, to the eyes of all a believing Christian priest. His published works, *La Religion d'Israel* and *Etudes évangeliques* propounded his acceptance of the German critics Wellhausen and Julicher. In 1902 he was censured by the Archbishop of Paris, Cardinal Richard. In the field of scriptural studies, Loisy had by now become a complete follower of the eschatological school of Biblical criticism.

Properly to evaluate the checkered career of the Abbé Loisy one must keep in mind the confused intellectual state of the Church. The modernists who were undermining dogmatic, moral and ascetical theology and Sacred Scripture had yet to be condemned. Tyrell

[8] *Ibid.*, p. 28.
[9] A brief survey of Loisy's life and work may be found in A. C. Cotter, S.J., "Alfred Loisy," *Theological Studies*, Vol. 2 (1946), pp. 242–251.

in England, Fogazzaro and Murri in Italy, Hébert in France were propounding new theories, new approaches in every facet of Catholic teaching. If one were not a specialist in every field how could he say that this interpretation was wrong, that was right? The Church was paralyzed, frozen by the seemingly unending flow of themes. The progress of modern knowledge in many fields seemed to overwhelm even the most brilliant.

Alfred Loisy was destined to be the line of demarcation, the historical point at which the Church would confront the modernist advance and turn it back on all fronts: Scripture, dogma, moral theology, ascetics, history. The German critic Harnack had published the *Essence of Christianity* in 1900, presenting the Jesus of the liberal school, that is, the doctrine that Jesus' teaching was the idea of God revealing Himself as the Father of all. Loisy, be it remembered, was a convinced eschatologist, and in turning upon Harnack he did so as an eschatologist rather than a believing Christian in the traditional sense. He flatly contradicted and seemingly refuted Harnack in a work called *L'Evangile et l'église*. Catholics, delighted with the rebuttal of Harnack, blinded to the implications of eschatology, greeted Loisy with open arms. Prepublication encouragement was given by Archbishop Mignot in France; Wilfred Ward in England praised it, as did Dom Amelli, the Abbot of Monte Cassino. Battifol, hesitating to suspect that its implications were true, coming from such a distinguished figure as Loisy, charitably spoke of it as "a work of mystification." [10] The Dominican Scripture scholar, Père Marie-Joseph Lagrange read it, understood it, and over the tumult of enthusiastic reviews called for its immediate condemnation.

When the shouting and the tumult of the modernist era passed it became evident that Lagrange had been right. In the cold light of reason, *L'Evangile et l'église* was a denial of the divinity of Christ, of the divine institution of the Church, of the hierarchy and the sacraments, and finally of the unchanging nature of Christian doctrine. Within a year, the new Pope, Pius X, issued the encyclical *Pascendi* against the modernists who then left the Church and with

[10] An interesting account of the reception accorded the work may be found in Maisie Ward's *Insurrection vs. Resurrection* (London: Sheed & Ward, 1937), pp. 161 ff.

them went Alfred Loisy. From the ashes of Loisy's discredited career the figure of Père Marie-Joseph Lagrange began to emerge.

Père Marie-Joseph Lagrange (1855–1938)

The life and work of Père Lagrange stands as one of the principal influences in the contemporary Biblical revival in France. Reaction to the critics, the direction of the Teaching Church, and the tradition of Biblical scholarship stemming from Père Lagrange have each in its own way served to give direction, substance and impetus to the Biblical movement as we find it in France today.

Lagrange was born in the little town of Bourg-en-Bresse in 1855, received his earlier education at Autun, and went to Paris as a young man to study law. After he received his doctorate of law he served the one-year compulsory military service required of all French youths, and in 1879 at the age of twenty-four entered the Dominican Order. He did his theological studies at the University of Salamanca in Spain, and was ordained in 1883. Five years later he was sent by his superiors to study oriental languages at the University of Vienna. Two years later, in 1890, he was in the Holy Land where he had been commissioned to open a school for the study of Scripture.

The choice of Palestine for such a school was extremely fortuitous. Of necessity, the geographical element, long missing from the abstract works of the Biblical critics, would now provide a new scientific element in the reconstruction of the human framework in which the Bible was written. The modest little school opened on the 15th day of November in 1890, and Lagrange began his lifework. In 1892 the *Révue biblique*, the scholarly organ of the school, began publication.

The life of Père Lagrange as he lived through these momentous days may be divided, like the Bible he loved so well, into the periods of the Old and New Testaments. He began work immediately on Old Testament criticism and its geographical background. During 1893 and 1897 he toured the Holy Land, and definitely located such Biblical sites as Sodom, Petra and Sinai. This establishment of authentic sites and the geographical reconstruction of the environment of the Jews mark a decisive point in the critical studies of the Pentateuch.

Lagrange journeyed to Europe in August of 1897 to deliver a paper on the "Sources of the Pentateuch" to the Scientific Congress of Catholics being held at Fribourg. From this period through the modernist crisis he was subjected to continual criticism and denunciation at Rome by the conservative and traditional Catholics who had rejected all criticism out of hand. In 1902 he lectured at the Institut Catholique in Toulouse, and the following year published these conferences in *Méthode historique,* destined to rank among the most lasting of his contributions.[11]

The year 1903 witnessed a turning point; he was directed by authority to turn his labors toward the New Testament. The life and death struggle with modernism had now passed to the battleground of the New Testament. Furthermore, the Pentateuchal question of origin and authorship had become too touchy. Many ecclesiastical authorities believed that Lagrange for this reason should leave the field of Old Testament and turn to that of the New. Despite the manifestations of displeasure with his work, Leo XIII appointed him a member of the Pontifical Biblical Commission in 1903, and in that year encouraged his publication of an up-to-date scientific commentary on Sacred Scripture in a series called *Etudes bibliques.*

His conferences on the Gospels and the Church (during 1917–1918 at the Institut Catholique in Paris) were published,[12] and he turned out many needed but less scholarly works as well. Among the more popular were: *The Gospel of Jesus Christ, The Meaning of Christianity According to Luther, Christ and Renan, M. Loisy and Modernism.* His scholarship was evident in his contributions to the *Révue biblique,* and the *Etudes bibliques,* as well as in the books: *Etude sur les religions sémitiques* (1903); *Le Messianisme chez les juifs,* and *Le Judaisme avant Jésus-Christ* (1931); *Historie ancienne du canon du Nouveau Testament* (1933); *La Critique textuelle du Nouveau Testament* (1935); *La Critique historique, les mystères: l'orphisme* (1937). In addition to these popular and scholarly works, Lagrange published a number of commentaries on the books of the New Testament: *Saint Mark* (1910); *Epistle of the Romans* (1916);

---

[11] Translated in English as *Historical Criticism and the Old Testament* (London, 1905).

[12] *The Meaning of Christianity* (London, 1920).

Epistle to the Galatians (1918); *The Gospel of St. Luke* (1921); *The Gospel of St. Matthew* (1923); *The Gospel of St. John* (1925); *The Synopsis Evangelica* (1926); and the *Evangile de Jésus-Christ* (1928).[13]

The encyclopedic mind of Père Lagrange was devoted over the years to almost every facet of Biblical criticism. He published studies on the Old Testament, the New Testament, the Hellenistic backgrounds of the New Testament, and the influence of the pagan mystery religions upon the growth of Christianity.

As a person Père Lagrange was revered by his fellow religious and by his students as a man of great sanctity. His confreres marveled at the scrupulous obedience he rendered to the daily tasks of religious life. The historian also finds in him a person of such stature as can come only from sincere and unswerving obedience to the Church and his superiors. At length, worn out by his labors in the fruitful presentation of the Word of God, and grown old in the land of the Bible, Père Lagrange died on March 10, 1938.

The Accomplishments and Significance of Lagrange

Père Lagrange brought to the study of Scripture, and to the Biblical movement as a whole a valuable sense of balance. He rejected the antisupernatural prejudice that lay at the basis of Biblical criticism up to that time, he dismissed the critics' arrogant *a priori* denials of the supernatural and the consequent possibilities of supernatural intervention in human history. At the same time, while adapting the tools of critical research and inquiry, he scorned the conservative approach to the Bible that had so long neglected the human elements necessarily involved in the very idea of God's Revelation to man. Pope Pius XII, in his encyclical letters *Divino Afflante* and *Humani Generis*, would in later years as we shall see reecho Lagrange's approach, an approach that was, if we might term it so, an "incarnate" one toward Scripture. For Lagrange, in Biblical studies one must always be carefully respectful both of the God who speaks and of the man who writes.

[13] *The Gospel of Jesus Christ* (Westminster, Md.: Newman, 1943). A complete bibliography of Lagrange's works and an interesting biography may be found in F. M. Braun, O.P., *L'Oeuvre du Père Lagrange* (Fribourg, St. Paul, 1943).

It is precisely because of his commitment to Thomism that Lagrange was able to take such a balanced view of the Bible. The Thomistic notion of instrumental causality, of God using human nature or man in a given time and place as the means of His Revelation, serves to keep the importance of God and man in proper perspective. Thus, Father Richard T. Murphy, in speaking of this approach of Lagrange, comments: "For a keen Thomist like Lagrange the Bible was a divinely inspired book containing the Word of God, but it was not merely a collection of Revelations. It was also a human work, written by human instruments writing freely and without constraint under the constant, efficacious influence of the Holy Ghost." [14]

In working with the Old Testament, Lagrange could state as early as 1896 in the *Révue biblique* the principle which animated his critical work, and to which he would continually return, that ". . . only by studying the sense of the terms, the character of what is proposed and the literary forms of the books . . . we can know the thought and intention of the author." For Lagrange, then, scriptural work begins with the proper recognition of literary forms. Poetry, parables, history in the oriental sense can all influence the proper interpretation of the documents of Revelation. Furthermore, the objections of natural science to certain allegations and phenomena in the Bible were dismissed by Lagrange. For him, as for St. Augustine sixteen hundred years before, the sacred author intended no book of science or properly scientific explanation of natural phenomena, but rather used the "science" of his day in the expression of the Divine Message.

The basic problem presented by the Biblical critics was their usage of the historical method in the destruction of the credibility of both Old and New Testaments. To this problem he turned in the 1902 Conferences at Toulouse, and the fruit of his thought is permanently enshrined in the *Méthode historique*.

In this brief work Lagrange presents a threefold solution to the problem of reconciling the historical method and traditional Christianity. In ascending order of importance these solutions are: first, a renewal of his dismissal of the objections of the natural sciences

[14] Richard T. Murphy, O.P., "Père Lagrange—A Memorial," *Père Lagrange and the Scriptures* (Milwaukee: Bruce, 1946), p. 182.

(and thus Lagrange struck what was to become the deathblow of concordism—those grotesque and extravagent theories by which the findings of science were alleged to be presented, at least confusedly, in the Biblical revelation). Second, Lagrange renewed his emphasis upon the importance of literary forms, and their proper recognition in the exegesis of the Bible (a point reemphasized and asserted by Pope Pius XII in the *Divino Afflante*). Third, one must always be aware of the progressive nature of the Revelation of the Old Testament. In this progressive concept of Revelation Lagrange stated that during the four great periods of Jewish history (Patriarchal, Mosaic, Prophetical and Post-Exilic) God's Revelation grew, developed and showed substantial advancement.

This solid work and the basis of faith upon which it was founded obviated many of the Old Testament difficulties of the critics. In addition, Lagrange "baptized" the many-document theory as a source for the Pentateuch. To the principles of the *Méthode historique*, Lagrange contributed to Old Testament studies his own research in the oral and written sources of the Old Testament, and developed as well a scientific geography of the Holy Land.

The *Méthode historique* may serve as well as a transitional point for a survey of Lagrange's contributions to New Testament studies. He reissued the work within a year, and the second edition of 1904 contains a telling criticism of Loisy and of the limits of the historical method as applied to the New Testament. The eschatologists and Loisy, no less than the liberals, were now the target of an offensive. Lagrange's preoccupation with Loisy and his school saw fruit in the *Le Messianisme chez les juifs*, and the *Le Judaisme avant Jésus-Christ*, in which Lagrange, while granting the existence of eschatological thought at the time of Jesus, nevertheless rejects the excessive and unproved claims of Loisy. Condemning both liberals and eschatologists to a continuing fruitless and insoluble search for the real Jesus, he commented: "Everywhere questions are raised, but nowhere are the answers acceptable to all."

The principles of historical method as applied to the New Testament, involved for Lagrange one basic consideration, and that was the acceptence of the environment in which those books were produced, and for him that environment was the Church. Always aware of the limitations of historical method, he had even in his earlier works insisted that ". . . environment should be taken into account; and it is precisely in the Church that we have the environment in which the Scriptures appeared." Lagrange returned to this point again in the 1917–1918 conferences at the Institut Catholique in Paris, published as *The Meaning of Christianity* in 1920. In that work he insisted upon the fact that, because of her unbroken tradition, the Church alone could properly interpret the New Testament.

It was the *Méthode historique* that guided Lagrange's many commentaries on the New Testament which began to appear after 1910. They reflected his work on the synoptic problem (that is, the problem of which of the first three Gospels is the oldest and which Gospels influence which) and the Johannine question (the disputes over the author, philosophy and theology of the fourth Gospel). For Lagrange the fourth Gospel was undeniably the product of a Jewish author, a surprising position in a day when the Biblical critics were simply dismissing it as Hellenistic, and a position which today commands the allegiance of most scholarly critics. The Greek influences on early Christianity, and the alleged formative influences of the Mystery religions (positions today severely restricted by the critics themselves) also came under the judicious eye and stern judgment of Lagrange.

From this survey of his work let us turn to an evaluation of it and of Lagrange in the Biblical revival of today. Not the least of Père Lagrange's contributions to the Church was the intellectual assistance he rendered to many on the verge of losing their faith. Difficult though it may be for the modern to conceive of such an intellectual attack as Modernism presented, the awful reality of threatened loss of faith loomed before the minds of intelligent Catholics at the beginning of the twentieth century. The work, the scholarship, the brilliant erudition and the enormous talents of Lagrange steadfastly held off for many the threat to their faith. Jean Guitton has written: "Thanks to him, sincere belief could become, or at least remain, 'a reasonable service,' when everything conspired against it." [15]

The refutation and resistance that Lagrange offered the critics

---

[15] Jean Guitton, "The Influence of Père Lagrange," *ibid.*, p. 170.

was basically on their own grounds and with their own weapons. Science, archeology, geography, literary criticism and the historical method were no less a part of his approach than of many of the Biblical critics. And in this, Lagrange baptized a scholarly tradition of Biblical criticism, making it respectable in and acceptable to the Church. Always a man of balance, he was well aware of the real limitations of the historical method in particular and of Biblical criticism in general. Many of his contributions have today found their way into papal pronouncements on Scripture (to which we shall return). The present eminent state of Biblical criticism in the Church owes its origins and its tradition to the initial efforts of Père Lagrange.

If for many Catholics he was instrumental in the preservation of their faith, and for many non-Catholics the first reputable Catholic Biblical critic since Richard Simon, he is at the same time an example to Catholic Biblicists today. He labored in the Church under the dangerous clouds of suspicion raised by many, a position not unknown to French scholar-priests today. For them, his tradition of scholarship despite opposition has become a real, living and influential force that renews their dedication both to the Church and to their work.

Finally, the importance of Père Lagrange to the field of Sacred Scripture must not be gauged by his writings alone, but by the works he so firmly established as well: the Ecole Biblique in Jerusalem, its journal, *Révue biblique*, and the studies, *Etudes bibliques*. The school that he founded, because of the quality of its students and the research and scientific approach practiced there, remains one of the greatest single influences on the contemporary Biblical scene. Today, under its very able director, Père de Vaux, the Ecole Biblique continues to serve as an enormous monument to its founder. Among its many products are the archeologist Vincent, the exegetes Braun, Boismard and Benoit, and the Biblical theologian Ceslaus Spicq. The school's translation of the Bible, the *Bible de Jérusalem*, with its critical notes has been called by many the greatest vernacular version of Sacred Scripture yet produced.

In 1941, four years after his death, the Reverend Richard Murphy stated succinctly the vindication of Père Lagrange's life and work:

"That he aroused criticism, that many sincere men believed him to be a dangerous radical was almost inevitable, for he was a scholar and a pioneer, and such things were to be expected. He bore them without bitterness. What does it matter, he used to say, if my reputation suffers a bit, if thereby the truth is spread? The passing years brought peace and international recognition and an ever widening circle of friends to the old master who did for modern criticism what St. Thomas did for Aristotle." [16]

Not only has Père Lagrange's work been vindicated, but his disciples have progressed beyond the positions he outlined in his works. In his spirit they have refused to stop their work with his conclusions. Biblical science progresses, for, as Father Semain has remarked: "Father Lagrange wished to be above everything else, a furrow and not a rut." [17]

The French Biblical Tradition and the Influences That Mold It

The Catholic Biblical movement which began with Leo XIII and the work of Père Lagrange continued to dominate the scene of French theology through the twentieth century. The Abbé Vigouroux, a contemporary of Père Lagrange, was among the first to use archeological evidence against the Wellhausen synthesis. Vigouroux began as well the massive encyclopedia of Scriptural studies, the *Dictionnaire de la Bible*. Lagrange and Vigouroux were joined by Prat and Durand in New Testament criticism during the modernist era and immediately after.

During the years that followed the modernist crisis much valuable work continued among the French until the Second World War. The Institut Catholique, the Catholic University at Paris and Lyon, provided scientific background in document and manuscript work, languages, archeology and oriental background. At the Ecole Biblique, Père Louis Vincent, disciple and student of Père Lagrange, attained international respect for his studies on the backgrounds of Sacred Scripture. Most of Vincent's work has been historical, geographical and archeological and has appeared in a wide number of

[16] Richard T. Murphy, O.P., *ibid.*, p. 188.
[17] As quoted by André Legault, C.S.C., "Anointings in Galilee and Bethany," *Catholic Biblical Quarterly*, Vol. XVI (April, 1954), p. 138.

periodicals. Ferdinand Prat worked on the life of Christ and Pauline theology.[18] In 1933 Jules Lebreton published an excellent life of Christ.[19] At Louvain, Van Hoonacker, Tobac and Coppieters attempted to reconcile the findings of the German critics with Catholic teaching. These men in turn exerted influence upon the scholars Lucien Cerfaux and the gifted Abbé Coppens.[20] Van Hoonacker's influence was continued as well through Regny and Charue, while at Ghent Canon Van Imschoot represented the best of these traditions.

The Biblical movement in France and Belgium, in addition to the work and tradition set by Lagrange and his contemporaries, has received three major and formative influences: first, that of contemporary non-Catholic critics; second the teaching of the Church; and finally, relationship to the contemporary liturgical movement.

Since 1920 modern Biblical criticism has come to be dominated by the German school of form criticism *(Formgeschichte)* founded by Martin Dibelius and Rudolf Bultmann. This school sought to go behind the written sources of the Biblical manuscripts to an investigation of the oral traditions which they manifest, thus complementing a purely literary criticism of Biblical texts. The method derives from the works of the German Hermann Gunkel (1862–1932) who taught at the universities of Göttingen and Berlin, and who had successfully applied it to the Book of Genesis and the Psalms. Form criticism rests upon two basic presuppositions: that many Biblical books (the Gospels preeminently) are not one basic personal work of the sacred author, but the redactions of previously existent and well known stories and sayings; and, secondly, that as such they are the creation of the community. This method has in modern times dominated the field of the New Testament, and has admittedly provided new insights on that period of oral tradition that immediately preceded the written documents. The method of

18 Ferdinand Prat, S.J., *Jesus Christ, His Life, His Teachings and His Work* (Milwaukee: Bruce, 1950), 2 vols. *The Theology of Saint Paul* (Westminster, Md.: Newman, 1946), 2 vols.

19 Jules Lebreton, S.J., *The Life and Teaching of Jesus Christ* (New York: Macmillan, 1957).

20 Joseph Coppens, *Les Harmonies des deux Testaments* (Tournai-Paris: Desclée, 1949).

such an approach is valid and usable, while its presupposition that the Gospels, for example, are solely the creation of the Christian community, is to be rejected. Bultmann's attempt to "demythologize" the New Testament is a literary attempt to arrive at historical judgment. This unwarranted dismissal of facts simply as forms is unacceptable for the Catholic and at least questionable for the objective critic, for the Biblical authors have asserted that they are "eyewitnesses" to the facts they narrate. Nevertheless, this demythologizing process "has successfully directed scholarly attention to the theme of Revelation and the insertion of God's Word into human history . . . [and] underscored the existential nature of Biblical thought." [21]

It is not strange that such critical accomplishment and progress as form criticism represents have had a singular influence upon the work of the French, for "all modern Catholic exegetes are indebted to the tremendous stream of non-Catholic works on Biblical subjects, which flow universally over the Western world, for their suggestive ideas, scholarly exegesis and broad and bold hypotheses. These when tested and examined by the touchstone of the Rule of Faith have yielded, and continue to yield, valuable lights and fresh illustration of the truth of God's Word." [22]

In responding to the work of the form critics the French have brought into being new and vital works on the Gospels. In 1955 the *Journées bibliques* held at Louvain saw a number of new approaches to the problem of the Gospels in the light of modern research. These studies were presented by Cerfaux, de Colages, Descamps, Levie, Rigaux and others, and the work has since been edited and published in book form.[23] Other works are available by the Jesuits Malevez and Marle on the method and findings of Rudolf Bultmann.[24] Utilizing solidly established form-critical techniques, Lucien Cerfaux's *La Voix vivante de l'évangile au début de*

[21] David M. Stanley, S.J., "Towards a Biblical Theology of the New Testament," The McAuley Lectures—1958 (West Hartford: St. Joseph's College, 1959), p. 271.

[22] Leonard and Orchard, "The Place of the Bible in the Church," *Catholic Commentary on Sacred Scripture* (New York: Nelson, 1953), p. 8, col. 6h.

[23] *La Formation des évangiles: Problème synoptique et formgeschichte* (Bruges: Desclée, 1957).

[24] René Marle, S.J., *Bultmann et l'interprétation du Nouveau Testament* (Paris: Aubier, 1956) and also L. Malevez, S.J., The Christian Message and Myth (Westminster: Newman, 1959).

l'église in 1956 is preoccupied with refuting the allegation that the
Church substituted her beliefs for historical truths.[25] Cerfaux takes
up a study of the Gospel of Christ as it is co-mingled in the apostolic
tradition and the personal witness to fact by each of the Evangelists.

If the French Biblical movement is shaped by influences outside
the Church, it is to no less degree directed by the authoritative
teaching of the Church. During the period of Modernism, and
immediately afterward, the decree *Lamentabili* and the encyclical
Pascendi of Pius X against the modernists provided the guidance and
effectively determined the road which the French were to follow.
The encyclical *Spiritus Paraclitus* of Pope Benedict XV in 1920
added little that had not been said by Leo XIII or Pius X. He
reiterated again the truth and historicity of the Bible, the need for
Biblical scholarship and the true norms of interpretation. A more
substantial step, however, was taken by Pope Pius XII in the encyclical *Divino Afflante Spiritu* in 1943—a step that denoted a sweeping change in attitude on the part of authority.[26]

Pope Pius XII spoke approvingly in the *Divino Afflante* of the
enormous strides taken by Biblical scholars toward a greater knowledge of the Bible and of the life and times of Christ, and it was his
desire "to ensure that the work not only proceed without interruption, but may also daily become more perfect and fruitful." [27]

The first major change to be noted in the attitude of Church
authority was one of pleasure at the real progress of the Biblical
scholars. The second was no less radical: that the scholars were not
to limit themselves simply to the Vulgate text but to use all the
modern sciences of textual criticism, ". . . since this branch of
science has attained to such high perfection." [28] This use of the
most ancient documentary sources is meant to hasten publication by
Catholics of ". . . editions of the Sacred Books and of ancient versions brought out in accordance with these standards, which . . .
unite the greatest reverence for the sacred text with an exact
observance of all the rules of criticism." [29]

[25] Tournai: Maredsous; Paris: Casterman, 1956.
[26] All references to the *Divino Afflante* from *Rome and the Study of Scripture, op. cit.*
[27] *Ibid.*, pp. 87–88.
[28] *Ibid.*, p. 90.
[29] *Ibid.*, p. 90.

These fundamental changes in attitude expressed by the Holy Father would no doubt have delighted the heart of Père Lagrange had he lived. But the Pope was not done with approving of so much of the work that Lagrange had accomplished. Attentive to the human problems involved in Revelation, he also reiterated Lagrange's point on literary forms:

. . . the inspired writer, in composing the sacred book, is the living and reasonable instrument of the Holy Spirit. . . . Let the interpreter then, with all care and without neglecting any light derived from recent research, endeavour to determine the peculiar character and circumstances of the sacred writer, the age in which he lived, the sources written or oral to which he had recourse and the forms of expressions he employed.[30]

The entire question of literary forms is expounded by the Pope in great detail and by many examples. The study of Biblical antiquities is approved and encouraged, and praise is given to the Catholic commentators on Sacred Scripture ". . . in no way deterred by difficulties and obstacles of all kinds, [who] strove . . . to make suitable use of what learned men of the present day, by their investigation in the domain of archeology or history or philology, have made available for the solution of new questions." [31]

One commentator remarked that the encyclical was a "breath of fresh air." Others hailed the encyclical from varying points of view: as a confirmation of the work of Père Lagrange, as the definitive end of the modernist era, as the dawn of a new day in the Biblical renewal of the Church. Each evaluation seems to be true, and yet none exhausts the historical importance of the encyclical. The contemporary Biblical revival in France and Belgium, among the scholars and on the popular level as well, owes much to the brilliant and progressive leadership displayed by the Holy Father.

A final word must be said about the relationship of the Biblical revival to another movement contemporaneous with it: the liturgical renewal. Aubert, in his survey of twentieth century theological thought speaks of the scriptural, liturgical and patristic revivals as

[30] *Ibid.*, p. 96.
[31] *Ibid.*, p. 100.

mirroring a new return to the sources of theological thought.[32] The Bible is no longer looked upon as a source from which one simply draws quotations to buttress theological arguments, but has been rediscovered as the Revelation of God, the source of all theology. But the growth of this Biblical revival and that of the liturgical one as a contemporary have not been a pure happenstance. As the liturgical movement, so vitally concerned with the Word of God and its proclamation in the worship of the people of God, grew and prospered, it became increasingly aware of its Biblical basis. As Père Louis Bouyer has pointed out, a theology of the liturgy is basically the same as that of Scripture: a theology of the Word, vitally related to the Biblical movement and dependent upon it for lasting roots.[33]

The Biblical Revival in France Today

Before any approach to the Bible, one must necessarily be equipped with the best textual version possible and with a reliable historical, geographical and cultural background of the times involved in the book of Scripture under study. Five major vernacular texts of the Bible are available throughout France and Belgium. Foremost of these are the Jerusalem Bible, and also Bonsirven's version of Crampon's Bible. The late Père Bonsirven, S.J., who held the chair of New Testament Exegesis at the Pontifical Biblical Institute in Rome, also contributed numerous works on Biblical background with studies of Judaism and the Talmud. Among the Belgian productions, the Maredsous Bible and the New Testament translation of Dom Bernard Botte are extremely popular with the scholar as well as with the man in the street.

The Jerusalem Bible, the production of the Ecole Biblique in Jerusalem, remains, however, the finest product of modern scholarship.[34] The reason for this excellence lies in the enormous progress made in recent years through archeology and the discovery of

[32] Roger Aubert, *La Théologie catholique au milieu du XXᵉ siècle* (Paris: Casterman, 1954).

[33] Louis Bouyer, C. Orat., *Liturgical Piety* (Notre Dame, Ind.: University Press, 1954), pp. 253–254.

[34] *La Sainte Bible* (Paris: Editions du Cerf, 1955). Other editions exist published by Desclée de Brouwer. A new editing and revision of text and notes is now appearing book by book.

ancient manuscripts, through philology and the exploration of the real meaning behind the usage of words, and through the advances made in the critical approach, both literary and historical. The translations of the Jerusalem Bible consistently brought to bear the full weight of these advances upon the accurate establishment of the text. The critical notes that accompany the translation provide excellent commentaries upon the text in line with the findings of modern research. Such names as De Vaux, Cazelles, Gelin, Duesberg and Boismard testify to the accuracy of its translation and the high quality and excellence of its introductions and textual notes.

Since the end of World War II the historical knowledge of Judaism from the second century B.C. through the time of Christ has been enormously enhanced by the document discoveries at Qumran in the Judean desert (popularly referred to as the Dead Sea Scrolls).[35] The incorporation of what is available in these finds has enhanced the Jerusalem Bible; however, the full meaning of these discovered texts will not be appreciated until they are completely collected, correlated and evaluated—a process that involves years of work. Under the direction of Jean Carmignac, The *Révue de Qumran* began publication in 1958. It will publish the international scientific advancements made in the study of the Dead Sea manuscripts.

Utilizing traditional findings and modern research based upon the Qumran discovery, Père de Vaux, the present director of the Ecole Biblique, published in 1958 the first volume of his *Les Institutions de l'Ancien Testament*, a work which is an extremely competent guide to the tangled backgrounds of the Old Testament.[36] The advances of Biblical geography have been collated and presented by Père du Buit, O.P.[37]

A number of splendid introductions to the Bible have been

---

[35] An ample revision in the English translation makes a current work on Qumran more valuable than the original French. The author is a Polish priest of the diocese of Warsaw. Milik, *Ten years of Discovery in the Wilderness of Judea* (Napierville, Ind.: Alec R. Allenson, 1959) as Vol. 26 in the series "Studies in Biblical Theology."

[36] Ronald de Vaux, *Les Institutions de l'Ancien Testament*, Vol. I (Paris: Editions du Cerf, 1958).

[37] Père M. du Buit, O.P., *Géographie de la Terre Sainte* (Paris: Editions du Cerf, 1959).

written in modern France and Belgium. Among the most popular are the works of Daniel-Rops, the introduction by Charue, as well as those of the Abbé Poelman and the work of Aigrain and Englebert.[38] A work of higher quality, widely praised and translated, is Dom Célestin Charlier's *La Lecture chrétienne de la Bible*.[39] The recently published *La Bible* of Père Jean Levie, S.J., containing a history of the scriptural movement in the Church, and the norms of exegesis has been judged by many as one of the most valuable introductions available.[40]

A word should be said about a work simply entitled *Introduction à la Bible*, co-edited by the late Sulpician, Abbé A. Robert, and Abbé A. Feuillet.[41] The first volume *Introduction générale—Ancien Testament*, appeared in 1957. Up-to-date and using evidence gathered from the excavations and studies, many of the French scholars of the caliber of Cazelles and Gelin contributed a series of essays on inspiration, interpretation, the norms of Biblical criticism, and the books of the Old Testament. The preface was penned by Bishop Weber of Strasbourg, a Scripture scholar himself. However, despite the general excellence of the work and the enthusiastic reception it received in scriptural circles, there were those who felt the work to be "dangerous."

The critics of this work were French—a sobering thought for many who view the French scene with pure optimism. The objection of these French integralists was that they felt the work to be entirely too critical, and too reliant upon the historical method. The tradition of conservative reaction that had plagued the work of Lagrange fifty years earlier is still a force to be reckoned with in France. There were other critics, of far more liberal and progressive propensities, who, while not objecting to the critical apparatus of

[38] René Aigrain and Omer Englebert, *Prophecy Fulfilled* (New York: McKay, 1958). Poelman, *How To Read the Bible* (New York: Kenedy, 1951). Also the works of Daniel-Rops: *Sacred History* (New York: Longmans Green, 1949); *The Book of Books, the Story of the Old Testament* (New York: Kenedy, 1956); *The Book of Life, the Story of the New Testament* (New York: Kenedy, 1956); *Jesus and His Times* (New York: Dutton, 1956); *Saint Paul* (Chicago: Fides, 1953).

[39] Dom Célestin Charlier, *The Christian Approach to the Bible* (Westminster, Md.: Newman, 1958).

[40] Jean Levie, S.J., *La Bible: Parole humaine et message de Dieu* (Paris-Louvain: Desclée de Brouwer, 1958).

[41] A. Robert and A. Feuillet (eds.) *Introduction à la Bible* (Tournai: Desclée, 1957–1959), 2 vols. An approved revision of Vol. I was published in 1959.

the *Introduction à la Bible* nevertheless felt that there was an excessive negligence displayed toward the theology of the Old Testament. For these men the lack of accent upon the theological meaning of the Old Testament was sufficient reason for refusing support to the work when it came under attack. The attack upon the work, and its limited success, was carried out by the conservatives.

Delated to the Holy Office, it is significant to note that no condemnation was issued, and furthermore there was no request for removal from circulation—in fact, as far as the Holy Office was concerned, no objection could be taken to the work. The conservatives, however, were not to be deprived of some consolation, and so they obtained in 1958 a directive from the Sacred Congregation of the Seminaries forbidding the use of *Introduction à la Bible* in the seminaries, either as a textbook or as a work to be used in preparing lectures on Scripture.

Must a Catholic feel in the light of these developments that there is something abhorrent in the work of Robert, Feuillet and their collaborators? By no means, for there has been no official reprobation of the work by the Church, but merely the judgment that at the present time those responsible for seminary education do not feel that such a work is suitable for the seminarist beginning his studies in Sacred Scripture. This attitude of praise and reservation has been adopted by others.[42] That the *Introduction à la Bible* is not at all what its detractors claim it to be is evident from the fact that after slight and extremely minor revision a new publication (1959) has met with full ecclesiastical approval.

Scholarly and theological exploration of the Old Testament has continued to move ahead. Work on Old Testament theology has been begun by Van Imschoot.[43] Cazelles, Gelin and Botte have contributed to a study of Moses and the Mosaic tradition in the

[42] Father McKenzie comments that Robert and Feuillet's work is in the Roman letter ". . . described as unsuitable because it does not meet the principles and method of sound pedagogy and for other reasons unspecified . . . [this] prohibits no one from reading the book or placing it in the library. Msgr. J. J. Weber also warns in the Preface that it is not a book which the teacher may place in the hands of the student with the simple recommendation to read. . . ." John L. McKenzie, S.J., in his review of the book and the action of the Sacred Congregation: "Book Reviews," *Theological Studies*, Vol. 20 (March, 1959), p. 108.

[43] Van Imschoot, *Théologie de l'Ancien Testament* (Tournai: Desclée, 1956), 2 vols.

shaping of Old Testament theology published in 1955.[44] Most of these competent critics collaborated on the Jerusalem Bible, and their introductions written at the time to each book of the Bible provide some of the finest, as well as the most up-to-date scholarship available on the Old Testament.

Studies of the formation of the Gospels because of the critical work of the form critics has not exclusively dominated the field of New Testament studies. Braun, Boismard and Bouyer have published works around the themes of the Johannine Gospel. In 1957 the age-old problem of the date of the Passion of Christ in the Synoptics and John was reopened with an exhaustive study by Miss Annie Jaubert.[45] An assistant professor at the Sorbonne, she studied at the Ecole Biblique, and utilized modern patristic studies, the Qumran findings and a complete investigation of the calendars of the period. As a result of her work she produced an entirely new reconciliation of the Gospel accounts.

Important works on the Gospels have been published by Pierre Benoit, O.P., Xavier Léon-Dufour, S.J., and Dom Jacques Dupont. Dupont, professor of Sacred Scripture at the Abbey of St. André, published in 1949 his dissertation: *Gnosis: la connaisance religieuse dans les épîtres de St. Paul,*[46] and he has worked on the Acts of the Apostles for the Jerusalem Bible. In 1954 he published his monumental study of the Beatitudes: *Les Béatitudes: le problème littéraire; le message doctrinal.*[47] No contemporary study of the Beatitudes could ever ignore this important work, and Dupont's place among the scholars of the New Testament is guaranteed by this work alone. Père Jean Galot, S.J., has published a fine study of the place of Mary in the Gospels marked by a penetrating examination of the Marian texts of the Gospels.[48]

Lucien Cerfaux, now professor emeritus at the University of Louvain, has for many years been a singular and formative influence

---

[44] *Moise, l'homme de l'alliance,* Cahiers Sioniens (Paris: Desclée, 1955).

[45] Annie Jaubert, *La Date de la Cène: calendrier biblique et liturgie chrétienne* (Paris: Gabalda, 1954).

[46] Dupont, *Gnosis* (Louvain: Nauwelaerts, 1949).

[47] Dupont, *Les Béatitudes: le problème littéraire; le message doctrinal* (Louvain; Nauwelaerts, 1954). A complete revision was brought out during 1958-1959.

[48] Jean Galot, S.J., *Marie dans l'évangile* (Paris: Desclée, 1958).

in the field of Pauline theology.[49] It is interesting to note in the work of such speculative theologians as de Lubac, Congar and others the frequent references on Pauline questions and interpretation to the works of Canon Cerfaux. Other modern contributions to the growth of Pauline studies have been made by Dupont (in his *Gnosis*), Benoit, Spicq, Cambier and the Franciscan Rigaux.[50]

Many of the finest productions of French scholarship in the field of Sacred Scripture have not been limited to the consumption of other specialists, but have been placed on the market for a wide popular reading. This has been accomplished through collections such as the *Lectio Divina,* and *Témoins de Dieu.* The work and writing of these men have thus been brought to an ever wider audience.

It is well also to note the important developments of the French scriptural scene in making the Bible known and loved by many. In Belgium, "Biblical Days" were organized by Canon Coppens at the University of Louvain. Retreats for clergy and religious have been given by eminent scriptural critics. In Brussels under Abbé Poelman, and in Louvain under Dom Botte, "Biblical Circles" have been established for a more fruitful and accurate study of the Word of God. At Liège, the *"Union des religieuses enseignantes"* was formed, particularly for nuns and sisters. The *Ligue catholique de l'évangile* in France coordinates and popularizes Biblical materials, as well as publishing the useful little quarterly *Evangile.* No periodical in France and Belgium has remained untouched by the Biblical revival, so that excellent articles on Scripture may be found in *La Vie spirituelle, La Maison Dieu, Lumière et vie, Lumen Vitae, Paroisse et litturgie,* and the *Nouvelle revue théologique.* The popular picture magazine *Fêtes et saisons* frequently publishes special Biblical numbers, and even diocesan magazines such as *Evangiliser* and *Esprit et vie* contain fine articles on Sacred Scripture.

In France among the many collections the *Témoins de Dieu* series

---

[49] Two of Cerfaux's finest works have been published in English, *Christ in the Theology of St. Paul,* and *the Church in the Theology of Saint Paul,* (New York, Herder & Herder, 1959).

[50] See the interesting collection of papers delivered at the 1952 *Journées Bibliques* at Louvain on the Pauline teaching on the Messianic hope by Rigaux and others (Coppens, Cerfaux, Descamps), *L'Attente du Messie* (Bruges: Desclée, 1954).

presents the life and work of great Biblical personages. In order to stimulate popular reading of the Bible the *Ligue de l'évangile* was established. A number of fine introductions on an extremely popular level are available in the series *Pas à pas avec la Bible*, Grelot's *Introduction aux livres saints*, and Joly's *Aux Sources bibliques*.

The observer of the contemporary scene cannot help but be struck by the power and undeniable impetus of the French Biblical movement. The popularization of the Bible by scholars themselves bears adequate testimony to the comprehension of the French Biblical movement, and also to the apostolicity that inspires it. The Abbé Moeller of Louvain has commented:

We think that the Biblical revival is not only deeply linked with a return of the Church to its sources but also with its universal missionary vocation. To the extent in which the Christian message will appear to the world in its Biblical clothing (and liturgical, for the Liturgy is "the Bible prayed, lived, communicated in by the Church"), to that same extent missionary expansion will be founded on its fundamental providential design. There is a harmony between the Bible and the modern world. Doubtless, the paradoxical, "scandalous," nature of the Divine Word remains; we must avoid the danger of minimizing it, as certain "preachers" are doing today. On the contrary, this paradox ought to give the world a shock. But in so doing it will awaken the deepest harmonies in the modern soul. The Bible reveals itself as much more in tune with the universality of the world's cultures than at first sight; it is far easier to transmit a concrete, existential thought, founded on the action of God with regard to man, than abstract systems. In the exact measure in which the Christian message is centered on the Bible lived in the Church, it is seen as fundamentally based on the intervention of God in history, through the Incarnation. At the same time the "unique" character of Christianity . . . will be clearly shown; Christianity will no longer be a philosophy, a doctrine, one system among others, but on the contrary the Divine response, in action, in the Person of the Incarnate Son, to the expectation of the peoples.[51]

The Development of Biblical Theology

Owing to a shift of emphasis among Protestants in Biblical criticism, and the insistence upon the theological value of Scripture by

[51] Abbé Charles Moeller, "The Bible and Modern Man," *Lumen Vitae*, Vol. 10 (Jan., 1955), p. 64.

Pope Pius XII, the Biblical revival in France and throughout the world has taken a new turn toward the construction of a Biblical theology. The scholars are now producing works centered about the great Biblical themes, and these in turn provide the groundwork for what is gradually developing into a Biblical theology.

The change of heart manifested by the German Biblical critics in their attempt to return the Biblical message of salvation has ". . . contributed to the present revitalization of European Protestantism. These scholars have managed, especially through their studies in Biblical theology, produced so abundantly and so competently in the last dozen years, to satisfy a deeply felt need for a more positive, dogmatic structure in renascent Protestant Christianity." [52] Foremost amongst European scholars marking this Protestant critical approach to the restoration of Biblical theology has been Oscar Cullmann, now Professor at the Sorbonne. Cullmann's influence has been felt strongly in the French Biblical revival.

Pope Pius XII, in stressing the theological value of the sacred text, gave timely direction to the Biblical movement. Catholic Biblical critics ". . . were so engrossed with countering the attacks of rationalist and modernist foes, that they had little time and no taste for the doctrinal exploitation of the inspired text." [53] Papal direction coupled with the influence of Protestant Scripture scholars has initiated this new movement in the Church.

In his work on twentieth century Catholic theology Aubert draws a parallel between two textbooks on dogmatic theology.[54] One lists the attributes of God in the conventional manner: Essence, simplicity, immutability and so forth. The other presents the same theme thus: The Most-High, the All-Present, the Unique, the Merciful One, the Father. The point that Aubert is making is that a new atmosphere for the study of dogma has been created. This he maintains is attributable basically to the Biblical revival. However, the Biblical movement has gone beyond the simple creation of a positive atmosphere for the study of theology and now aims at the construction of a theology of the Bible.

The series *Témoins de Dieu, Etudes bibliques, Lectio Divina,*

---

[52] Daniel M. Stanley, S.J., *op. cit.,* p. 269.
[53] *Ibid.,* p. 269.
[54] Roger Aubert, *op. cit.*

Bible et vie chrétienne represents the first steps taken toward a Biblical theology. The initial works of the movement appeared in the early 1950's. Abbé Descamps published in 1950 his *Les Justes et la justice dans les évangiles et le christianisme primitif*,[55] and Père Guillet in 1951 produced the *Thèmes bibliques: études sur l'expression et le développement de la révélation*.[56] These two works heralded the beginnings of Biblical theology among the French. The mid-1950's witnessed three eminent publications: Van Imschoot in Belgium published his two volumes on a theology of the Old Testament in 1956.[57] The following year Bonsirven published a study of New Testament theology around the central theme of the Kingdom of God.[58] Bonsirven's work was highly praised and well received. In 1958 the extremely capable Dominican, Père A. M. Dubarle, Professor of Scripture at the Dominican house of studies at Saulchoir, published a work for the *Lectio Divina* series dealing with a Biblical-theological approach to the question of original sin.[59]

The basic work, however, has been that done by the key figure in the field of Biblical theology among the French: Père Ceslaus Spicq, O.P. He was born in 1901, studied at the Ecole Biblique in Jerusalem, and at Le Saulchoir. From 1928 to 1953 he held the New Testament chair at the University of Fribourg. In 1950 he called attention to the new trend beginning to emerge in Biblical studies in an article on *L'Avènement de la théologie biblique*.[60] Choosing the notion "love-*agape*" as a basis and central theme for Biblical theology he began publication of a series of works about this theme in 1955 with *Agape: prolégomènes à une étude de théologie néo-testamentaire*.[61] In this work he advanced the definition of charity as a cordial love impregnated by respect. The work was firmly based upon linguistic research and analysis of the Greek classics, the Septuagint and ancient Jewish traditions. Carrying his analysis of *agape* into the New Testament he published two volumes

---

[55] Descamps, *Les Justes et la justice* (Louvain: Presses Universitaires, 1950).
[56] Guillet, *Thèmes bibliques* (Paris: Aubier, 1957).
[57] Van Imschoot, *Théologie de l'Ancien Testament, op. cit.*
[58] Bonsirven, S.J., *Le Règne de Dieu* (Paris: Aubier, 1957).
[59] Dubarle, O.P., *Le Péché originel dans l'Ecriture* (Paris: Editions du Cerf, 1958).
[60] Spicq, O.P., "L'Avenement de la théologie biblique," *Revue des sciences philosophiques et theologiques*, Vol. 35 (1951), pp. 566 ff.
[61] Louvain: *Studia Hellenistica*, 1955.

in 1958 and 1959 on *Agape dans le Nouveau Testament*.[62] The work of Spicq gives promise upon completion of being a theological landmark signifying the first flowering of Biblical theology.

Père Spicq, writing in the *Révue des sciences philosophiques et théologiques* in 1958, went even further on the question of Biblical theology than he did in his article of eight years previous.[63] He draws attention in this article to the great need of a unifying theme for Biblical theology. Although, he admits, that it is Christ, both the event and the doctrine of Christ, that constitutes a recapitulation of both Old and New Testaments, he questions the reduction of all Biblical theology to a Christology. For a central notion, it is not surprising that Spicq advances "love-*agape*." For him, *agape* is expressive not only of the central mystery of God but also of the theme of all Scripture, the reciprocal relations of God and man. It would be erroneous to think, however, that Spicq ignores the many tasks that would be required for such a construction as a Biblical theology envisages. But, for him, it is this "love-*agape*" concept that will provide a theme of harmonious construction.

The work of Spicq's fellow Dominican, Marie-Emile Boismard, and of Père Louis Bouyer of the Oratory, have also been significant contributions to Biblical theology.[64] Both have concentrated upon the Johannine writings and contributed to the *Lectio Divina* series. Boismard writes frequently for the *Révue biblique*, and has worked on the Fourth Gospel and the Apocalypse for the Jerusalem Bible. He is at present continuing his research at the Ecole Biblique. Bouyer has also published a study of the concept of "Wisdom" in the Old Testament, and in 1958 Yves Congar contributed to the growing lists of Biblical-theological works with a study of the Presence of God.[65]

[62] Paris: Gabalda, 1958–1959.

[63] Spicq, O.P., "Nouvelles réflexions sur la théologie biblique," *Revue des sciences philosophiques et théologiques*, Vol. 42 (1958), pp. 200 ff. Abridged in English as "The Work of Biblical Theology," *Theology Digest*, Vol. 7 (Winter, 1959), pp. 29–34.

[64] Boismard, O.P., *Saint John's Prologue* (Westminster, Md., Newman, 1956); also *Du Baptême et Cana* (Paris: Editions du Cerf, 1958). Bouyer, *The Meaning of Sacred Scripture* (Notre Dame, Ind.: University Press, 1958); and also *Le Quatrième évangile* (Tournai: Casterman, 1955).

[65] Bouyer, *Le Trône de la sagesse* (Paris: Editions du Cerf, 1957). Also Yves Congar, O.P., *Le Mystère du temple ou l'économie de la présence de Dieu à sa creature de la Genèse à l'Apocalypse* (Paris: Editions du Cerf, 1958).

Thus it is that it is only in the past few years that the concept of Biblical theology itself has been worked out. "It is, first of all, theology in its own right, not the raw materials from which systematic theology can be constructed. It is a branch of positive, as distinct from, scholastic theology . . . a synthesis which, while remaining within Biblical categories of thought, exposes in the language of today the various aspects of the Christian reality, expressed with graduated clarity by the inspired writers of the New Testament." [66]

The first steps toward a Catholic Biblical theology have been taken in modern France and Belgium. Nor can one say that this growing concept is not "traditional" in the very best sense of that term, for as Father MacKenzie has remarked, a Christian of the first 1500 years would not understand such a term as Biblical theology, and would have asked, "What other kind of theology is there?" The first fifty years of the Catholic Biblical movement, the work of scholars throughout the world, has provided the necessary tools for this magnificent development in the approaches to Biblical theology. There is no doubt that this will constitute the major preoccupation of French theologians in the years that lie ahead.

2. THE LITURGICAL MOVEMENT

The liturgical movement that persists in contemporary France is a movement that began in the nineteenth century and continues with unabated fervor to the present day. The Abbot Guéranger and the Benedictine restoration at Solesmes in 1872 certainly mark the beginning of the modern liturgical revival; however, it would be inaccurate to consider the movement itself as the singular product of the Franco-Belgian complex.[67] Although it had its beginnings among the French it was soon adopted by the Germans, and received from them sound theological and historical foundation. The strength lacking in the unfortunate weakness of scholarship displayed by Guéranger was supplied by the Germans, and the move-

[66] David M. Stanley, S.J., *op. cit.*, pp. 277–278.
[67] A brief treatment of the historical development of the liturgical movement may be found in Oliver Rousseau, O.S.B., *The Progress of the Liturgy* (Westminster, Md.: Newman, 1951).

ment itself received at the turn of the century firm direction from the Holy See.

A few short years after the restoration of Solesmes, the Abbey of Mont-César was established at Louvain in Belgium, a house destined to exert great influence and orientation upon the liturgical movement. From too great a concern for accidentals and ritual considerations of liturgy the movement has progressed consistently through the years to become today a primarily pastoral one. It has come to signify an interest primarily concerned with the restoration of the full Christian life to the Christian people. This liturgical revival might be characterized as theologically sound, built upon the fountainheads of Scripture and the Fathers, and marked by dynamic social implications.

Those disparate elements and groups of liturgists from the period of Guéranger to Pius X were galvanized by his pontificate into the forerunner of contemporary pastoral liturgy. Saint Pius X in his *Decree on Frequent Communion*, and the *Motu Proprio on Sacred Music* definitely shaped the movement as a primarily pastoral one, having as its object the complete participation of all according to their function in the Church.

After Pius X came the moving influence of Dom Lambert Beauduin. Beauduin had been a parish priest and later a monk at Mont-César, and in addition to his natural talents brought to the movement theological ability. Beauduin founded the Belgian Pastoral Liturgical Movement, and through the years his work found capable assistance in the projects of Dom Caspar Lefebvre and the Abbey of St. André-les-Burges.

At the Abbey of Maredsous two great contributions were made to the liturgical movement. The first of these was the spiritual writing of Dom Columba Marmion. Basing retreats, conferences, and sermons, which he later collected and edited, on the solid base of dogma, Scripture and liturgy, Marmion began a trend of spiritual writing based on the sources of the Christian life.[68] Maredsous' second contribution was the establishment of the *Revue bénédictine* which was to provide examples of exacting scholarship for the

[68] The well known uniform translation and publication of Dom Marmion's works has been done by Herder of St. Louis, Mo.

liturgical movement. French and Belgian scholarship was complemented by the Germans, Casel and Herwegen, and the Benedictine foundations at Maria Laach and Beuron. Today the intellectual heritage of the liturgical movement is ably represented by the research work in liturgy carried out by Dom Bernard Botte, and the superior of Mont-César, the talented Abbot Cappelle.

During this period of Belgian and German contributions the French, Church historians, for the most part, brought to the liturgical movement the important results of their study and research. In the early twentieth century Abbé Duchesne, Msgr. Battifol, Dom Cabrol and Dom Henri Leclercq were responsible for a number of significant works. The most important of these was Duchesne's *Les Origines du culte chrétien*, which included an ordinal believed lost to history, as well as an extremely penetrating and critical study of the first historical stages of Christian worship. Of equal value was the monumental *Dictionnaire d'archéologie et de liturgie* begun by Dom Leclercq with the assistance of Cabrol.

Today scientific studies in the liturgy, of practical value as well as of intellectual importance, are published in the series *Etudes liturgiques* and *Lex Orandi* published by Editions du Cerf. The periodical La *Maison-Dieu* is devoted to one liturgical theme in each issue, calls upon some of the greatest theologians for its contributors and has deeply enriched the field of contemporary liturgical study.

Depth has also come from the Biblical field, and both the Biblical and liturgical movements have interacted upon each other. Thus, much of a specifically liturgical value can be found in the Biblical periodical *Bible et vie chrétienne*. Other periodicals such as *Lumen Vitae* and *La Vie spirituelle* carry scholarly articles of liturgical interest.

As has been remarked it is the accent of pastoral liturgy that dominates the contemporary scene. The Abbey of Mont-César publishes the periodical *Questions liturgiques et paroissiales* specifically for the clergy. The *Bulletin paroissial liturgique*, begun by Dom Caspar Lefebvre, has since become the *Paroisse et liturgie* and exercises enormous influence upon the clergy of France and Belgium.

In pre-World War II Belgium the Abbey of Mont-César organized liturgical weeks. Today, the Abbey provides courses in liturgy for the pastors and students at Louvain, and also annual liturgy courses for seminary professors from all over the world. In France, in addition to the Liturgical Institute established at the Institut Catholique in Paris, there are annual meetings of theologians, historians, liturgists, canonists, and Biblical and patristic experts. In these meetings they are joined by priests in the active work of parishes, missions, retreats, and chaplaincies. The collaboration achieved by both groups at these annual study meetings in Vanves are sponsored by the French organization Centre Pastorale Liturgique.

The Centre Pastorale Liturgique itself is modeled upon the lines indicated by Dom Beauduin, and serves as the central unifying force for the liturgical movement in France. It is interesting to note that in the CPL not only are the Benedictines active but, equally, the Dominicans, Jesuits, Oratorians, secular clergy and even laymen. Among the most active are the Dominican Roguet, Canon Martimort, and Père Concoeur. The basic activity of CPL is to translate the fruits of the liturgical movement to the people. Missals are published in great variety for every possible type of person and in great numbers. The popular monthly *Fêtes et saisons* frequently presents an attractive presentation of a liturgical theme prepared by CPL. Pamphlets, records, filmstrips and extremely artistic movies are also made available by CPL. The liturgical revival therefore makes effective use of the arts. Not only are these products of the CPL to be found in abundance, but there exists the extremely able periodical *Art d'église* (formerly *Artisan liturgique*) from the Abbey of St. André. In the field of music there is the popular revival of Gregorian chant. The music of the Psalter is used in the admirable compositions of the Jesuit Père Gelineau. Good music is promoted by *Musica Sacra* published at Malines. Nor are the catechetical fields left untouched by the liturgists; two periodicals are published devoted to catechetics and the liturgy: *Notre catéchèse* and *Croisade liturgique à l'école*.

In both Belgium and France the liturgical movement has constantly received encouragement, assistance, and direction from the episcopacy. There exist episcopal committees for the pastorate and liturgy which have been an essential and directive force in the growth of the movement. This direction is exemplified in the excellent *Directoire pour la pastorale des sacraments*, issued in 1951,[69] and the *Directoire pour la pastorale de la messe* in 1956.[70]

If one were to estimate the contemporary contributions of theologians to the field of liturgy one would have to include practically every major voice in French theology. De Lubac, Congar, Spicq and others have expressed a liturgical orientation in many of their works. The tradition of exacting research begun by Duchesne is represented today by the scholarly contributions left us by Msgr. Michel Andrieu, who was Dean of the Theology Faculty at the University of Strasbourg. He has published authoritative studies on the Roman Ordinals and the Roman Pontifical.[71] On the contemporary scene three men stand out for extremely important contributions, each on a different level: Dom Bernard Botte, Père A.-M. Rouget, O.P., and Père Louis Bouyer.

Dom Botte works on a particularly high level of scholarship, contributing to various periodicals, and he has recently prepared a new version of Baumstark's study of comparative liturgy by overhauling it in line with the most modern research.[72] His lasting contribution has been his translation of the Roman Mass in collaboration with Miss Christine Mohrmann, a world-wide Latin authority.[73] Père Roguet writes on an entirely different level. His excellent studies on the Mass and the sacraments are written for popular consumption.[74] There is no doubt that Roguet succeeds enormously well in the specific field he has chosen; the popular rendition and translation of the very best in liturgical scholarship.

Père Bouyer occupies a level somewhere between the two. While scholarly and scientific in liturgical research, he is preeminently a patrologist and theologian, and aims at being understood. His work is a classical example of the French technique of *haute vulgarisation*.

[69] Paris, 1951.

[70] Paris, 1956.

[71] Michel Andrieu, *Les Ordines Romani du haut moyen-âge* (Louvain, 1931); also *Le Pontifical romain au moyen-âge*, "*Studi e testi*" (Vatican City: Biblioteca Apostolica Vaticana, 1938–1941).

[72] Anton Baumstark, *Comparative Liturgy* (Westminster, Md.: Newman, 1958).

[73] Botte and Mohrmann, *L'Ordinaire de la messe* (Paris: Editions du Cerf, 1953).

[74] A.-M. Roguet, *Holy Mass: Approaches to the Mystery*, and *Christ Acts Through the Sacraments*, both Collegeville, Minn: Liturgical Press, 1953.

One of the great products of the liturgical revival is certainly Bouyer's *Liturgical Piety*.[75] This work was delivered in substance as a series of lectures in America at the Summer School for Liturgy at the University of Notre Dame. In fact it was written in English by Père Bouyer and appeared in the United States before its French edition. The book has had a wide and enthusiastic reception and there are few who do not make it a *sine qua non* on any reading list in liturgy. It is firmly based on a historical and scriptural sense, and offers an outline for a theology of the liturgy. After examining with skillful insight the history of the liturgical movement, Bouyer makes tentative advances toward a definition of liturgy. His examination of liturgy extends back to Old Testament rites, the Last Supper, the early Christian service and relationship with the mystery religions, and the growth of Christian liturgy. He bases liturgy upon a theology of the Word of God and the concept of covenant and community. In turn fruitful insights are gained in examining the sacraments and liturgical year in this aspect.

Finally, we must not neglect to point out that the liturgical movement in France, as elsewhere, is solidly based upon the work of two pontiffs. Its initial pastoral direction was received from the teachings of St. Pius X, and implemented by the work of Dom Lambert Beauduin. The modern driving force within the liturgical movement dates from the *Mystici Corporis* of Pius XII. When in 1950 Pope Pius XII issued the *Mediator Dei* on the sacred liturgy the French and Belgian liturgists could look upon it as their great vindication, and at the same time as their contemporary inspiration. In a later chapter we shall return to the work of the pontificate of Pius XII and its influence upon the French.

It is well one also be aware that there is no monolithic French mind entirely dedicated to the liturgical revival. There are in France, as elsewhere, many closed minds, diffident personalities for whom pastoral liturgy, like the Biblical revival it depends on, is simply the product of extremism and of little real value for religion. The few apologists that the French have had in the English-speaking world have unfortunately labored too long and too hard to create their

---

[75] Bouyer, *Liturgical Piety, op. cit.* An earlier work, now dated because of changes is his study of the Holy Week liturgy, *The Paschal Mystery* (Westminster, Md.: Newman, 1949).

representations of the "French spirit" as opposed to or different from the American one. No nation has a monopoly on sound theological approaches based upon the sources, and there are conservative and even reactionary elements in all nations. Perhaps on the whole the French have progressed far ahead of the American Church in the use of the sources, but they, as well as we, have a significant number of individuals serving to check, and occasionally effectively block, the progress that paradoxically lies in a return to the sources. Thus, for example, in 1959 a distinguished French liturgiologist in a study of the *Ceremoniale episcoporum*, which was valuable in some respects, nevertheless could openly lament the growth of pastoral liturgy and the entire liturgical movement. For him, liturgy connotes the baroque conceptions of splendor and ceremony that dominated the churchmen of the seventeenth, eighteenth and early nineteenth centuries. His lack of sympathy with the directives of the liturgical movement is not an altogether unusual one in the country that more than any other has come to symbolize the progress of the liturgy.

3. THE PATRISTIC REVIVAL

For modern French theologians the works of the Fathers of the Church have assumed their rightful place in the theological framework. Thus the modern theologian no longer looks back to the patristic age for its purely apologetic value, but for its properly theological value as a source of Christian theology. Aubert remarks that "the Biblical revival and the liturgical movement tend to complete themselves by a patristic renaissance."

This contemporary renewal of patristic studies among the theologians of all nations as well as the French finds its source in the monumental nineteenth century collection of the Abbé Migne: the *Patrologia Latina* and the *Patrologia Graeca*, enormous collections and collations of the texts of the Fathers. However, this French interest in patristics is not simply a nineteenth century phenomenon that may be dated from the time of Migne.[76] Migne's work is only

---

[76] A survey of Migne's life and work may be found in A. C. Cotter, S.J., "Abbé Migne and the Catholic Tradition," *Theological Studies*, Vol. 7 (1946), pp. 46–71.

the continuation of the older and perduring tradition among the French. Patristics never really died in France as an important theological influence, but this tradition was rather the heritage of the earlier Gallican spirit. Patristics was historically for the French the necessary instrument in the development of a theological continuum while the French Church remained removed from Roman influence.

Among the first patrologists in the contemporary French revival was Dom Germain Morin of Maredsous, who devoted his talents of textual criticism toward an accurate establishment of texts. Although Migne had collected the documents, these remained but raw material that had to be reworked by scholars, of whom Morin was the first. Still others took up the work of editing and critically evaluating the patristic sources. This has become a tradition of scholarship among the French, and today the names of Palanque, de Plinval, Marrou, Courcelles and Audet are known to every theologian working with the sources. The Benedictines, Leclercq and Dechant, have devoted much time and research to the medieval "fathers" in a direct line of descent from the earliest Fathers of the Church.

Much of this contemporary work done in patrology owes a debt of gratitude to the Institut de Recherche et d'Histoire des Textes, which was established by Félix Grat in Paris in 1937. Today among its directors may be found Abbé Richard, and among the many successful projects that it has supported, the enormous bibliographical work *Prosopographie chrétienne du Bas-Empire* by Henri Marrou. Canon Draguet of Louvain is working on oriental sources and is largely responsible for the *Corpus Scriptorum Christianorum Orientalium*, which began in 1903 under Chabot and whose publication is under the joint sponsorship of the University of Louvain and the Catholic University of America. Others in the Oriental Language Department of the Institut Catholique in Paris have labored in the field of patristics and the Eastern Church. At the Institut, Canon Bière, Dom Mercier, Dom Lanne, Abbé Velot, Abbé Maries and Antoine Guillaumont are carrying out original research and critical publication of texts in the original Georgian, Armenian, Coptic, Syriac and Ethiopian documents.

At Steenbruge in Belgium, the Benedictines of the Abbey of

Saint Peter have begun work on a collection destined to be a "new Migne." It is their intention to reedit all of Migne, and bring it up to date with the most accurate texts and bibliography available. Their first great step toward this goal was taken in 1950 with the publication of Dekker's *Clavis Patrum Latinorum*. In France, the Franciscan Père Hamman has undertaken what he modestly terms a "supplement to Migne." Both the work of Hamman and the Benedictines at Steenbruge are inspired by the researches of half a century. It is their intention to correct what are now obviously inaccurate allegations of authorship, and to include in the collections available to scholars hundreds of texts which were previously unknown to Migne or only recently discovered.

The series *"Sources chrétiennes"* has included a number of critically established and accurately translated texts for Iranaeus, Tertullian, Gregory of Nyssa and other Fathers. Père Audet has given us the most accurate text and commentary yet available for the oldest of non-Biblical Christian documents, the *Didache*.[77] The work of Marrou, Sagnard, Refoule, Drouzey, Bardy and others is making available to the Christian faithful the writings of the earliest Fathers of the Christian faith. Danielou and Bouyer, eminent patrologists in their own right, have popularized these findings, and draw upon patrology in their works as a source for a more fruitful Christian life.

It is certainly fitting that in any discussion of patrology among the French that we mention that most versatile and prolific theologian, Père Jean Danielou, S.J. In 1942, in collaboration with Père Henri de Lubac, he founded the *Sources chrétiennes* for the translations of Greek and Latin Fathers. Since 1945 he has edited the bibliographical bulletin of patristic studies for the *Recherches de science religieuse*.

Père Danielou has accomplished in a few short years a significant amount of work and is looked upon as one of the most thoughtful and provocative of modern French theologians—faculties that happily spring from a deep familiarity with the Fathers. He is, as well, blessed with the ability to present difficult themes to a large audience attractively. The patristic revival in modern France has a most ade-

---

[77] Jean-Paul Audet, *La Didache* (Paris: Gabalda, 1958).

quate spokesman and representative in the figure and accomplishments of Père Danielou.

In concluding this survey of the return of theologians to the sources of theology a number of observations must be made. It is evident that non-Catholic scholarship has served to occasion the Biblical movement. However, the purely negative power of reaction was not sufficient to propel this movement forward toward such depths or for such a length of time. The reason that lies behind this depth and intensity must be found in the interest of the Teaching Church, in the encouragement and direction of the Popes, and in the work and example of Père Lagrange.

Closely allied to the Biblical movement is the liturgical revival. The progress of that movement marked by the restoration of the importance of Sunday for the Christian, the Paschal liturgy and the temporal cycle over the sanctoral one, indicates a preoccupation with the theological foundations of the movement. This theological foundation seems to lie in a sound exegesis of the Word of God. To the movements of the Bible and the liturgy has been joined the French tradition of patristics with its great Christocentric themes and ideas so familiar to the other two.

The progress of the sciences, the accentuation of community and the proper place of individualism have created a mental milieu more favorable to the threefold renewal than the hinderances it faced in the closed conservative and individualistic traditions that have sprung up since the Middle Ages. The Word of God to His people, written in Scripture, proclaimed in liturgy and commented upon in the works of the Fathers of the Church, this same Word of God, as we have seen, both implies and confirms a social and corporate view of the phenomenon of man. The theology of the sources represents the paradox—progress by going back. The theology of the sources today is a reaction to the sentimental anthropomorphism that has been at the same time the heritage of medievalism. Coupled with the progress of the secular sciences, the theology of the sources has come to dominate every field of theological endeavor. It is this fact that constantly recurs in any survey of theology in France today.

IV

✿

THE THEMES OF THE
THEOLOGIANS

When we speak of the work of the theologian we use that term in its widest possible reference. Those scholars specializing in the Sacred Scriptures, the writings of the Fathers, and the progressive history of Christ's Church are no less theologians than the speculative student of dogma who attempts to synthesize all the data of Revelation. The demands and implications of Revelation in man's moral life, and in the economic, social and cultural orders are theological as well in the best sense of that word. The traditional axiom that "nothing is alien to theology" is nowhere more widely manifest than in the breadth of the contemporary theological movement in France. Up to now we have tried to survey the work of the theologians of the sources, now we shall turn to the work of "theologians" in a more properly theological and traditional sense. Some of these are dogmatic theologians in the traditional sense, and others are theologians exploring the implications of Revelation for modern man. Some of these men reflect upon the essential elements of Revelation, their relationships and synthetic construction into a "theology"; others examine the new fields opened by the mind of modern man through science and research, attempting to relate them to the absolute facts of Revelation.

One must be aware in dealing with various schools of theology and theologians of the complex sources of their thought, and the skein of interrelationships that affect the development of theological thought. The theologian may be brought to face a problem because of some external attack upon traditional belief, or simply because of the presence of some historical fact, or again because of the intellectual milieu in which he finds himself. Within theology itself there are the influences of previous work, or of necessities that face the Church, and finally the Teaching Authority of the Church herself. Thus, for example, the definition of the doctrine of the Assumption has led to an increased theological speculation concerning other privileges and dignities of the Mother of God.

In dealing with the French theological revival we find the constant interplay of ideas and theological problems stimulating and provoking still further ones. Thus, for example, in no small way the liturgical revival stimulated work in an adjacent but necessary field, Sacred Scripture. In turn both have influenced and impelled patristic studies, and in time received back from patristics reflections upon scriptural exegesis and the meaning of liturgical forms. Another example: consideration for the needs of Catholic Action in France has led to increased reflection upon the position of the layman in the Church, and upon the Church herself. This work in turn brings the problem of ecumenicism to the fore, and this, being no small problem in itself, reflects Protestant difficulties both with regard to the historical facts of heresy and with the twin problems of the Church herself and Marian dogma. The considerations of Catholic Action might, on the other hand, lead one to the considerations of liturgy and Scripture as the fundamental sources for spiritual life. Thus Scripture, liturgy, patristics, and dogma, moral theology and ascetics become inevitably intertwined.

We must conclude therefore that the simple divisions of theology by the traditional theologians themselves, as well as those devised by chroniclers of theological thought, and those divisions we adapt for this survey cannot do justice to the enormous complexity of contemporary theological thought, whether it be French, German, or that of any other nation. We have chosen, however, in this case to divide this chapter along the lines indicated in the work of five modern French theologians, and according to the theological themes they have explored. Work parallel to theirs in these thematic schemes have also been referred to.

1. ALBERT DONDEYNE–FAITH AND REASON

In a previous chapter some attention has been given to the philosophical movements of the modern day, and to the immediate development of the Thomist revival.

It is not a great step from the philosophical reflection upon the phenomenon of being to the "being" of phenomena. The Christian theologian is not simply a metaphysician or natural theologian but the contemplator of the revealed Mysteries of God, of the supernatural order of the divine economy. Thus, to his philosophical basis the theologian brings faith, and from these follows his construction of a theological system. *"Fides quaerens intellectum,"* for theology must use philosophy and philosophical concepts, and it is ever dependent upon reason as well as faith and upon the constructs of reason.

The Church and the theologian cannot ignore philosophy, and cannot be indifferent to doctrines which, as Albert Dondeyne remarks, "either exaggerate or minimize the powers of natural reason, that is to say, the two extremes of rationalism and fideism in all their forms." [1]

There are some Christian thinkers in both France and Belgium for whom the Thomist revival is itself a problem. While even the most traditional and conservative of Thomists would not say that philosophic speculation ended with St. Thomas, nevertheless some traditionalists have been rather hidebound in their deliberate ignoring of and casual treatment of modern thought. The widespread influence of Scientism, Phenomenology and the forms of Existentialism confront the theologian not only without but also—at times—within the Church. Dondeyne quotes M. Marrou in 1956: "There is at the moment among young priests and religious [he is speaking of France] a polite indifference, to say the least, in regard to traditional theology and its conceptual armory. . . ." Thus for some Thomism does not seem to be "relevant" to modern man, and it was toward these that Pope Pius aimed his strictures in the encyclical *Humani Generis.*

[1] Albert Dondeyne, *Contemporary European Thought and Christian Faith* (Pittsburgh: Duquesne University Press, 1958), p. 131.

The problem may be approached in another fashion. There are those who seek to work with the data of Revelation in a theological framework, but they come to this work committed to other than the Thomist system of philosophy (for example, Phenomenology or Existentialism) or perhaps to no system whatsoever. In performing the work of the theologian, in attempting to synthesize, they relate the various data of Revelation with the traditional teaching of the Church. Perhaps in attempting to relate to man according to the peculiarities of the particular philosophy to which he is committed, he conflicts with what is traditionally accepted by the Church or with theological conclusions the Church has taught. For these men there is an unbearable tension in that they inevitably seem to come into conflict with an accepted *a priori* datum of Revelation, namely: the inerrancy of the Church of Christ, to which they are committed as well.

The continued historical repetition of this almost certain path to error has led the Church not to the imposition of Thomistic philosophy as of itself a *sine qua non*, but rather to her adoption of Thomism as the realist philosophy most in accord with the data of Revelation and the truths of human reason. The Catholic does not look upon Thomism as an imposed or built-in system of philosophy and theology, of reason and belief, but rather as that system historically proved most adequate to the *fides quarens intellectum*.

The traditional problem of the proper relationships of philosophy and theology remain for the French a real intellectual problem. The current theological attitude among the French is one of working within the Thomist system—widely understood. Thus, at the present time they do not look upon the problem as one of choice between Thomism or some other, but rather of what they prefer to call "a crisis for Thomism." Facing the powerful influences of the modern philosophies which reflect the strivings of modern man there is a widespread attempt to harness the positive good, the true insights and the real advances made by these philosophies to the perennial system of Thomism, and to the traditional teachings of the Church. Foremost among contemporary Christian thinkers attempting to grapple with the problems of the "Thomistic crisis" is Abbé Albert Dondeyne.

Dialogue and Synthesis

At the present time Abbé Dondeyne is Professor of Philosophy at the University of Louvain. Born at Lo in Belgium on May 10, 1901, he is a secular priest, a graduate of the university and a professor there since 1936. Most of his work has appeared in French and Flemish, although the best of these have been published in English. Most of his essays in French periodicals have been gathered up, reworked and edited for his outstanding contribution, *Foi chrétienne et pensée contemporaine*. Of greater brevity, but marked by the excellence of his thought, was his essay on "The Existence of God and Contemporary Materialism" for Jacques de Bivort de la Saudée's *Essai sur Dieu, l'homme et l'univers* in 1950.

The substance of Dondeyne's thought is to be found in the *Foi chrétienne*, his significant contribution toward the realignment of Thomism and modern thought. In this work he not only outlines the problems presented to contemporary theologians by modern philosophers, but he faces as well many "approaches" that may be taken to realign modern thought with the accepted philosophy of the Church and with its inerrant theological teaching. For Dondeyne the question is not a cavalier alignment of "their" arguments and "our" answers, but rather a sympathetic and complete understanding of the position to which these thinkers are committed, and, consequently, an examination of the possibilities that remain to be completely explored by which their grasp of truth might be fully broadened and extended to an acceptance of the totality of truth.

Dondeyne's thought and work are therefore dominated by one driving consideration: the necessity of communication, sympathy and approach by the Christian toward his contemporaries. Thus the themes he treats are those of the moderns: the questions of God and man and reason; the problems of liberty, freedom and humanism; and the fundamental basis from which these questions spring, that is, the personalist emphasis of the existentialists. Christian faith, if it is to demonstrate persuasively the power of truth, must enter into dialogue, into a willing relationship with contemporary thought. Such a meeting is not the simple setting against each other of two divergent positions, rather, as Dondeyne remarks:

Dialogue is a common effort of many, directed toward a mutual understanding and a mutual enrichment. But to understand one another means first to learn from one another, and to learn from one another means to show oneself responsive and open. Nothing is more dangerous to the human spirit than to believe that one has understood everything and that one has no more to learn from anyone. By taking up this attitude, one renders oneself impervious not only to the thought of others but even, in a sense, to one's own thought, since it is only by confronting ideas with one another that the mind begins to awaken and that the unreflecting anonymous consciousness gives way to the reflective personal one. From this stems the necessity of dialogue for every man who thinks, and for the Christian, in particular. To be open to the problems posed by modern thought is, for the Christian, not only the best means of attaining to an understanding of his age but also a way to deepen his own faith and to make it bear a more efficacious witness." [2]

In his monumental work, *Foi chrétienne*, Dondeyne reflects this willingness to meet the contemporary thinker, and in that work he places himself squarely in the Thomist tradition. From this basic position he meets the problems posed for the Thomist by phenomenological Existentialism. Thomism and Existentialism are compatible and contributory one to the other; the objectionable features of existentialist relativism and atheism, he states, are accidental and may be shown to be purely accretions to the basically sound intuitions that Existentialism has achieved. There is, he states, a need for a new synthesis of Thomism and the sound achievements of the existentialists, ". . . a Christianity which proved incapable of effecting the synthesis between faith and those partial truths and genuine values that it encounters in the world, would be doomed to failure right from the beginning. This, in turn, underlies the importance of a philosophy (and, *a fortiori*, of a theology) that is living and contemporary, one which takes account of the aspirations of the modern world and speaks its language." [3]

This synthesis of Thomism and Existentialism must be pressed by the Thomist. He has the warrant of tradition: "As against those who feared that Christian piety would be corrupted by pagan phi-

[2] *Ibid.*, p. 5.
[3] *Ibid.*, p. 199.

losophy, St. Thomas, urged on by a great respect for human reason and boundless confidence in the unity of truth, firmly held to the belief that the synthesis of faith and reason was not only possible but necessary for the survival of both." [4] Furthermore, this synthesis is to be based only upon those positive principles of the dialogue as he has expounded them. The question of the synthesis and mutual reexamination is pressed by Dondeyne upon his existentialist contemporaries as well, for such a "reappraisal may be of considerable value to existential phenomenology as well as to Thomism." [5]

The objection is not infrequently heard from the traditional scholar that he has no need, being in possession of the truth, to run after novelties, and to examine every shifting current in modern thought. Dondeyne comments: "the mere fact that our time has seen the appearance of a philosophy about which it has been said that 'it is identical with the very striving of modern thought,' is an event which forces us to reflect. It invites the philosopher to give new thought to old problems. Such an event cannot be attributed to a mere taste for novelty." [6] Furthermore, Dondeyne speaks of Thomism as a living and "open" philosophy. "A Thomism shut in on itself can never be a living philosophy, capable of answering the needs of contemporary thought . . . a living and contemporary Thomism is not something existing once and for all, but something always to be achieved." [7]

Existentialism and God

In grasping the meaning of modern philosophy, for Dondeyne, one must also grasp the dynamic implications of existence. "Human 'existence' is the central reference point of the new philosophy, and this 'existence' is essentially temporal." [8] Because of phenomenological reflection upon human existence a sense of the historical dimension of things dominates the modern mind, a sense that provides for the modern a principle of discrimination: namely, that "there is a better world waiting to be built, greater justice waiting to

[4] *Ibid.*, p. 132.
[5] *Ibid.*, p. 4.
[6] *Ibid.*, p. 134.
[7] *Ibid.*, p. 164.
[8] *Ibid.*, p. 35.

be achieved . . .", and thus "the sense of being-in-history becomes the motive force of humanity in moments of crisis bringing new vitality to their new humanism." [9]

This concept involves for the existentialists a serious theological implication. Belief in God, they allege, clouds this sense of being-in-history, and it leads to rigidity of thought and the death of all reflection. Thus the Christian is supposed to be wrong for he places "the foundation of truth and morality outside of experience" in God.

Is it true that belief in God and in after-life stifles in us any feeling for man or for history? This is the all-important question which the modern world puts to the Christian conscience, and particularly to the Christian moralist, whether he be philosopher or theologian. This question must be taken seriously. It is not to be dismissed as an idle objection cooked up to disconcert believers. It is by no means a simple task to reconcile belief in a Divine, immutable revelation with a healthy and vigorous humanism that respects the historical character of human life. The bringing together of time and eternity, and even more the entry of the eternal into history (which is, after all, the essence of the Christian religion, centered as it is around the mystery of the Incarnation of God), pose multiple problems both in theory and in practice.[10]

In addition to this, Dondeyne states, in the light of God's existence life takes on meaning in God's sight, and "our historical existence becomes completely consistent when it is seen as the object of God's love." [11] The atheism of the contemporary existentialist is based upon an idea of God implying a duality between being and thought, in which being is conceived of as being completely impenetrable, or "the-other-than-consciousness." This he points out is a fundamentally epistemological problem, one in which the existentialist himself will not press forward because of an inevitable idealism. The objection then is one of idealism, and simply speaking a meaningless and contradictory one for the existentialist.

When writers like Sartre or Merleau-Ponty declare that the existence of God is irreconcilable with the contingency of history and the autonomy of human freedom, what they have to say has nothing to do with

[9] *Ibid.*, p. 39.
[10] *Ibid.*, p. 40.
[11] *Ibid.*, p. 65.

the God of Abraham, Isaac and Jacob, the God of love preached by St. John. They are attacking a notion of their own making, conceived in the likeness of a manufacturer of paper-knives, or an Absolute Knower reached on the basis of notional evidence or of an immanent dialectic. If God be revered as Word and Love, His co-existence with human liberty ceases to be an insoluble antinomy. For the function of the Word is to bring a message which will waken us to true liberty, and the function of the Spirit is to liberate us for love since He cannot love without inspiring us to love in return. [12]

Dogma and Faith

A reexamination of the Faith, and its dogmatic formulas is demanded in the light of the attraction and dynamism existentialism manifests. The Faith is not a moribund collection of abstract propositions, such as the modern frequently envisions it when he speaks of the "dogmas" of Catholicism, or the "dogmatism" of Christian thought. Dondeyne once again recalls the traditional understanding these formulas of faith have, for they stand "for the religious mystery that is the object of faith, or more precisely the knowledge that we have of this mystery thanks to revelation, as well as the propositions in which this knowledge is expressed." [13]

Faith, therefore, cannot be a blind adherence which would stifle further reflection upon the object of faith, but would rather demand such reflections. Faith cannot terminate in a dogmatic proposition, but rather through such propositions it terminates in an adherence to God Himself.

To say that faith reaches out to God Himself and to the work of His redemptive love through the dogmatic proposition, is to proclaim once more the intentional character of the attitude of believing . . . with Faith dogmatic formulae do not constitute its final object, but the intention of faith in some ·way animates these formulae. Through them the soul throws itself open to God Himself.[14]

God, therefore, cannot be a concept valueless for us, deprived of real meaning. He is God-for-us, not simply a theory proposed in

12 *Ibid.*, pp. 65–66.
13 *Ibid.*, p. 177.
14 *Ibid.*, p. 177.

opposition to the materialist or atheist. God is not simply a dramatic *deus ex machina* concluding a purely rational argument, although His existence may be arrived at through reason. Rather than a term He is a reality. Thus Dondeyne can comment in his essay on "God and Contemporary Materialism":

If this were the only meaning and significance of theism our argument with the materialist would lose much of its seriousness. Fundamentally a God who is postulated merely as a final explanation of the universe hardly concerns us. We scarcely care whether the world was set in motion by an "initial shove" given it by God, as Descartes believed, or whether physical movements are the effect of a transformation of energy that constitutes and defines matter. The universe of electrons, neutrons and protons that gives us being may itself be given being and kept in existence by a creative God: but unless that God is a God-for-us, the fact represents no value or aim for us; it makes little difference to our situation in the world and sheds little light on the great agonizing question: is life, or is it not, worth the pains of living? [15]

The reality of God and the meaning of faith confer meaningful implications for the Christian. In commenting on religious education and the modern world Dondeyne stresses the coordinate of temporal action to faith, of a true humanism that is intrinsically involved in the Christian conception of faith. For Christian faith is inseparable from the love of God which is identical with the love of neighbor. The Christian has an earthly vocation, and Christianity is also a humanism. "What Christianity contributes to the world is a particular sensitivity to the infinite dignity of the human person and the values which constitute his personality; respect for life and death, an extremely delicate sense of truth, chaste and faithful love, a very lofty conception of liberty, responsibility and work, the sense of the radical equality of all men above the differences of race or social conditions.[16]

Albert Dondeyne has done much to bridge the gap between the modern mind and the traditional presentation of Christian thought.

[15] Dondeyne, "The Existence of God and Contemporary Materialism," *God, Man and the Universe* (New York: Kenedy, 1954), p. 9.
[16] Dondeyne, "Religious Education and the Modern World," *Lumen Vitae*, Vol. 12 (1957), p. 39.

He has reminded the Catholic philosopher and theologian of the necessary conditions for true dialogue, and he serves for his contemporaries as a witness to the "openness" inherent in the traditional philosophy preferred by the Church. Bringing within the scholastic tradition the vibrant and youthful enthusiasm of the existentialists, and their dynamic intuitions into old truths, Dondeyne reinvests Christianity with an urgency for the modern world. For the Christian intellectual he has set forth a plan of work and a spirit of approach that has come to dominate many of his contemporaries in France and Belgium:

The intellectual who is a Christian, particularly if he be a philosopher or theologian, has the obligation of trying to meet this demand for sincerity and of manifesting the living testimony of a faith whose implications are fully accepted and which is, therefore, open to all the problems of our time. This faith will, of course, involve a sincere adherence to religious dogma, but it must also know how to avoid all appearance of dogmatism. It is evident that, to accomplish this mission, the intellectual must live in continual contact with the world. He will have to be "present everywhere in regions of intellectual conflict"; he must get used to "looking at the problems of men and nature in the new dimensions in which they henceforth pose themselves." (Pius XII) If he is not capable of seeing the unbeliever's point of view and of taking seriously the difficulties that the unbeliever feels bound to raise against the Faith, he will do immense harm to the Christian cause; for he will give the impression that Christian belief is a dogmatic attitude which cannot be reconciled with the respect for the complexity of problems and the desire for absolute sincerity which are the mark of the modern mind. It is vitally important that Christians should pursue their dialogue with modern thought in sincerity and fidelity. It is mainly by the conflict of ideas that human thought passes from the stage of prereflective, anonymous and dogmatic contentedness, to the reflective, personal and free awareness which alone can show forth the truth in all its persuasive power.[17]

Contemporary Developments

As we have remarked, theism and atheism constitute an initial theological problem for the contemporary theologian in France.

---

[17] *Contemporary European Thought, op. cit.,* p. 203.

A further problem in the very outset of any treatment of theology is posed as well in the relationship of human reason to faith, and the consequences of the attitude adopted by the theologian will be most evident in his treatment of what has been traditionally called apologetics. The traditional approach of theological manuals to apologetics has been in this manner: the philosophical possibility of Revelation, the criteria for determining authentic Revelation, the validity and historicity of Scripture, the historical recognition of a *de facto* Revelation from the miracles and claims of Christ, and, finally, the constitution and prerogatives of the Church founded by Christ.

Two significant works, critical of the approach offered by the manuals, appeared in 1945 and 1946. In 1945 the Abbé Roger Aubert, of Louvain, examined with great detail the problem of the act of faith, pointing out that there exists today a certain excessive rationalistic approach to the truths of the Faith.[18] While he would not simply reject the traditional apologetic of the theologians, he emphasized that there was room as well for the affective approach, so dear to the French since Pascal and so effectively personalized in the figure of Cardinal Newman.[19]

The Jesuit, Jean Levie, in 1946 went a step further with certain theological and historical criticisms of the manual approach.[20] Traditional apologetics he found to be guilty of five undemonstrated assumptions, as well as an ignorance of the value of the affective approach. For Levie apologetics cannot be removed from theology proper, and, in their traditional approach, theologians since the sixteenth century ignore the following facts: First, the traditional preamble to faith is not totally independent of Revelation; second, the preamble to faith cannot be completely grasped by the unbeliever; third, the manuals suffer from a historical positivism that ignores the interest and meaning a particular event has for its recorder; fourth, the traditional presentation of the preamble to faith demands an unattainable objectivity that ignores the religious or nonreligious orientation of the inquirer; fifth, each of the steps of

---

[18] Roger Aubert, *Le Problème de l'acte de foi* (Louvain: Editions Warny, 1948).

[19] An example of this approach may be found in Jean Mouroux, *The Meaning of Man* (New York: Sheed & Ward, 1948).

[20] Jean Levie, S.J., *Sous les Yeux de l'incroyant* (Paris: Desclée, 1946).

the apologetic argument cannot be self-enclosed, but "each argument is of value in the exact measure that it shows and makes known the center of intelligibility: the Whole Christ in His Church." [21]

Levie's work has been widely discussed and fairly well received.[22] The problem, because of its obvious implications for the catechetical apostolate, is frequently discussed in the periodical *Lumen Vitae*, and many major theologians in France today have since commented in much the same manner as Levie. The relationship of reason to faith, and its consequences in harmonizing the conclusions of revealed religion with philosophical investigation, method and conclusions dominate the work of Levie's fellow Jesuit, Père André Marc.[23]

2. HENRI DE LUBAC—GOD AND THE CHURCH

Père Henri de Lubac has become for many not only one of the most penetrating theologians in modern France but the symbol of the theological revival itself. When conservative critics sought to check the rapidly expanding theological movement in France after World War II de Lubac became a prime target of criticism. It would be incorrect to assume that he has taken to himself any leadership over contemporary theology, titular or otherwise, and yet even a cursory examination of his work and method display the various qualities that mark the modern theological revival. First of all, de Lubac's theological inquiries are solidly based upon the accurate exegesis of Scripture and upon an enormous erudition in the Fathers. He also brings to theology today a sympathetic attitude toward those outside the Church baffled by the mystery of the supernatural that underlies religion. An inveterate humanist, his concern for human personality and dignity make him an understanding participant in the theological dialogue seeking to reconcile the differences that separate modern man from the Church.

[21] *Ibid.*, p. 57.

[22] See the fine treatment of Levie's thesis in Joseph L. Roche, "The Postulates of Traditional Apologetics," *Conference Bulletin of the Archdiocese of New York*, Vol. 34 (1957), pp. 21–35.

[23] Père André Marc has long labored at a Thomism incorporating modern contributions. See his *Raison philosophique et religion révélée* (Paris: Desclée, 1955), and his synthesis, *L'Etre et l'esprit* (Paris-Louvain, Desclée de Brouwer, 1958).

Born in 1896, Henri de Lubac entered the Society of Jesus in 1929, and during the 1930's made his debut upon the theological scene with a number of articles on the problem of the supernatural. He assumed, during the thirties, and still maintains the professorship of the history of religions on the Jesuit theological faculty at Lyon-Fourvière. His contributions have always been marked by a patristic-historical approach to theological problems. He published his first major work in 1937, *Catholicisme*, on the corporate destiny of mankind, and this underwent four editions within ten years.[24] He became in the early 1940's a co-editor with Père Jean Danielou of the *Sources chrétiennes*, a series of definitive translations of the Fathers. He also became a cooperator in the *Théologie* series undertaken by the Jesuit theologians of Lyon-Fourvière, and contributed an introduction to Danielou's *Platonisme*, the second work of the series. De Lubac contributed the third volume of this series in 1943 with *Corpus Mysticum: l'eucharistie et l'église au moyen-âge.*[25]

Corpus Mysticum serves as an excellent introduction to the strong historical bent that de Lubac usually follows in his presentations. The work was a historical-theological inquiry into the real meaning of the phrase "*Corpus Mysticum.*" In it he traces the earlier application of the phrase by some of the Fathers and early theologians to the Eucharist, and then the gradual transference of the term as applying to the Church. The Dominican theologian Père Nicolas, while admitting the masterful sweep of the work and its undoubted contribution toward an understanding of the history of the phrase, nevertheless took sections of the work as mirroring a theological relativism. Although the work was highly praised by such scholars as the medievalist Glorieux and the theologian Chenu, it is noteworthy that Nicolas's criticism of "theological relativism" was to return again to plague de Lubac.

The most controversial of all de Lubac's works, the *Surnaturel*, was published in 1946 as the eighth in the *Théologie* series.[26] The *Surnaturel* became an immediate center of controversy, the most pressing objections of the critics being brought against de Lubac's

[24] Henri de Lubac, *Catholicism* (New York: Sheed & Ward, 1946). This translation was from the tenth French edition.

[25] *Corpus Mysticum* (Paris: Aubier, 1943).

[26] *Surnaturel* (Paris: Aubier, 1946).

conclusion that the beatitude of the Beatific Vision was the natural end of man. In the same year he published a shorter work on missiology, *Le Fondement théologique des missions*.[27] In this work, based upon the theme of the Church, de Lubac put forward a fundamentally theological basis for the missionary activity of the Church. This basis lay, he said, "in the nature of the Church." The very nature of the Church is charity—a universal, world-wide, outgoing and expansive charity. Charity is love, a love-communicative-of-itself, because that is the essence of love. Thus missionary activity as such is an essential element of the Church. For de Lubac the missions reflected an especial aspect of the Mystery of Christ and the Church, namely, the undeniable and irresistible power of charity.

In 1947 de Lubac revealed much of himself in the collection of *Paradoxes* which he published.[28] The *Paradoxes* were written in the style of the *Pensées* of Pascal, and within a few years he published a second volume of these intensely personal thoughts.[29] During these years, 1945–1950, he tells us that "I felt, too strongly for comfort, the gathering of those dangers which have in some cases, unfortunately, since become only too clear to all." [30] He tells us that he had become alarmed at the adverse influences attacking the Church on all quarters, and the threat this posed to the "sense of the Church" in men of "the utmost nobility of character and the profoundest loyalty." [31] Thus he produced his *Méditation sur l'eglise*, translated as *The Splendour of the Church*, his reflections on the Church, so that others might come to realize "The pricelessness of that good which consists, quite simply, in belonging to the Church." [32]

These years also witnessed the production of a number of works on questions relevant to humanism, basically with regard to the alleged necessity for an atheistic basis for humanism demanded by the Marxists. These works consisted of a study of Proudhon, and

---

[27] *Le Fondement théologique des missions* (Paris: Editions de Seuil, 1946).
[28] *Paradoxes* (Paris: Editions de Seuil, 1947).
[29] *Further Paradoxes* (Westminster, Md.: Newman, 1958).
[30] *The Splendour of the Church* (New York: Sheed & Ward, 1956). Introduction, p. xi.
[31] *Ibid.*, p. xii.
[32] *Ibid.*, p. xii.

one of Feurbach, Nietzsche and Compte.[33] He also published minor works on Buddhism,[34] the knowledge of God,[35] and a competent patristic study of the typological interpretation of Scripture in the Church.[36]

If history and patrology mark the method of de Lubac's presentation, so also the basic content of his thought is marked by a unifying vision of God, man and the Church. The progress reflected in his work touches upon the manifold principal elements of the Divine Plan: the supernatural, the basis of human dignity in the Divine Plan, and man's supernatural fulfillment in the corporate nature of the body of the saved—the Church. It is to these major themes, the pivotal ideas in his thought, that we must now turn. But in any such examination of de Lubac's thought we must always realize his own fundamental attitude as regards the facts of faith: that de Lubac, the theologian, "takes a humble pride in his title of believer, above which he places no other." [37]

Natural and Supernatural

During the 1920's and 1930's the relationship between the natural and supernatural orders became one of the central questions of discussion by the theologians. This was basically owing to the philosophical influence of Blondel. Strongly influenced by the neo-Augustinian attitude of Blondel, the Jesuits Rousselot, Maréchal, and de Broglie made tentative advances to a new approach toward the entire presentation of the supernatural. The practical meaning of these new considerations was demonstrated by de Lubac in 1934 and 1936 in articles in the *Nouvelle revue théologique* in which he pointed out that contemporary thought was seeking the basis for a true humanism, and was a quest for a philosophy of the human person. Later in the 1940's, de Lubac would return to the problem

[33] *The Un-Marxian Socialist* (London: Sheed & Ward, 1948); *The Drama of Atheist Humanism* (New York: Sheed & Ward, 1950).
[34] *Aspects of Buddhism* (New York: Sheed & Ward, 1954).
[35] *De la Connaisance de Dieu* (Paris: Editions de Témoignage, 1958), and *Sur les Chemins de Dieu* (Paris: Aubier, 1956). Trans. as *The Discovery of God* (New York: Kenedy, 1960).
[36] *Histoire et esprit* (Paris: Aubier, 1950).
[37] *Further Paradoxes, op. cit.*, p. 121.

of the natural and supernatural orders, and the implications such theology would have upon the formation of a Christian humanism.

With the publication of the *Surnaturel* in 1946, de Lubac presented his historical study of the concept of the supernatural, of the doctrines and ideas intimately related to it, and the historical development of this concept in the Church. By no means did he intend to publish a definitive work, but rather a set of notes that might make an approach toward an ultimately definitive work in the field. The theme of the *Surnaturel* has been summed up for de Lubac since the time of St. Thomas in his teaching on "the natural desire for the Beatific Vision." The book is divided into four sections. In the first, he presents a comparative study of Augustinianism and Baianism, and he concludes that the idea of a "system of pure nature" and an absolute dualism between nature and the supernatural as two closed orders begins in this historical period of the Church. The second section is devoted to the problem of the impeccability of angelic spirits in the theology of St. Thomas, and the third section to the origins of the word "supernatural" itself. It is the fourth section, a series of historical notes and a discussion of the natural desire for the Beatific Vision, that produced the controversial reaction to de Lubac's presentation.

The importance of the question of the natural desire for the Beatific Vision according to de Lubac is that it implies the entire question of the relationship of the natural and supernatural orders. Since the time of St. Thomas the theologians have concentrated their approach to the supernatural in their practical discussion of the existence in man of a natural desire for the Beatific Vision. St. Thomas himself taught the existence of such a desire according to de Lubac, and it is to a presentation and defense of this proposal that de Lubac turned. The existence of such a desire in human nature has God for its author. *De facto* man has sinned, and through the work of Christ has been saved and destined for the supernatural order. There does not exist, and cannot exist a question of a state of pure nature, or a consequent purely natural end for man. But in addition to this, the gratuity of the supernatural order, that is, man's supernatural end, as the free gift of God must be maintained.

A major critical objection, and one of the most telling, against de Lubac's presentation of the Beatific Vision as the natural end of man was that St. Thomas never taught such a doctrine. A semantic problem developed over the question of what exactly St. Thomas did teach, and the Thomist experts fell over themselves to get into print destroying the historical basis of de Lubac's approach to the supernatural. More serious theological objections were entered by the theologians. Basically, they maintained, that if de Lubac were to sustain his thesis he would destroy not only the gratuity of the supernatural order, but the distinction between the natural and supernatural as well. De Lubac did not emerge from the debate unscathed, even two subsequent articles on the supernatural did not salvage his position.

The magnitude of the opposition that de Lubac met was unexpected. The Jesuits Danielou and Bouillard, and de Solages of the Institut Catholique alone took de Lubac's position in the argument. Almost every major theologian in France, and throughout the world, soon entered his objections. The dispute became so intense in the period of 1947–1950 that, as we shall see, the *Surnaturel* became more than a question of theology but a symbol of all that was to be resisted in the new theological revival.

It is unfortunate that the legitimate boundaries of theological dispute were so flagrantly transgressed in *"l'affaire Surnaturel."* De Lubac's presentation, although weak in its reconciliation of his propositions and the traditional teaching of the Church, never approached the sensational either in content or intent. Throughout the debate, especially in the rejoinders to his critics, de Lubac maintained a deliberately professional tone directed toward a solution of the problem raised. The same cannot be said of all his critics, since for a few of them the question of the supernatural was to be treated as polemic rather than theology. Admittedly few, yet at times these few made petty little inferences against the person and loyalty of de Lubac in what were ostensibly theological refutations. In fact, since Pope Pius XII's encyclical *Humani Generis*, not a few have alleged de Lubac as the object of one of the Pontiff's censures.[38] While de Lubac may not have escaped some severe and legitimate objections,

[38] De Lubac maintains that he was misunderstood and that this censure does not apply to his position.

he certainly did emerge from the debate not only as a thought-provoking and penetrating theologian, but as a courteous and respectable disputant as well.

Christian Humanism

Because of the intellectual atmosphere of modern France, the theologian faces not only the question of the supernatural, but of theism itself. Contemporary atheism is not always (as is sometimes supposed) a simple question ultimately based upon the moral deficiencies or immoral proclivities of the atheist. It has flowered in eighteenth century rationalism, nineteenth-century Marxism, and twentieth-century positivism into a full-blown intellectual difficulty. Atheism has been seized upon as a necessary position for the establishment of a lasting humanism. In *The Drama of Atheist Humanism*, de Lubac examines this necessity for atheism as found in Feuerbach, Nietzsche and Comte.

A brilliant analysis of each of these men in turn is presented not only with the exposition of their positions, but with the penetration of their thought in a sympathetic manner. Thus with de Lubac we have not simply the considerations of the critic, but those of a man who can become deeply involved in his examination and presentation of these men, and who at the same time can bring to the work a skilled theological ability, distinguishing the good they represent from the error that is to be rejected.

In the threefold analysis that de Lubac makes, Feuerbach is in his opinion the essential link between the idealist Hegel and the materialist Marx. It is Feuerbach's explanation of God in psychological terms that firmly establishes the Marxian adaptation of the Hegelian dialectic. Thus Feuerbach's God, which is abstract humanity, has come to modern man in the Marxian state—the embodiment of humanity. Feuerbach was a humanist, and so also in their turn were Nietzsche and Comte, each replacing the traditional God with man, each seeking a positive basis for a total philosophy that would preserve human value. As Feuerbach replaced God with humanity, Nietzsche replaced Him with an emerging superman, and Comte, "by far the most dangerous" (because of a root denial of individual dignity), replaced him with a religion of humanity and common sense. Each of these men in their turn plays the role of savior and savant in the development of atheistic humanism.

To these men de Lubac contrasts the figures of Kierkegaard and Dostoevski: to an atheistic humanism he contrasts the two moderns most symbolic of theistic humanism. The reason for this is made quite clear. The inevitable and inexorable result of Feuerbach, Nietzsche and Comte is a humanism that becomes inhuman, a new religion of man that ignores the essential dignity of each individual man. To establish a basis of humanism the Living God is a necessity —the traditional concept of the personal God is an absolute requirement for any true humanism. As in the *Surnaturel,* de Lubac turns again to an old consideration of his, and places it in his study of Kierkegaard and Dostoevski, that there can be no religious vacuum for man.

In 1947 he presented a long historical consideration of the founding figure of French social thought, Pierre Proudhon. De Lubac here displayed considerable regard for Proudhon's agnosticism. "He no more gives up seeking than humanity itself gives up." Proudhon is a more respectable figure for the humanist, because Proudhon's acknowledged agnosticism "is not something purely negative. It takes on a positive value when it becomes acknowledgment of mystery." [39] Proudhon, the atheist humanist, unlike his predecessors, remains a negative witness to the mystery that attracts humanity itself, and remains transcendent to it.

The contemporary challenge of Marxism, the self-proclaimed savior of any true humanist value, leaves the Catholic face to face with the most powerful enemy of all. The dream of a stateless and classless society proposed by Marxism, the inevitable free state of natural man in such a society to which history carries forward the human race, is for de Lubac precisely that, a dream. "In a nontranscendent society, the reduction of man to his 'social relationships' will work inevitably to the prejudice of personal inferiority, and will beget a tyranny of some kind, however novel." [40]

In the face of a growing movement for a philosophy of humanity, for a firm intellectual basis for humanism and individual value, de

[39] *The Un-Marxian Socialist, op. cit.,* pp. 291–292.
[40] *Catholicism, op. cit.,* p. 200.

Lubac., in complete sympathy with such desires, demands the necessary consideration of man's spiritual nature, "The happiest and
most perfect form of social existence would be the most inhuman
of conditions if it were not ordered to the spiritual life, just as the
latter would be, in a final analysis, only a mystification if it retired
into itself in a sort of refined egoism." [41] De Lubac comments on
the Marxist claim somewhat pointedly: "Marx's social, historical
man has only two dimensions, but the sense of the Eternal, the
consciousness of the Eternal Presence which he must regain, will
repair his loss." [42]

In itself then, and for itself alone, humanism is not Christian, and
since a religious vacuum is impossible it cannot acquire essential
value apart from God who bestows upon it the dignity and value
which it requires. For de Lubac, the essential demand of conversion,
the spiritual law of loss in order to find death and resurrection,
binds the humanist desire. "Christian humanism must be a converted
humanism . . . if no one may escape from humanity, humanity
whole and entire must die to itself in each of its members so as to
live transfigured in God." [43]

True humanism therefore demands God as its basis, for without
Him atheistic humanism becomes hypocrisy and a mockery of individual dignity. Lasting humanism demands the Christian fact, and
the Christian fact implies a true humanism.

If there be no man without humanity, much less still is there any humanity without men. By calling us back inwards, the Gospel is at the
same time calling us back to the truth of human relationships, that truth
fatally betrayed by all ideologies and political systems.[44]

The Church

The fundamental factor that gives unity to de Lubac's vision of
man and humanism is the Church. The reality of God's work in
our attainment of the end of man, beatitude, is focused upon the
Church. Human community, the *consortium* of the faithful is a real

---

[41] *Ibid.*, pp. 200–201.
[42] *Ibid.*, p. 201.
[43] *Ibid.*, pp. 206–207.
[44] *Further Paradoxes, op. cit.*, p. 38.

part of our beatitude; mankind, de Lubac tells us, has a corporate destiny in the Church. Thus he refers to St. Thomas: "The end of a reasonable creature is to attain to beatitude, and that can only consist in the kingdom of God, which in its turn is nothing else than the well ordered society of those who enjoy the vision of God." [45]

The demand for community essential in humanism, the supernatural end of each man destined by God, these are concepts fulfilled and united in de Lubac's vision of the Church:

God did not make us to "remain within the limits of nature," or for the fulfilling of a solitary destiny; on the contrary, He made us to be brought together into the heart of the life of the Trinity. . . . But there is a place where this gathering-together of all things in the Trinity begins in this world; a "family of God," a mysterious extension of the Trinity in time, which not only prepares us for this life of union and gives us a sure guarantee of it, but also makes us participate in it already. The Church is the only completely "open" society, the only one which measures up to our deepest longings, and in which we can finally find our whole shape. . . . For us, according to the mode which suits our earthly condition, the Church is the very realization of that communion which is so much sought for. She guarantees not only our community of destiny but also our community of vocation. . . . [46]

In confronting the Church, in subjecting this awesome Mystery of the Church itself not only to our faith but also to our reflection and thought, we come close to the heart of the fundamental mystery. Thus "today we are at the beginning of an attempt at an unfolding which is at once analytic and generalized—an attempt to grasp the mystery in its totality." [47] For the theologian a point must be reached in his personal development in which one particular mystery comes to the foreground of the reflexive landscape—and today that mystery is becoming for many the Church. This fulcrum of further reflection "becomes a species of vital centre round which, for practical purpose, all the others organically group themselves . . . it becomes the standard around which is fought out and decided the crucial battle for orthodoxy." [48] In de Lubac's work this central

---

[45] *Catholicism, op. cit.*, p. 60.
[46] *Splendour of the Church, op. cit.*, pp. 174–175.
[47] *Ibid.*, p. 3.
[48] *Ibid.*, p. 8.

theme, this decisive focal point has become the Church. "It certainly seems as if the present day has brought about the moment for carrying out a labour of this kind apropos that particular section or aspect of the total Christian mystery, that particular member of the 'body of truth,' which is the mystery of the Church." [49]

The meaning of the Mystery of the Church is that it is fundamentally Christ:

The Church is the sacrament of Christ; which means, to put it another way, that there is between her and Him a certain relation of mystical identity. Here again we encounter the Pauline metaphors and the rest of the biblical images, which the Christian tradition has continually explored. . . . Head and members make one single body, one single Christ; the Bridegroom and the Bride are one flesh. Although He is the Head of His Church, Christ does not rule her from without; there is, certainly, subjection and dependence between her and Him, but at the same time she is His fulfillment and "fulness." She is the Tabernacle of His presence . . . the Temple in which He teaches . . . the ship and He the Pilot . . . the deep ark and He the central mast. . . . She is paradise and He its tree and well of life. . . . Practically speaking, for each one of us Christ is thus His Church.[50]

Thirteen years before, de Lubac had expressed these thoughts, this same theme, that as Christ is the sacrament of God, the Church is the sacrament of Christ:

If Christ is the sacrament of God, the Church is for us the sacrament of Christ; she represents him, in the full and ancient meaning of the term, she really makes him present. She not only carries on his work, but she is his very continuation, in a sense far more real than that in which it can be said that any human institution is its founder's continuation. The highly developed exterior organization that wins our admiration is but an expression, in accordance with the needs of this present life, of the interior unity of a living entity, so that the Catholic is not only subject to a power but is a member of a body as well, and his legal dependence on this power is to the end that he may have part in the life of that body. His submission in consequence is not an abdication, his orthodoxy is not mere conformity, but fidelity. It is his duty not merely to obey

[49] *Ibid.*, p. 9.
[50] *Ibid.*, pp. 151–153.

her orders or show deference to her counsels, but to share in a life, to enjoy a spiritual union.[51]

De Lubac's vision of the Church is closely related to the theme of history so frequently discussed by contemporary historians, philosophers and theologians. Viewing human history from the insight of the Church as the extension of the Incarnation, the Church as the working out of the Divine Plan, he places himself firmly in that camp of the theologians of history which is called "Incarnational." These theologians stress the Person and Work of Christ as the meaning of all human history in contrast to the "eschatological" theologians for whom stress is more properly placed on the fact that human history is now drawing to an end, the last days. Thus de Lubac, keenly perceptive of the scope and dimension of human history and of the necessity the theologian faces in meeting the problem of human history, writes:

Amid this universal chorus Christianity alone continues to assert the transcendent destiny of man and the common destiny of mankind. The whole history of the world is a preparation for this destiny. From the first creation to the last end, through material opposition and the more serious opposition of created freedom, a divine plan is in operation, accomplishing its successive stages among which the Incarnation stands out as chief. So in close connection with the social character of dogma there is another character, equally essential, and that is the historic. For if the salvation offered by God is in fact the salvation of the human race, since this human race lives and develops in time, any account of this salvation will naturally take a historical form—it will be the history of the penetration of humanity by Christ.[52]

This Incarnational theology of history envisions for de Lubac the specific commitment of the Christian to the world and to history. He cannot be passive or "withdraw" from the world, and Christian humanism is firmly based upon this "law of the Incarnation":

The Word of God submitted himself to this essential law: He came to deliver us from time, but by means of time. . . . That is the law of the Incarnation and it must undergo no Docetist mitigation. Following

---

[51] *Catholicism, op. cit.,* p. 29.
[52] *Ibid.,* p. 69.

Christ's example, "loyally and with no cheating," every Christian must acquiesce in that state of engagement in time which gives him part and lot in all history, so that his connection with eternity is not unrelated to a past that he knows is immense and a future the length of which is hidden from him.[53]

The constant problem and "scandal" of the human element in the Church, according to de Lubac, have led many erroneously to distinguish the "visible Church" and the "Mystical Body of Christ." "Some thinkers have even found themselves led into this situation without actually so intending, through a lack of grip in their theological reflection." [54] In contrast to this, the doctrine of the Mystical Body of Christ, so explicitly drawn out by Pope Pius XII in an encyclical devoted to it, is to be strongly urged. And yet despite this official proclamation of the Church, because of the sometimes apparent irreconcilability of human weakness and the Divine Nature of the Church, some still preserve this distinction, holding discussions on the Church as a "sociological reality" or on her "sociological situation." Such distinctions he warns are sound in theory and sometimes useful in practice, but they "nevertheless ignore the subtle unity between the human and divine, a union so delicate that if we push ahead with our own critique without due caution we very often run grave risk of behaving like the son who insults his mother." [55] Rather must one remember "that the human element itself as something essential to the structure and life of the Church as Christ willed her to be, is divine in its foundation." [56]

De Lubac's view of human history and the Church, his brilliant insight into the nature and meaning of the phrase, "the Church is the Mystical Body of Christ," is laden with valuable implications for the working theologian. Not the least of these is the theme sounded so well by Dondeyne, that if the Church is by nature "open" to the world, so also should be its theologians: "Christianity transformed the old world by absorbing it. . . . If indeed Christianity is divine, entirely divine, it is in one sense human, the more human for being the more divine, and by penetrating into the very fabric of human history—yet without rending it—it has come to transform mankind and to renew the face of the earth." [57] Thus as Jesus took the elements of His Body from our race, so also with His Church, for humanity provides it with a body, and as the Church grows the human contribution must increase. Thus the Fathers of the Church "were fond of emphasizing, sometimes to excess, the points of similarity between Christian beliefs and the teachings of the philosophers . . . they never understood the 'purity of Christianity' in a purely negative sense adopted by some of their defenders." [58]

This openness to the world on the part of the Church and the theologians is simply on the one hand to insist on the truth, and on the other hand to adapt whatever can be assimilated. But this is admittedly a tortuous road, not easily followed, "a systematic persevering effort that love alone makes possible." [59] In addition, de Lubac spells out for the theologian further obligations that bind him, his necessary unity with the Church, and the spirit that must animate any man who works with the Revelation of God entrusted to the Church:

In a true man of the Church the uncompromisingness of the faith and attachment to Tradition will not turn into hardness, contempt or lack of feeling. They will not destroy his friendliness, nor will they shut him up in a stronghold of purely negative attitudes. . . . He will not give way to the spirit of compromise. . . . He will refuse to develop a craze over one single idea, like a common- or garden-fanatic, since, like the Church, he believes "that there is no salvation save in balance." . . . He will take great care that some generalized idea does not gradually come to take the place of the Person of Christ . . . his total and unconditional faith will not come down to the level of a sort of ecclesial nationalism. . . . He will hold himself apart from all coteries and all intrigue, maintaining a firm resistance against those passionate reactions from which theological circles are not always free, and his vigilance will not be a mere mania of suspicion . . . he will not show himself hostile on principle to legitimate diversity.[60]

As we have seen, Henri de Lubac has brought to theology not only the skillful patience of the historian and the solid reflections of the patrologist but the incisive appreciations of a delicate mind.

[57] *Catholicism, op. cit.*, pp. 146–147.
[58] *Ibid.*, p. 147.
[59] *Ibid.*, p. 149.
[60] *Splendour of the Church, op. cit.*, pp. 184–186.

De Lubac leaves his reader not only with these subtle appreciations of the great themes of Christianity, but with a demonstration of how to penetrate these mysteries more deeply. As the years have developed his style of presentation, so also they have brought his thinking and reflection more consistently upon the Mystery of the Church. Toward the Church have converged the meaning of the theological themes he has touched: nature and the supernatural, the end and destiny of man, modern ideology and humanism, Christ and human history. The Church is, for de Lubac, the form that humanity must put on to be itself, and it is the "Splendour of the Church" that is constantly illuminated in his writing.

To see in Catholicism one religion among others, one system among others, even if it be added that it is the only true religion, the only system that works, is to mistake its very nature, or at least to stop at the threshold. Catholicism is religion itself. It is the form that humanity must put on in order finally to be itself. It is the only reality which involves by its existence no opposition. It is therefore the very opposite of a "closed society." Like its Founder it is eternal and sure of itself, and the very intransigence in matters of principle which prevents its ever being ensnared by transitory things secures for it a flexibility of infinite comprehensiveness, the very opposite of the harsh exclusiveness which characterizes the sectarian spirit. . . . The Church is at home everywhere, and everyone should be able to feel himself at home in the Church. Thus the risen Christ, when He shows Himself to His friends, takes on the countenance of all races and each hears Him in his own tongue.[61]

Contemporary Developments

The Mystery of the Church has become for many, if not most of the contemporary theologians the touchstone of their thought and work. A significant theological development is evident in the work of Msgr. Charles Journet, Professor at the Grand Séminaire in Fribourg. Like de Lubac, and Congar he has made magnificent contributions which have served to orient modern theology into a full-blown ecclesiology. His monumental work has been the *L'Eglise du verbe incarné*.[62] This work is a speculative reflection upon the

[61] *Catholicism, op. cit.*, pp. 153–154.
[62] The first volume of the projected two-volume translation of *L'Eglise du verbe incarné* has appeared: *The Church of the Word Incarnate* (New York: Sheed & Ward, 1955).

Church considered in the light of the traditional four types of causality. With his work widely translated and favorably received, Journet, a theologian of obvious talents, has established himself as one of the great living ecclesiologists.

Among other works he has produced is his early work on ecumenism, *L'Union des églises et le christianisme*, dealing in a sympathetic manner with the problem of the reunion of the various Christian denominations with the Church established by Christ.[63] There is also the slim but fascinating volume translated as *The Dark Knowledge of God*.[64] Journet's *Introduction à la théologie*, published in 1947, has also been translated and remains as a fine introduction to the many questions that face the modern theologian.[65]

Like most theologians actively engaged in publishing the fruit of their thought, Journet has not always succeeded in what he set out to do. In 1953 he replied to Oscar Cullmann who had written an extremely fine theological and apologetical work on St. Peter and the Roman primacy from the Protestant point of view.[66] It must be candidly admitted that this reply of Journet's was not of the stature and ability that has characterized his previous work, or of the work of Cullmann which he was criticizing. While he certainly succeeded in indicating the broad lines of reply that could be made, nevertheless he failed to come to grips with the problem in all its detail and wealth of reference as proposed by Cullmann. In 1957 Journet published an important work on the Mass, in which he was concerned with the crucial problem of identity in the Mass with the Sacrifice of the Cross.[67] Again, in the view of some, he did not quite come to grips with the problem involved. While presenting a tentative approach based upon the presence of Christ, he nevertheless failed to demonstrate sufficiently a solution for the problem of identity involved.

In the work of de Lubac, Congar, Journet, and in the earlier works of Masure and Mersch, the Church herself has become the object of patient reflection and thought. Since the Second World War, great popularity has been accorded to the posthumous works

[63] Paris: Desclée, 1929.
[64] *The Dark Knowledge of God* (London: Sheed & Ward, 1948).
[65] *The Wisdom of Faith* (Westminster, Md.: Newman, 1952).
[66] *The Primacy of Peter* (Westminster, Md.: Newman, 1954).
[67] *La Messe: présence du sacrifice de la croix* (Bruges: Desclée, 1957).

of the Jesuit, Yves de Montcheuil.[68] De Montcheuil was Professor of Dogma at the Institut Catholique in Paris, and an advisor to a number of Catholic Action groups. His books were the fruit of conferences with these groups. In 1944 he was killed by the Gestapo. His finest work, *Aspects of the Church*, is a study of the Church, her interior life, and her relationship to the world and man.[69] It would be erroneous to attribute to de Montcheuil any enormous importance as a speculative theologian; however, his figure and work have exercised an enormous influence within France since the end of the war.

3. YVES CONGAR, O.P.–THE CHURCH AND THE CHURCHES

If one were to look within the French Church today for the spirit of Lacordaire, no finer example of abiding faith in the Church could be found than in the Dominican, Yves Marie-Joseph Congar. Like Lacordaire before him, whom he admires intensely, and like de Lubac his contemporary, Père Congar has long labored under a cloud of suspicion and distrust. He has distinguished himself and his work by a constant, faithful and abiding trust in the Church of Christ.

Yves Congar was born in Sedan on April 13, 1904, and after completing his secondary schooling he entered the Dominican order. He was for many years and is now Professor of Theology at the Dominican House of studies at Le Saulchoir. During the war he was interned at Colditz and Lubeck, and resumed his theological post after the war. A prolific writer, his work has appeared in numerous periodicals since 1936, and in a number of books that have become landmarks in the theological revival in modern France.

His first major work, *Chrétiens désunis*, appeared in 1937, and marked the first public expression of a new theological orientation toward the ecumenical movement.[70] A collection of his articles on the Church, Christian unity, the theology of St. Thomas and the problem of dogmatic development which appeared during the 1930's

---

[68] Yves de Montcheuil, S.J., *For Men of Action* (Chicago: Fides, 1954); *Guide for Social Action* (Chicago: Fides, 1954).

[69] *Aspects of the Church* (Chicago: Fides, 1954).

[70] Yves Congar, O.P., *Divided Christendom* (London: Bles, 1939).

were collected and published in 1941 as *Esquisses du mystère de l'église*. To these were added a later article on the Holy Spirit and the work reappeared under the same title for the *Unam Sanctam* series in 1953.[71] Soon after the war he published two minor works: one a memorial on the Resistance, and the other, *La Catholicité en marche*, in 1948.

In 1950 he began the most fruitful years of his publishing career. In that year appeared his monumental *Vraie et fausse réforme dans l'église*.[72] Three years later the widely acclaimed study of the theology of the laity, *Jalons pour une théologie du laïcat*,[73] and a small work on the race question for UNESCO appeared.[74] The year 1958 saw a monumental work on Biblical theology, a study of the presence of God among His people during the various stages of history, *Le Mystère du temple, ou l'économie de la presence de Dieu*.[75] A number of articles have appeared in various periodicals, frequently in the now defunct *La Vie intellectuelle*, and in the continuing *Vie spirituelle* and the *Bulletin thomiste*. A collection of these have been published in book form.[76] He has also contributed the articles on "Schism" and "Theology" to the *Dictionnaire de théologie catholique*. At present he is working on what he hopes will be his *magnum opus* in theology, a complete treatise on the Church tentatively entitled *L'Eglise, peuple de Dieu et corps du Christ*.

The Church

The basic theme that marks the work of Congar is the same as that of de Lubac, the Church of Christ. The Church is envisioned in no narrow juridical attitude only, but animates the work of Congar because it is the continuing mystery of God-with-men. "It is no longer a question of presence only, it is of the *dwelling* of God in the faithful. All personally, and all together, in their very

[71] *Esquisses du mystère de l'église* (Paris: Editions du Cerf, 1953). Translated as *The Mystery of the Church* (Baltimore: Helicon, 1960).

[72] Paris: Editions du Cerf, 1950. Parts of the work have appeared in English in the periodical *Cross Currents*. See Chap. I, n. 2.

[73] *Lay People in the Church* (Westminster, Md.: Newman, 1956).

[74] *The Catholic Church and the Race Question* (Paris: UNESCO, 1954).

[75] Paris: Éditions du Cerf, 1958.

[76] *Christ, Our Lady and the Church* (Westminster, Md.: Newman, 1957).

unity, are the Temple of God because they are the Body of Christ animated and united by His Spirit." [77] Throughout his work, however, Congar specifically limits his vision to study the elements of this Church, most especially those human elements that go to make up the Mystical Body of Christ throughout time, and this always in view of the great unifying theme of God-man in the Incarnation.

The initial theme of this chapter, the necessary "openness" of the Church to the modern world, finds its echo in the work of Congar. In the *Esquisses du mystère de l'église* he comments with regard to the Church's catholicity that it is "the universal capacity for unity." The implications for Congar go far beyond just the theme of "openness" but as well to the formation of a theological basis for ecumenicism and for missiology: "Such a catholicity implies that every human value can, while keeping its proper reality, its difference in value and its own specific nature, be "recapitulated" in Christ, that is to say, it can be reanimated by His Spirit and assumed into the unity of His Body which is the Church." [78] Thus the Church is not only essentially open to human values but it is also her mission to reanimate these values with the Spirit of God.

Each Christian, as a member of the Church, not unlike the theologian, must share this approach of openness by the Church to the modern world. In the *Mystère du temple* he comments: "If Christ is the principle and the end of the Church-Temple, Christians are at once the matter of construction and the constructors of it. One of the common traits of the great Biblical images of the Church is that all are actively interested and integrated, some having a particular responsibility or function." [79] The layman, then, must also be aware of the implications inherent in this conception of the Church:

The vocation proper to lay people, corresponding to their state as such, is to make their way to God while doing this world's work . . . the lay person has to live for God without being dispensed from doing the work of the world; his particular Christian calling is to bring glory to God and the reign of Christ in and through that work: to be the Church—not the Church inert, present but not present in a world

[77] *Le Mystère du temple, op. cit.,* p. 281.
[78] *Esquisses du mystère de l'église, op. cit.,* p. 122.
[79] *Le Mystère du temple, op. cit.,* p. 197.

wherein she would have nothing to do, but—the Church active, there where the clergy are not, in ways the clergy cannot be, namely, in temporal affairs and daily events, doing the work of the world and of history. That is why Pope Pius XII said that the laity do more than belong to the Church, that they *are* the Church, *in as much as* she is "the society of those who, under the supernatural influence of grace, in the perfection of their personal dignity as sons of God and in the harmonious development of every human inclination and energy, build up the mighty framework of the community of men." [80]

The Human Element in the Church

While Congar has reached his most respected status as a theologian of the Catholic viewpoint on ecumenicism, to which we shall shortly turn, it is significant to note that he contributed major works that are studies of the precisely human elements of the Church. These are studies of the possibilities of and conditions for true and lasting reform within the Church, and of the place and nature of the layman in the Church.

It has been said that it was his *Vraie et fausse réforme dans l'église* that produced clouds of suspicion under which Congar was forced to labor, and there seems to be no doubt that the work was highly controversial from many points of view.

The problem to which this work was addressed was that of reform, of the true dissatisfaction that a Christian may feel within the Church, and of the sincerity that frequently lies at the bottom of such dissatisfaction. "Sincerity has always been a requirement of the Christian character, but in modern man there is an irrepressible need for sincerity, especially in matters of worship and in his relations with God." [81] Many parts of the work are precisely on questions that touch ecumenicism, with the historical framework in which heresies appeared and their relationship to a necessity of reform at the time among the purely human element of the Church. There is, of course, the necessity of touching upon the delicate question of relationships with the central authority of the Church located in the Roman primacy. Here he was most insistent upon the question of having at Rome an authentic representation of the wide human diversity that constitutes the Body of the Church; for

[80] *Lay People in the Church, op. cit.,* pp. 374–375.
[81] *Vraie et fausse réforme, op. cit.,* p. 50.

Congar, such insistence was not a matter of decentralizing ecclesiastical administration, so much as of "enabling central authority to avoid isolation." [82] The human element of the Church must never be lost sight of, the Church is in a sense "theandric" like her head, Christ.

That there are within the Church two general tendencies or elements, the component parts of which are not always found in their entirety, is also faced by Congar. He has dared to express in print what is no doubt a real division of outlook among men within the Church. There are those of a "liberal" outlook who are most insistent upon viewing the human elements operative in the Church, and there are those, whom he labels "integralists," of a more conservative, authoritarian frame of mind. Neither the Christian progressive nor Christian integralist has, so Congar believes, other than the interests of the Church in mind, but they do clash in the realms and order of ecclesiastical policy. It was his description of what he regards as "integralism" that more than any other factor won him undying opposition from certain churchmen:

This accustoms both priests and faithful to a certain lack of initiative even where life would demand that it be taken. Pushed to its extreme limit, it would end up by conceiving religion as something completely ready-made, entirely determined from on high and extrinsic to the personal decisions of conscience, and the "*sentire cum Ecclesia*" would become a mechanical docility complying with complete and meticulous regulations, admitting no margin for personal decision or adaptation. . . . It is because one is not sure of himself, and feels himself overwhelmed by the culture and dynamism of a world he knows principally from afar, that one is timid and sets up barricades. An Innocent III, a Leo XIII, a Pius XI, on the contrary, have been boldly openhearted and enterprising because they dominated their times by their intelligence and strong personality. There is something other than chance to be found to account for the fact that a timid and defensive Christianity easily becomes a religion of women and children which is afraid of mature men and scarcely pays any attention to them. It is not an accident, either, that in a regime of rigorous authority and strict regimentation the clergy has above all the tendency to seek security in what has already been accepted and to like "ready-made" recipes.[83]

[82] *Ibid.*, p. 303.
[83] *Ibid.*, this translation from the *Cross Currents* translation, *op. cit.*. p. 82.

Congar's response to the growing interest in the place of the layman in the Church is to be found in his *Jalons pour une théologie du laïcat*. An admirable theological treatise, the *Jalons* is based solidly upon Scripture, tradition and the teaching of the Church. Congar relates the position of the layman to the Church and its various functions: its royal (ruling), prophetical and priestly functions, and its teaching office and apostolic mission. The work is marked as is the *Vraie et fausse réforme dans l'église*, not only by an accurate and detailed usage of Scripture but by abundant historical examples. This latter element, present most significantly in these two works, provides excellent and factual illustrations for many of the points he wishes to make. Since the *Jalons*, other major works have followed to constitute a significant corpus of works on a theology of the laity.

Divided Christendom

The meaning of Père Congar's fruitful explorations of the Mystery of the Church in its specifically diverse and human aspects as well as the total Mystery, is to be found in the constant theme of ecumenicism which he propounds. The ecumenical movement has no more thoughtful Catholic theologian than Père Congar. His first major work, *Chrétiens désunis*, was devoted to a study of ecumenicism; it still remains as one of the great early books in the Catholic theology of ecumenicism. Congar has traveled widely and written many articles in periodicals for those interested in the problem. It is frequently alluded to, and historical references of a more properly ecumenical nature mark the *Vraie et fausse réforme dans l'église*. It is to an ecumenical consideration of Continental Protestantism that he returned in the more recent *Christ, Our Lady and the Church*.

There is not to be found in Congar's work a lyrical approach to ecumenicism, nor the romantic attitudes of some, nor the simple emotional exhortations "to come together." He has treated non-Catholic Christendom in an admittedly sympathetic manner, but always with the theological approach. This is what has marked his specific contribution to modern ecclesiology, the firm theological base upon which he places Catholic interest in the ecumenical movement.

In a divided Christianity, the foremost elements that the Catholic must seek to reunite are those of Eastern Orthodoxy and Western Protestantism. In *Chrétiens désunis*, Congar's statement of the differences that lie between these two bodies and the Church of Christ is marked by a sense of history, by the method of historical appreciation that so strongly characterizes his other works. In addition to these historical insights, a remarkable sense of the meaning of Sacred Scripture and the sources of theology give theological depth as well as historical breadth to his treatment of the problem.

In facing the Orthodox schism, which he places in its root cause at 330 A.D. when the Imperial seat of government was transferred to Byzantium, he reminds us that the final break with Rome and the consequent separately developed traditions of the East "have affected also Eastern ecclesiological thought. From the first the Eastern mind envisaged rather the divine realities at the heart of the Mystery of the Church than its earthly aspect and human implications; it saw more clearly the inward unity of faith and love than the practical demands of ecclesiastical communion." [84] It would be, he states, blindness indeed to attempt to reunite the Eastern to the Western Church on such oversimplified grounds as the *"filioque,"* while being unaware of the traditions and attitudes that have become the warp and woof of Orthodoxy.

In like manner Western Protestantism must not be simply considered as a product of bad will, a deliberate and malicious rending of the unity of the Church. The real religious spirit and feeling of Protestantism that have served to carry it through the history of the last three centuries must be faced and appreciated. "It seems fairly clear that the Reformation, in the circumstances outlined, in conflict with some of them and helped by others, was in essentials a religious movement, an attempt to revive religion by a return to the sources." [85] The appreciation of the positive factors historically involved in heresy and schism is necessary for any real approach to the problem, and it is this appreciation so eloquently demanded by Congar which later marks the outstanding contributions of Louis Bouyer and George Tavard to the Catholic ecumenical approach.

[84] *Chrétiens désunis* (Paris: Editions du Cerf, 1937), p. 14. The reader is warned that the English translation, *Divided Christendom*, is badly translated in parts. References here will be to the French edition.
[85] *Ibid.*, p. 22.

In both these major cases of Christian division the common obstacle to full reunion with the one Church of Christ, and perhaps the greatest obstacle is the continued division itself.[86] The historical development of a continuance of separation becomes in itself the major problem:

Thus the persistence alone of separation has become a heavy stone rolled over the mouth of the sepulchre where unity was entombed by the first misunderstandings. While separation has lasted reproaches have gained force, differences have multiplied and taken root, controversies, prejudices and passions have piled up and have become a historic tradition and inheritance. It would be easy to give instances, some of which would appear incredible if the witnesses to them were not above suspicion. We have only to think of that ensemble of active prejudice to be found in all non-Catholic countries. . . . We, on our side, have most of all got into the way of doing without our separated brethren. . . . Each Christian group has followed its own lines and evolved in its own way. This is a fact of importance. . . .[87]

The Church and the Churches

It is not enough to place the Catholic ecumenical attitude toward separated Christians upon the consideration and appreciation of the Orthodox or Protestant difficulty. For Congar, Catholic ecumenicism must rest upon the theology of the Church; it must find not only its principles but its dynamism in the proper conception of the Church. It is the Catholic Church that alone possesses complete unity, a unity communicated by the unity of God Himself:

The ground of the Church's existence is the communication to the many of the life of the Father. It is because there is only one God that there is only one Church, one with the very oneness of God, outside whom she does not exist. Because we participate in one life, which is the life

---

[86] This point is taken up again especially with regard to the Orthodox in Congar's contribution to "*1054–1954 : L'Église et les églises*" (Chevetogne: Editions de Chevetogne, 1954), 2 vols. This is an excellent two-volume work on the Eastern Church and the Orthodox Schism including many distinguished contributors such as Cerfaux, Dupont, Danielou and Capelle. Congar's essay has been translated and printed separately in English as *After Nine Hundred Years* (New York: Fordham University Press, 1959).

[87] *Chrétiens désunis, op. cit.,* pp. 29–30.

of God, we are one with God, and one among ourselves, in Christ. . . . The life of God in glory and beatitude becomes, by grace, a "common good" pertaining to God and those whom He calls to share it. And this *bonum commune* constitutes a society absolutely unique, which is the Church.[88]

From the unity of the Church of God flows her uniqueness. They are obviously not the same: one is to be without division, the other to be the only one of a kind. "Now if the Church is no less than the communication of the life of the Blessed Trinity, she is necessarily one with the oneness of God Himself, and therefore unique as God is unique, one sole Church, as there is and because there is, one sole God, one Lord, one Father, one Faith." [89] In line with the unity and uniqueness of the Church certain consequences are evident, that the unity of the Church, derived from above, cannot be broken by the secession of any member; that there can be no salvation except in the Church. This Church, one, unique, indivisible, and necessary, is the Mystery of union in Christ, and through Christ to God:

Thus we approach God only in Christ, we are sons only in Christ, we inherit only in Christ, we share in the blessings of the covenant only in Christ, we are conformed to the life of God only in Christ. . . . The Church is the visible reality of the Lord, His "*soma*," a Christophany: she is His own Body and His Flesh which He animates.[90]

Catholicity, or universality, of the Church and of her mission, follows from these considerations. As Christ our Head is Him in whom every man is assumed and incorporated, His Church cannot but be catholic or universal. "Its oneness is given by God precisely to restore into unity all the diversity of His creation . . . its catholicity is precisely this capacity of unity to save, to fulfill, to bring back all humanity. . . . The Church is catholic exactly as she is one, in the same degree and by the same principle." [91]

From these properly theological concepts the Catholic in facing

[88] *Ibid.*, pp. 63–64.
[89] *Ibid.*, p. 72.
[90] *Ibid.*, pp. 74–75.
[91] *Ibid.*, pp. 121–122.

the modern ecumenical movement "gives a categorical refusal, in so far as ecumenicism implies that the Church of Christ does not actually exist in this world, and that there has been some sort of failure and a break in the living continuity which by grace and the gifts of the Spirit links her with the historic incarnation and redeeming work of her Lord." [92] The Catholic may not accept the erroneous theory or faulty conceptions of the Church that his non-Catholic contemporary advances as a basis for the ecumenical movement. The Catholic reason for taking an active interest in the movement is different, and must be radically different from that of the non-Catholic. But it is in no sense a less real commitment to the attempt to settle the problems that division has created.

Père Congar states that the Catholic facing the challenge of the Orthodox schism, having firmly established his own theological position, will find many points of doctrinal agreement with the Orthodox. However, despite agreements, the attempts to establish accord and agreement are destined to stumble upon the theological problem of the Church herself:

It is obvious that Catholics are in full agreement with the substance of the Orthodox affirmations about the fellowship of the Holy Ghost and the Mystical Body of Christ. . . . But if we hold all the positive content of this ecclesiology in common with the Orthodox, we add something to it, or rather, we feel that they take something away from it. What we add and what they reject are the elements proper to the Church Militant, the conditions due to the present state of the Church on earth, *ex hominibus.* . . . To say that God calls us, sanctifies and saves us corporately in the Church, does not only mean that He unites us mystically in Him by giving the same life to all, but that He has instituted for us on earth a saving and sanctifying community, analogous to a human society. For the very reason that it comes under the law of human life the Mystical Body manifests itself as a society on human lines: the Church, in becoming the Church Militant, realizes her inner nature, which is the fellowship of the divine life, under the appearance of a visible society hierarchically constituted. We cannot speak absolutely of the Church Militant here on earth as we can of the glorified Church. Now it seems to us that Orthodox ecclesiology does not lay sufficient stress on the human side of ecclesiastical reality. Orthodox theologians,

[92] *Ibid.,* p. 177.

indeed, often define the Church in terms which are as applicable to the Church Triumphant in heaven as to the Church on earth, so far removed are they from the conditions actually imposed on the latter.[93]

If the fundamental theological difficulty that faces Catholics and Orthodox lies in the sphere of ecclesiology, the differences that are basic to the Catholic-Protestant division are based upon the Incarnation. "The Incarnation is the key to the whole mystery of the Church and the sacraments. In the degree to which Protestant- ism can school itself in a profound and realistic contemplation of the Mystery of the Incarnation will it return. . . ."[94] It is to this theme Congar returned twelve years later in the collection, *Christ, Our Lady and the Church*, in which he attempts to show that the Protestant difficulties with the Catholic theology of Mary and the Church "are closely bound up with each other, and that our failure to agree about them has its roots in a divergence about Our Lord Himself. . . ."[95]

Protestant problems with regard to Mary and the Church are closely related to the work of salvation through the Incarnation, "the one brings it about, the other communicates it to men and permeates the world with its effects."[96] Thus the Church on earth follows this law of the Incarnation, "human and corporal from one end to the other, and divine from one end to the other; theandric, as is Christ."[97] Protestantism is afflicted with the thought of Luther, of his compelling vision of the transcendent God, so that the con- cept of created instrumentality is lost.

Luther will have it that *everything* in the work of salvation must pro- ceed from God alone and be solely God's doing; for this a transient gift only would be needed from Him. There can be no return to God in which man is the active agent, no re-ascent in which man's cooperation, moved and made possible by a gift of God, would have some sharing in producing the result. He is insistent that God in fact operates all our deeds in us. . . . The conception he developed too of the part played

93 *Ibid.*, pp. 266–268.
94 *Ibid.*, p. 344.
95 *Christ, Our Lady and the Church, op. cit.*, p. 5.
96 *Ibid.*, p. 15.
97 *Chrétiens désunis, op. cit.*, p. 86.

by the humanity of Christ in the economy of salvation is not uninfluenced by it. The humanity of Christ plays no part in the causality of the Redemption in Luther's thought. . . . The Sacred Humanity united to the Divinity without confusion or division is the instrument of our salvation, and the means by which all grace is communicated to us. This is why our Lady, by her intimate association with the sacred Humanity, and the Church in consequence of it, play the part our teaching assigns to them.[98]

If Congar's strictures on the proper evaluation of the humanity of Christ, the role of Mary, and the work of the Church are sharply aimed at the theology that divides Catholicism and Protestantism, in no less a manner is he critical of excessive Catholic "tendencies" by individuals which serve to strengthen the Protestant error by reaction. "It may also be that some expositions of our Lady's place show her too exclusively endowed, in herself and on her own behalf, with unprecedented privileges; as if for instance God had willed in honoring man in Jesus Christ to honor woman in Mary." [99]

The divisions of Christendom, which it is the desire of ecumenicists to heal, must find not only sympathetic treatment on the part of Catholics but theological awareness as well. If Congar has brought to contemporary theology a theological awareness of the problem of a divided Christendom, he has also brought a sense of urgency and hope to Catholics engaged in the dialogue with their separated brethren:

Of re-union, as of the Second Coming of the Lord, we can only say that God alone knows the time, and it is in vain for us to try to determine the day or the means. Since it is something which of itself is quite beyond our power, and can only come about through the omnipotence of God, it must be for us, above all, an object of hope and of prayer. Our sin and wickedness have entombed the unbroken unity of Christendom, and oppressed by the humanly insurmountable obstacles in the way of its restoration to us we begin to ask, like the holy women at the sepulchre, "Who shall roll away for us the stone at the door of the Tomb?" Yet perhaps the angels of God already have been given a mission which we cannot foresee.[100]

[98] *Christ, Our Lady and the Church, op. cit.,* pp. 28–29, 31.
[99] *Ibid.,* p. 39.
[100] *Chrétiens désunis, op. cit.,* pp. 344–345.

Controversy

Père Yves Congar's status today as one of the greatest theologians of ecumenicism has not been attained without a certain opposition. Dispute has frequently centered about his theological proposals, and no small amount of antagonism has been created by his "attitude" toward separated Christians. On this latter point there is a common opinion among his critics that Congar goes too far in accentuating the human deficiencies in the history of the Church, and that his sympathetic approach has the "tendency" to minimize either the content or importance of Christian dogmas disputed by the dissidents. Yet his critics have not produced any solid evidence for these allegations.

Theological controversy has been aroused by Congar's treatment of the position of non-Catholic Christians vis-à-vis the Church. Taking as his initial position the theological certainty of the Church as humanity reconciled with God, the Church then because of her unity with Christ derives from Him the principles capable of reconciling with God every man and all humanity. These principles are "an ordered fullness, living and organic" rather than essentially diverse; yet "they are multiple, because of the complexity of that humanity which they have to reach and permeate and vivify into a people and a Church." [101] These principles are ordered one to the other, but they can be realized in separation "not indeed in the Church as such . . . but in us, the members of the Church, who may be unequally inspired by her soul and live by only a part of her energies." [102] Therefore, it follows that non-Catholic Christians can share some of these principles as members of the Church:

There is perfect membership of the Church—and so of Christ—in one who lives according to all the principles of the new life of reconciliation with God which Christ has fully given to His Church. But there is imperfect membership of the Church, and of Christ, in one who lives only by one or other of the principles of the new life. It is because the benefits of the New Covenant are many that it is possible to belong to the Church in varying degree and to claim membership of it on various grounds.[103]

101 *Ibid.*, p. 283.
102 *Ibid.*, p. 284.
103 *Ibid.*, p. 284.

As a matter of fact, the valid Baptism conferred by many non-Catholic Christian communities makes the child a real member of the one Church of Jesus Christ. However, "Catholic though he be by the grace of that Baptism, he will in fact find himself in an objective Christian milieu which is impoverished and distorted, a confessional or ecclesiastical order which is not the full and true life of the Church of Christ. . . . In short, he will not find the whole of the living principles ordained by God to bring all humanity in fellowship with Himself." [104]

Such a consideration leads to definite conclusions. The Protestant or Orthodox Christian who is separate from the one true Church because of morally invincible ignorance is not in the real sense a "heretic." Such a non-Catholic Christian "even if he professes material heresy, cannot be called a heretic . . . they are more rightly called separated brethren." [105] He will never find in his sect all the principles of life in Christ, but in virtue of those he does discover (Baptism, charity and sacramental grace if there are valid sacraments) he is to that degree a member of the Church. Such separated brethren belong to the Church insofar as they belong to Christ; and, on the other hand, it may never be forgotten that "the good dissident, so long as he remains dissident, will never enter, whatever he may do, into complete enjoyment of all the benefits entrusted to the people of the New Covenant for the realization of their communion with God." [106]

There are Catholic theologians, actively engaged in the ecumenical movement, for whom the non-Catholic dissident is not a member of the Church. These theologians—and their numbers are not insignificant—deny to Christians not living under the ruling and teaching power of the Pope and the bishops of the Catholic Church any real membership in the Church. Thus, on this particular point strong exception has been taken to Père Congar's position.[107] As Congar

---

[104] *Ibid.*, p. 289.

[105] *Ibid.*, pp. 290–291.

[106] *Ibid.*, p. 293.

[107] See the Rev. Edward F. Hanahoe, S.A., *Catholic Ecumenicism* (Washington, D.C.: Catholic University Press, 1953). See also George Tavard's contribution toward the settlement of this problem in "Catholicity and non-Catholic Christians," *Downside Review*, Vol. 77, no. 249 (Summer-Autumn, 1959), pp. 205–216.

limits the membership in the Church to individual dissidents living by one or more of the principles of reconciliation in Christ and not to their sects, these theologians deny membership in the Church to both individuals and sects.

Père Congar's approach to the non-Catholic Christian is, as we have seen, basically that of a theologian with sympathy and historical appreciation. But, as he has pointed out, the Catholic theologian must also turn his attention to the properly theological principles that govern the cooperation of Catholics with non-Catholics in the modern pluralistic state. Thus, he states, this question is one of the most urgent tasks facing the theologian today. And it is upon this highly debated question of Church-State relationships that Congar has taken the position of separation of Church and State, based ultimately on theological grounds.[108]

The primary theological principle that is involved in Catholic–non-Catholic relationships in the pluralistic state is this, that the supernatural end of the human race is known and accomplished only through the revelation proposed and interpreted by the teaching authority of the Roman Catholic Church. In the modern world the Church must not attempt to induce man and society to subordinate themselves to this end by the medieval way of subordination to the Church's power of jurisdiction, but rather the Church must show to each man the demands of the Truth. For Congar, "the sword of the Church is the Word of God."

The Church, in fearlessly facing the modern world, is to fulfill her mission of reconciling man and society with God, and of unifying and vivifying all members of the Body of Christ with the Spirit of Christ; and, the more surely she acts upon the basis of the theology of her own constitution, the closer she draws to the theology that is the source of her strength. The separation of Church and State which he envisions is arrived at, as are many of the answers the theologians propose to difficulties, if the theologian utilizes sound historical information as well as strictly dogmatic facts. Thus, Congar sees the medieval thesis of Church-State unification as only one of the "hypotheses" realized in history, not one to which the theologian is bound because of an absolute dogmatic value.

[108] See his essay on pluralism in *Tolerance et communauté humaine* (Paris: Casterman, 1951), pp. 191–223.

Contemporary Developments

The awareness of the Church, and the continuing examination of the meaning of the Mystery of the Church by the theologians is represented by new and significant approaches to a theology of the laity. Thus their work is symbolized by the *Jalons* of Père Congar. In addition to these theological reflections the growing importance of Catholic Action, and the papal encouragement and approbation given it in the past thirty years, give ample evidence of an awareness on the part of the Church of the importance of the lay apostolate.

In 1955 Msgr. Léon J. Suenans, the Bishop of Malines in Belgium, wrote on the work of the laity in *L'Eglise en état de mission*.[109] Msgr. Gérard Philips, Professor of Dogmatic Theology at the University of Louvain, in 1955 produced a capable treatise on the theology of the laity in a scholarly and yet extremely clear and popular work.[110] Most of the major theological periodicals have taken up the theme in frequent articles; among the more articulate are the Dominicans Plé, Grangette and Servand in *La Vie spirituelle: supplement*.

Aside from this theological examination of the place of the laity, it might be noted here that fascinating aspect of the French Church —the place of the laity among the theologians. As it is not unusual to find in the sciences a large number of priests, by the same token, it is not unusual to find laymen among the theologians. Jean Guitton, layman, professor, Catholic intellectual, is basically a philosopher. He has brilliantly approached the traditional apologetic problem in his two books: *Le Problème de Jésus: Divinité et Résurrection*, and *Le Problème de Jésus et les fondements du témoinage chrétien*, and other important works.[111] Other laymen, such as the distinguished humanist Gustave Thibon, and the historian Henri-

---

[109] Bruges: Desclée, 1955.

[110] Gérard Philips, *The Role of the Laity in the Church* (Chicago: Fides, 1955).

[111] These two works were collated and translated as *The Problem of Jesus* (London: Burns, Oates, 1955). See also the translations *The Virgin Mary* (New York: Kenedy, 1952), *The Modernity of Saint Augustine* (Baltimore: Helicon, 1959), and his biography of the priest who influenced a host of modern French intellectuals, *Abbé Pouget* (Baltimore: Helicon, 1959).

Irenée Marrou touch in their influential works many of the problems that have traditionally perplexed theologians.

The Ecumenical Movement

In the developing theology of the Church that preoccupies the modern theologian in France today, there has been significant advance in the field of ecumenicism. Ecumenicism has become one of the most distinctive contributions to theological thought by the French, and many of their works are marked by an "openness" to the problems posed by ecumenical thought and the ecumenical movement in the Protestant Church. The field is marked by many fine contributions, especially, as we have noted, those of Yves Congar. Charles Journet devoted one of his earliest works to a sympathetic consideration of the problem of the reunion of the various Christian denominations with the Church established by Christ.

Among modern ecumenical contributions, one of the most significant has been that of Père Louis Bouyer, professor at the Institut Catholique. Bouyer had been a Lutheran minister and a student of Oscar Cullmann at the Sorbonne. In 1954 he published *Du Protestantisme à l'église*.[112] The theme of the book was that the valid and valuable religious insights of the Protestant experience could only find their full flowering and meaning in the tradition from which they were drawn—Catholicism. For Bouyer reunion is not the question of the "conversion" of a Protestant but his fulfillment.

The French theologian, George Tavard, published *A la Rencontre du protestantisme* in 1953, and prepared a revised edition for English translation in 1955.[113] The book created some small furore because of its sympathetic approach to the Protestant ecumenical movement. Although not completely representative of American theologians and their positions, nevertheless the distinguished American ecumenicist, Edward Hanahoe, severely criticized Tavard, and was upheld by another American theologian of importance.[114] Despite this opposition from some Americans, Tavard has taken up residence

112 Louis Bouyer, C. Orat., *The Spirit and Forms of Protestantism* (Westminster, Md.: Newman, 1956).

113 Rev. George H. Tavard, A.A., *The Catholic Approach to Protestantism* (New York: Harper, 1955).

114 Rev. Joseph C. Fenton, "Appraisal in Sacred Theology," *American Ecclesiastical Review*, Vol. 134 (1956), pp. 24–36.

in the United States and continues to write well and frequently on a sympathetic and understanding approach to non-Catholics.[115]

Mention should also be made of the excellent work by Gustave Thils of Louvain in 1955: his *Histoire doctrinale du mouvement œcumenique*.[116] Thils has been, of the French and Belgian ecumenicists, one of the most respected and accepted in theological circles.

The ecumenical movement that so marks the French theological approach to the Church is not a comparatively contemporary one, an immediate situation without root. There has been since the very beginnings of the modern theological revival a strong ecumenicism in France and Belgium. In 1890 Père Fernand Portal entered into conversations with Lord Halifax looking toward the corporate reunion of the Anglican Church. In 1896, Pope Leo XIII's decision against the validity of Anglican Orders, in the encyclical *Apostolicae Curae*, ended all further discussions with the Anglicans of that time. However, between 1921 and 1927 the Malines Conversations were held under Cardinal Mercier. These also proved fruitless as regards the corporate reunion of the Anglicans. It would be senseless to think that because of the eventual termination of both attempts without a reunion that nothing was gained. Certainly each of the parties concerned received at least understanding and sympathy for the position of the other, and these are the materials for a real charity.

During the 1930's the Abbé Paul Couturier continued friendly relations with the Protestant bodies of France. He strongly influenced the Protestant monastic communities established at Taizé and Grandmaison. Couturier could witness before his death in 1953 the Church Unity Octave firmly established among Protestants as well as Catholics. They were praying, in his words, for the "visible unity of the Kingdom of God, such as Christ wants it and through the means He will choose." This was a prayer which did not exclude the Catholic belief that such a unity already existed in the Apostolic See. Since his death, Père Villain has carried out Couturier's work and written an eloquent tribute about his predecessor.[117]

---

[115] George Tavard, A.A., *The Church, the Layman and the Modern World* (New York: Macmillan, 1959).

[116] Louvain: Editions Warny.

[117] Villain, *L'Abbé Paul Couturier, apôtre de l'unité chrétienne* (Paris: Casterman, 1957).

The ecumenical movement is also marked by an appreciation and understanding of the work of modern Protestant theologians. The Jesuit scholar René Marle has published a trenchant study of Rudolph Bultmann.[118] The most eminent of the new theologians of Protestantism, Karl Barth, has been the object of an exhaustive study by Henri Bouillard, S.J.[119] In Protestant circles Bouillard has been brought to task for approaching Barth in a nonecumenical spirit. However, de Lubac has written in defense of Bouillard that true ecumenicism does not ignore the truth, or the properly theological approach. For de Lubac, if there are to be approaches to unity that are sincere and lasting, they must be based on fact no less than charity.

The renewal in the sources of theology, particularly in the fields of patristics and Church history have created interest in the problem of the Catholic attitude toward the Orthodox Churches. In 1926, Dom Lambert Beauduin founded the Priory of Union at St. Emay in Belgium in response to the request of Pope Pius XI for men to devote themselves to the problem of East-West reunion. Beauduin began publishing in 1927 the quarterly periodical *Irenikon* dealing with liturgical and historical problems attendant on the Orthodox position. In 1939 the priory was transferred to Chevetogne in Belgium and was soon raised to the status of an abbey. At Chevetogne a wider interest in the reunion of all separated Christian groups was created.

At the present time Chevetogne has become one of the most important influences within the entire ecumenical movement. One commentator has called it "a place of reconciliation, . . . of prayer and quiet . . . of study; a great library is consecrated to the work of reunion. Cultivating the traditions of the Western and Eastern Churches within the one community, it is a living example of the enrichment possible when the different Christian traditions unite within the one faith." [120]

Papal approval of the organizational work of *Unitas* in Rome

<hr>

118 René Marle, S.J., *Bultmann et l'interprétation du Nouveau Testament* (Paris: Aubier, 1956).

119 Henri Bouillard, S.J., *Karl Barth* (Paris: Aubier, 1957), 3 vols.

120 John M. Todd, *Catholicism and the Ecumenical Movement* (London: Longmans, 1956).

under Père Charles Boyer, S.J., of the Gregorian University, was given in 1945. Among others working in the field of ecumenical relationships are the Belgian Dominicans under Père Jérome Hamer, and the French Dominicans at the ecumenical center, Istina, under Père C. J. Dumont. Dumont published in 1957 an extremely important collection of his articles on the ecumenical problem, and was one of the official Catholic observers appointed by the Holy See to the Protestant World Conference held at Lund.[121]

Nor is the ecumenical spirit limited to the separated Christian groups. Considerable work has been done toward evaluating, interpreting and appreciating the Jewish question by Abbé Paul Demann in Paris. Demann's group publishes a series under the general title of *Les cahiers sioniens*. The Eastern and Oriental religions have been approached. The Benedictines have established a monastery in Algiers among the Moslems, and sponsor Islamic-Christian theological conferences.[122] The Jesuits de Lubac and the late François Taymans have published excellent studies on the question of Buddhism, and others such as Monchanin and Le Saux on approaches to the Hindus.

The whole phenomenon of ecumenism among the French is worthy of examination. Tavard lists as major causes of this trend within the Church: The theological awakening of our century, the return to the Bible, the liturgical renewal, and the accession of the laity to responsibility. From without, he sees the immediate and permanent threat of a new dictatorship forcing a choice between Christian or Marxist unity. We might safely state that the future of the ecumenical movement within the Church seems assured, certainly in view of the forthcoming Council announced by Pope John XXIII and in his discreet and kindly invitation to other Christian groups to attend the Council. Père Congar's *Divided Christendom* recalls to us the two conditions for ecumenism: patience and respect for delay. And they are never more necessary than today for the successful fruition of the ecumenical movement.

[121] Père C. J. Dumont, O.P., *Approaches to Christian Unity* (Baltimore: Helicon, 1959). Under Dumont the Istina center publishes the periodical *Vers l'unité chrétienne*.

[122] Peter Beach and William Dunphy, *Benedictine and Moor* (New York: Holt, 1960).

4. PIERRE TEILHARD DE CHARDIN—
THE CHURCH AND SCIENCE

It is difficult for the American reader, or for that matter the English-speaking reader to appreciate properly the figure of Pierre Teilhard de Chardin, a French Jesuit, although a uniform English translation of his works is now about to be published. The importance of Teilhard de Chardin may be measured both by the content of his work and also by his contemporary influence. He is probably one of the most discussed and influential French thinkers today.[123] Although he died in 1955, somewhat under a cloud for his rather novel and striking theories, he remains as one of the predominant figures in contemporary French Catholic thought. The invocation of his name and his elaborate constructions have provoked numberless appreciations and criticisms.[124]

Père Teilhard de Chardin was born in 1881 in Auvergne in France. At the age of eighteen he entered the Society of Jesus, taught at Cairo and devoted himself to the study of geology and paleontology. Ordained in 1912 he continued these studies, served in World War I, and afterward became Professor of Geology at the Institut Catholique in Paris. He received his doctorate from the Sorbonne in 1922, and a year later went with Père Licent on a

---

[123] An excellent introduction to the thought of Teilhard de Chardin is the fine work of Abbé Claudè Tresmontant, *Père Teilhard de Chardin* (Baltimore: Helicon, 1959) and that of Nicolas Corte, *Pierre Teilhard de Chardin* (New York: Macmillan, 1960). See also Lawler, "Chardin and Human Knowledge," *Commonweal*, Vol. 68 (April 11, 1958), pp. 40 ff.; Poulain, "Christ and the Universe," *Commonweal*, Vol. 69 (Jan. 30, 1959), pp. 460 ff.; Towers, "The Significance of Teilhard de Chardin," *Blackfriars*, Vol. 46 (March, 1959), pp. 126-129; Russo, "The Phenomenon of Man," *America*, Vol. 103 (April 30, 1960), pp. 185-189. The following translations of his work are now available: *The Phenomenon of Man* (New York: Harpers, 1959), *The Divine Milieu* (New York: Harper, 1960); also the shorter pieces: "The Psychological Conditions for Human Unification," *Cross Currents*, Vol. 3 (Fall, 1952), pp. 1-5; "Building the Earth," *Cross Currents*, Vol. 9 (Fall, 1959), pp. 315-330.

[124] Tresmontant, *op. cit.*, prints the most extensive bibliography on Teilhard de Chardin. To these should be added the highly critical series by Grenet, "Services et dangers des écrits du R. P. Pierre Teilhard de Chardin," *Ami du clergé*, Vol. 69 (Jan., 1959), pp. 51-58, 65-76; and Fehlner, "Teilhard de Chardin: Ambiguity by Design," *Homiletic and Pastoral Review*, Vol. 60 (May, 1960), pp. 709-717.

scientific expedition to China. He returned in 1924, and soon lost his teaching post at the Institut Catholique because of his views on evolution and the problem of original sin. Thus, removed from his post at the Institut, he returned to China and Père Licent in 1926, and later participated in the Black Expedition that unearthed the skull of "Peking man." He stayed in China until 1946, unable to return to France because of World War II.

After his return to France in 1946, Père Teilhard de Chardin was advised not to write or publish after a number of articles and lectures expressed his rather radical positions. There seems no doubt that many of his theories and opinions were circulated in mimeographed form for the private use of a number of the French clergy and intellectuals. Some of these positions on evolution and original sin became untenable after the 1950 encyclical, *Humani Generis,* in which there were a number of explicit references to evolution, polygenism and original sin.

Under the auspices of the Wernner-Gren scientific foundation he came to the United States in 1951, and worked closely with that group until his death in 1955. According to Julian Huxley "he was prevailed upon to leave his manuscripts to a friend. They therefore could be published after his death, since permission to publish is required only for the works of a living author." [125] The concept implied toward ecclesiastical authority is hardly one that could not be questioned.

Since his death, the French editions of his work have been published, and of these the most important is the *Le Phénomène humain.* In *The Phenomenon of Man* Teilhard de Chardin presents in bold strokes his vision of reality, and the convergence of the forces of material and spiritual energy which compose the evolving human race. Although intended as a scientific study of man, in scientific terms, the work is fraught with theological implications to which we shall return. His correspondence during his first trip to China composes the *Lettres de voyage. Le Milieu divin* indicates his ascetical attitudes toward the world and science, drawing out the implications for the Christian scholar. *La Vision du passé,* and *L'Appari-*

[125] Teilhard de Chardin, *The Phenomenon of Man* (New York: Harpers, 1959). From the Introduction by Sir Julian Huxley, p. 25.

tion are for the most part well organized representations of a number of past articles, highly technical and additionally difficult because of Teilhard de Chardin's unique vocabulary constructions.

The Evolution of Man

Père Teilhard de Chardin's presentation of his theory begins with two major assumptions that are basic to its entire construction. First, it envisages only a scientific examination of the phenomenon of man, measured and observable by the physical scientist. Secondly, the process of evolution is not to be regarded as a theoretical approach but as an unquestioned fact. For Teilhard de Chardin evolution is more than fact, it is the basic condition of reality itself. Evolution cannot be regarded merely on a biological level but as the meaning and form of both material and spiritual energy present in the world.

In addition to these two basic assumptions, there is a necessary corollary. The evolutionary processes of reality cannot find their proper evaluation and definition simply through observation. They must be considered because of their progressive nature in reference to their direction, their ultimate term, their final end.

The evolutionary trends of reality and life converge toward man. This convergence is toward man on the simple biological level first, and later toward man in the philosophical sense, that is, as a thinking and willing creature. This final convergence upon philosophical man is caused by the complexity of forces and race development. Thus, de Chardin sees this process of evolution of man as a growth of the animal with a brain as the term of the evolution of multicellular units, and then of the evolution of primitive man, and finally of man the social being in history.

Is the origin of man singular? Is there a set of first parents? or are there many primary ancestors? Monogenism or polygenism? De Chardin, as a scientist, states:

Man came silently into the world. As a matter of fact he trod so softly that, when we first catch sight of him as revealed by those indestructible stone instruments, we find him sprawling all over the Old World from the Cape of Good Hope to Peking. Without doubt he already speaks and lives in groups; he already makes fire. After all, this is surely what we ought to expect. As we know, each time a new living form rises up before us out of the depths of history, it is always complete and already legion. Thus *in the eyes of science,* which at long range can only see things in bulk, the "first man" is, and can only be *a crowd,* and his infancy is made up of thousands and thousands of years.[126]

The mental subjective activity of man, of conscious and thinking mind, evolves from the convergence and intensity of the disparate trends of reality. Convergence produces complexity, and this complexity (which, simply speaking, is the increasingly detailed organization of life structures) becomes the necessary matter for the evolutionary emergence of the thinking, conscious man.

Teilhard de Chardin maintains that this evolutionary product, this man, this existing, thinking, conscious product has now increased in numbers, perfected communication, and consequently produced still further complexity. Such complexity leads to a new intensity of evolutionary activity, for man's complex organization and communication now guide the evolutionary progress of man to a higher level.

Man's present position and his knowledge lead inexorably to a new stage in evolution:

It was only in the middle of the nineteenth century, again under the influence of biology, that the light dawned at last, revealing the *irreversible coherence* of all that exists. . . . The distribution, succession and solidarity of objects are born from their concrescence in a common genesis. Time and space are organically joined again so to weave, together, the stuff of the universe. That is the point we have reached and how we perceive things today. . . . What makes and classifies a modern man is having become capable of seeing in terms not of space and time alone, but also of duration, or—and it comes to the same thing —of biological space time; and above all having become incapable of seeing anything otherwise. . . . Obviously man could not see evolution all around him without feeling to some extent carried along by it himself. Darwin has demonstrated this. . . . The consciousness of each of us is evolution looking at itself and reflecting. . . .[127]

Thus, man must in his present situation, in order to acquire the value of evolutionary progress, reflect upon himself, and he becomes aware of the laws that bind him.

[126] *Ibid.,* p. 185.
[127] *Ibid.,* pp. 217–218, 220.

Man is not the centre of the universe as once we thought in our simplicity, but something much more wonderful—the arrow pointing the way to the final unification of the world in terms of life. Man alone constitutes the last-born, the freshest, the most complicated, the most subtle of all the successive layers of life. This is nothing else than the fundamental vision and I shall leave it at that. But this vision, mind you, only acquires its full value—is indeed only defensible—through the simultaneous illumination within ourselves of the laws and conditions of heredity.[128]

Evolution has now reached this given point. The necessity of examining evolution in the terms of its direction and eventual completion leads Teilhard de Chardin from this scientifically based consideration to the eventual convergence of the evolutionary forces. These forces are now accentuated in man's intense mental activity, in man's organized society, and in man's progress in the arts of communication. This accentuation and complexity point to the convergence of these forces to a point tentatively labeled "Omega." The Omega point is visualized as the term of all evolutionary process.

For reflection to continue to progress and to function there is required above it a pole which is supreme in attraction and consistence. "By its very structure the noosphere (i.e., the sphere of mental activity that transforms life) could not close itself either individually or socially in any way save under the influence of the centre which we have called Omega. That is the postulate to which we have been led logically by the integral application to man of the experimental laws of evolution." [129] Furthermore, Omega is conceived of as already existing and operating at the core of the thinking mass, it is the conscious pole of the world that animates evolution in its lower stages, and can therefore "only act in an impersonal form and under the veil of biology." [130]

The process of evolution is for Teilhard de Chardin one that may be called *cosmogenesis*. The final emergence of man to point Omega is called *Christogenesis*. This latter completion of the process envisions the integration of human personality to the life

[128] *Ibid.*, p. 223.
[129] *Ibid.*, p. 291.
[130] *Ibid.*, p. 291.

and work of Christ. This concluding step in the evolutionary process lies yet beyond the present mind-conscious-of-itself, and it is one of incorporation, of entirety and wholeness with other men and life itself.

The summary presentation of such a breath-taking vision cannot of course do adequate justice to Teilhard de Chardin's systematic organization of scientific fact, or to his daring interpretation of the "wholeness" of reality, the world and man. He sees "modern man" as man at his present peak, the position that evolution has thus far reached. Now that man realizes evolution, evolution has thus become conscious-of-itself. This very fact is the condition for the present progress of evolution.

Every line of Teilhard de Chardin seems to bristle with a boundless optimism, and so evolution is presented as it must be—the vision of man beyond our present stage. It is conceived of as the creative act of God inherent in reality, and man, who is now evolution-conscious-of-itself, begins to return to God, to his center. This present condition of man looks to an eventual combination of the personal and the collective, not to a pantheism but to the inevitable fact of man gathered up in one in Christ.

In commenting on this presentation, the distinguished scholar Martin D'Arcy observes:

. . . Teilhard de Chardin sees the consummation of history in what he calls man's power "of reflection" and in the convergence of multiple minds into a new culture by dint of their discoveries of the wonders of the universe and of history. There will come a time, he thinks, when mankind will be sustained by the presence and conserving power of Christ, who is both God and man. The scientific apparatus he uses may be at times more an embarrassment than a help, but the Christian philosopher has found an ally, if an unexpected and strange one.[131]

There is implied in Teilhard de Chardin's vision of the world a new Christian attitude toward the intellectual life. Human activity has a particular value in the plan of God, and the Christian must cooperate in this order with God's designs as best he can. The Christian intellectual cannot "retreat" from the world but must

---

[131] Martin D'Arcy, S.J., *The Meaning and Matter of History* (New York: Farrar, Straus & Cudahy, 1959), p. 256.

become ever more engaged in human activity, for through his work and activity the "Incarnational mission" of Christ is ever more accomplished. *Le Milieu divin* is devoted to the explication of this position of the Christian intellectual.

In *Why We Believe*, Msgr. Léon Cristiani introduces the figure of Teilhard de Chardin to the reader with the comment "With him we are not dealing with a philosopher, nor is he a very trustworthy theologian." [132] Any commentary upon Père Teilhard de Chardin or his work or the theological implications of that work must inevitably arrive at this conclusion.

In his preface to *The Phenomenon of Man* de Chardin is most insistent upon this point: "If this book is to be properly understood, it must be read . . . purely and simply as a scientific treatise." And yet he was quite aware of the implications and basis that the work provided others: "Beyond these first purely *scientific* reflections, there is obviously ample room for the most far-reaching speculations of the philosopher and the theologian." [133] Science, philosophy, theology are not, therefore, to be envisioned as separate and distinct spheres of human knowledge that never meet, that are within their own borders destined forever to remain completely within their confines without relationship to one another, but rather they inevitably draw together and relate to one another in the intensive examination of any given phenomenon:

During the last fifty years or so, the investigations of science have proved beyond all doubt that there is no fact which exists in pure isolation, but that every experience, however objective it may seem, inevitably becomes enveloped in a complex of assumptions as soon as the scientists attempt to explain it . . . like the meridians as they approach the poles, science, philosophy and religion are bound to converge as they draw nearer to the whole. I say "converge" advisedly, but without merging, and without ceasing, to the very end, to assail the real from different angles on different planes.[134]

Teilhard de Chardin's vision is one which, therefore, includes both science and theology. His work must be examined by the theologian

---

[132] Msgr. Léon Cristiani, *Why We Believe* (New York: Hawthorn, 1959), p. 109.
[133] *The Phenomenon of Man, op. cit.,* p. 29.
[134] *Ibid.,* p. 30.

as well as by the scientist; first, because his approach to total reality contains theological implications, of which he was well aware; and, secondly, because he himself sought in his work a synthesis of religion and science. He sought, and to a degree achieved, at least in the theoretical order, the approach to such a synthesis.

The tension [of science and religion] is prolonged, the conflict visibly seems to need to be resolved in terms of an entirely different form of equilibrium—not in elimination, nor duality, but in synthesis. After close on two centuries of passionate struggles, neither science nor faith has succeeded in discrediting its adversary. On the contrary, it becomes obvious that neither can develop normally without the other. And the reason is simple: the same life animates both. Neither in its impetus nor its achievements can science go to its limits without becoming tinged with mysticism and charged with faith. . . . Religion and science are the two conjugated faces or phases of one and the same act of complete knowledge—the only one which can embrace the past and future of evolution so as to contemplate, measure and fulfill them. In the mutual reinforcement of these two still opposed powers, in the conjunction of reason and mysticism, the human spirit is destined, by the very nature of its development, to find the uttermost degree of its penetration with the maximum of its vital force.[135]

It is precisely upon this point that we touch the real significance of Teilhard de Chardin. Although a paleontologist, archeologist, geologist, although an extremely skilled and competent scientist, he did not remain purely on the level of the scientific observer content to leave only a record of his findings. His scientific knowledge became the basis for his attempt to construct the outlines of a synthesis based on evolution. He wanted to create the total picture with a meaningful relationship between the facts of faith and of modern science. He was obsessed with a deep sense of totality, of the meaningfulness of every fact within the cosmos. Thus, he sought as a scientist and as a Christian thinker to penetrate both the natural and supernatural orders, and to establish the internal harmony of both orders. Christianity became in this attempted synthesis the crown and achievement of evolution.

The last fully integrated presentation of Christianity, the last perfected harmonization of reason and faith as known to the Chris-

[135] *Ibid.*, pp. 283, 284–285.

tian was the attempt of St. Thomas Aquinas. Thus, Teilhard de Chardin and his work have been elevated to a position of great importance by modern Christian intellectuals, for implicitly or explicitly they see in him the St. Thomas of the Age of Science. Teilhard de Chardin cannot then be judged solely by the scientist, who for the most part holds his work in high esteem, but he must also face the exacting scrutiny of the theologian. It is one thing to speak of the "vision" of Teilhard de Chardin, of his integrated view of the cosmos, but the separate theological facts of revelation, the components of this view, and his use of them must also be subjected to the critical eye of the theologian.

Theology and Père Teilhard de Chardin

As we have seen, some doubt has been cast upon the strictly theological facets of Teilhard de Chardin, and, as we shall see, there are sufficient grounds for theological hesitancy when faced by his "vision." Many of the questions, and more so the objections of theologians concern not picayune points but center about basic facts, about theological certainties derived from the spheres of both natural reason and supernatural revelation.

Where in his outline of the irresistible forces of evolution does Teilhard de Chardin place the age-old problem of human freedom? The observer is left with the uncomfortable feeling that the traditional concept of man's freedom emerges dangerously imperiled. It would seem that the forces of compression, organization and interiorization which for de Chardin bring about "hominization," are also in his view by no means "necessary, inevitable and certain." He expresses this reservation:

But, in virtue of its very nature, as we must not forget, the arrangement of great complexes . . . does not operate in the universe (least of all in man) except by two related methods: (1) the groping utilization of favorable cases (whose appearance is provoked by the play of large numbers) and (2) in a second phase, reflective invention. . . . The cosmic energy of involution . . . finds itself intrinsically influenced in its effects by two uncertainties related to the double play—the chance at the bottom and freedom at the top. . . . In the case of very large number (such, for instance, as the human population) the process tends to "infallibilise" itself, inasmuch as the likelihood of success grows on the lower side (chance) while that of rejection and error diminishes on the other side (freedom) with the multiplication of the elements engaged.[136]

Thus, within the vastness of numbers and the complexity of the total cosmos the process becomes irresistible, despite the element of free will. The Christian, he assures us, has the positive guarantee of the final success of hominization "by the 'redeeming virtue' of the God incarnate in His creation." [137] The answer it seems is two-fold: the Christian is led to see the problem in the traditional setting of grace and freedom, while on the scientific level, he appeals to the past irreversibility of the evolutionary process, and then reasons toward its likely completion.

The objection of a possible pantheism is deliberately avoided by Teilhard de Chardin in his statement that the universal center of unification "must be conceived as pre-existing and transcendent." [138] The positive state of unification is "obtained not by identification (God becoming all) but by the differentiating and communicating action of love (God all *in everyone*). And that is essentially ortho-dox and Christian." [139]

Nevertheless, one facet of this objection may be pressed. If the forces of evolution in this temporary uncharted future do fuse certainly upon the Omega point, and if the Omega point is essentially God-working-in-the-world, the personality of Christ, where then does the distinction between the natural and supernatural orders lie? If evolution is, as it were, to cross the "barrier" that demarcates man's natural state and the gratuitous supernatural order, then is there really such a state as that traditionally designated by the term "supernatural"? The problem is of Teilhard de Chardin's own creation, and it is fraught with implications contrary to the traditional Christian position.

The final, and perhaps the most telling objection to the "vision" and "synthesis" of Teilhard de Chardin is that it lies in unavoidable conflict with the ordinary teaching of the Magisterium, the Teaching Authority of the Church as expressed by Pope Pius XII in *Humani Generis*. The conflict lies in two major positions, intrinsi-

---

136 *Ibid.*, pp. 306–307.
137 *Ibid.*, p. 307.
138 *Ibid.*, p. 308.
139 *Ibid.*, p. 308.

cally related, evolution itself and polygenism (the theory that states man had many "first" parents).

Polygenism does not seem to be impossible for Teilhard de Chardin, certainly at least not in the scientific order. "Monogenism in the strict sense of the word seems to *elude* science as such by its very nature. At those depths of time when hominization took place, the presence and the movements of a unique couple are positively ungraspable, unrevealable to our eyes at no matter what magnification." [140] He even goes so far as to state that monogenism is at least, therefore, a possibility: ". . . one can say that there is room *in this interval* for anything that a trans-experimental source of knowledge might demand." [141] This problem in *The Phenomenon of Man* remains at least unanswered, and we are encouraged to have patience and wait. However, it does seem that in numerous lectures and in unpublished notes, Teilhard de Chardin accepted polygenism as a necessary scientific deduction for any evolutionist.

As we have seen, Teilhard de Chardin held evolution as a fact, and also a condition of human existence. Pius XII, in *Humani Generis*, states: "Some, however, rashly transgress this liberty of discussion, when they act as if the origin of the human body from pre-existing and living matter were already completely certain and proved by the facts which have been discovered up to now and by reasoning on those facts, and as if there were nothing in the sources of divine revelation which demands the greatest moderation and caution in this question." [142] The teaching of the Church as expressed by the Holy Father is not one of opposition to the scientific theory of evolution—it is rather one of caution. You cannot, says the Pope, state evolution as an absolute fact, completely certain and proved. Such an attitude as Teilhard de Chardin manifests toward evolution, whereby he goes even further than seeing it as a fact, but also as the ultimate scientific explanation of the life forces is most certainly in opposition to the cautions of the Pope. It would be very rash and temerarious to be so apodictic about evolution in view of the explicit statement of the Pope.

The question of polygenism is treated more strongly still by the

[140] *Ibid.*, p. 185.
[141] *Ibid.*, p. 185.
[142] Pius XII, *Humani Generis*, N.C.W.C. translation, paragraph 37.

Pope. "When, however, there is question of another conjectural opinion, namely polygenism, the children of the Church by no means enjoy such liberty." Therefore, one cannot hold or profess the polygenistic hypothesis, no matter what his views on the evolutionary theory. It seems that in many instances Teilhard de Chardin exceeded this point. The fact of natural descent in man from Adam is necessary for the preservation of the traditional teaching of original sin. "Now it is in no way apparent how such an opinion can be reconciled with that which the sources of revealed truth and the documents of the Teaching Authority of the Church propose with regard to original sin, which proceeds from a sin actually committed by an individual Adam and which through generation is passed on to all and is in everyone as his own." [143]

It is to be noted that the Pope did not explicitly and positively state that polygenism as such is not possible because of the truth revealed in Scripture. He states two points: first, that there is to be no freedom to discuss and propound polygenism. Secondly, that the reconcilability of original sin and polygenism is not at all evident. In fact, he states such a reconciliation, is "in no way apparent." It is precisely here that Teilhard de Chardin meets great difficulty in explaining any such possible scientific affirmation of polygenism. He must explain, if it is a scientific fact, its theological correlative: original sin, its fact, its occasion, and its transmission.

On more than one point then there is conflict between Teilhard de Chardin and the Church. His published works avoid many of the problems that his theological critics have alleged exist. And can the attitude of leaving his works to be published by those outside the Church, without *nihil obstat*, or *imprimatur* of the Church, be the attitude of a capable theologian? While appreciating the many-faceted genius of Père Teilhard de Chardin, we must also be on guard lest the very breadth of his vision carry us away, becloud the necessary examination of the component facts of his "vision."

Père Teilhard de Chardin has been most fortunate in having for an apologist, Msgr. Bruno de Solages, the Rector of the Institut Catholique in Toulouse. De Solages, himself a theologian of some competence, in meeting the inevitable theological objections toward

[143] *Ibid.*, paragraph 37.

this theory of evolution, comments: "This exposé of totality, essentially done from the phenomenalistic point of view, is therefore by definition incomplete, since it does not study reality in all its profundity; it is not therefore a substitute for metaphysics or, *a fortiori,* for theology." [144] Msgr. de Solages, obviously aware of the real theological difficulties in Teilhard de Chardin's work, nevertheless ably defends the presentation of such a synthesis as de Chardin's:

It follows that the author is not supposed to be treating, in these writings, those strictly theological questions which could be raised at various points. For that would be precisely to confuse his perspectives. Indeed, to demand that he not make any cosmological statements except on condition that he should propose the solution of all the theological problems which these new perspectives would raise, would be a presumption, for two reasons. First of all, theological problems cannot be solved except by use of theological method, and it is to professional theologians that we must look for such solutions. Secondly, to demand that a thinker should not present his own synthesis except on the condition that he shall have already answered all the questions which could be raised, would be to demand the impossible. Only the naïve—in this life—believe that their systems provide all the answers.[145]

The work that de Chardin has left us may some day provide the pattern for the synthesis he so earnestly hoped for. It will provide the theologian with many vexing problems. It cannot be underestimated for its originality, strong scientific basis and the evident spirit of faith that it represents. However, there must always be present to the Christian intellectual the real problems presented by his work. There can be no wishful thinking away of his conflicts with the Magisterium. Although he may be the enigmatic figure of contemporary Christian thought Père Teilhard de Chardin must remain for the theologian a man whose work, while admired, is never simply accepted without the serious qualification that the Church, the authentic Teacher, demands.

[144] Msgr. Bruno de Solages, "Christianity and Evolution," *Cross Currents,* Vol. 1 (Summer, 1951), pp. 30–31.
[145] *Ibid.,* p. 31.

5. JEAN DANIELOU—THE FATHERS AND THE CHURCH

The most prolific of the theologians writing in France today is Jean Danielou. It seems that there is no end to the books and the multitude of articles that he produces, and one can only feel sorry for that researcher in the future to whom must fall the lot of compiling his bibliography. The one strain that marks Danielou's work is his constant use of the early Fathers of the Church. He is one of the most distinguished of the theologians of the sources, patristics being his continual superstructure for theological reflection. Most of his major work has been translated into English, and his popularity and fame are not limited to the borders of France, but are to be found wherever theology is taken seriously.

Danielou was born in Paris in 1905, and pursued his higher education at the Sorbonne from which he received his degree in philology in 1927. Two years later he joined the Society of Jesus, was ordained in 1938 and saw military service in World War II. He received his doctorate in theology from the Institut Catholique in Paris for his work on the spirituality of St. Gregory of Nyssa. Concurrent with this work for the degree in theology he also studied at the University of Paris which awarded him a doctorate of philosophy. In 1944 he succeeded Père Jules Lebreton, a famed fellow Jesuit, as the Professor of the History of the Primitive Church at the Institut Catholique. As one might expect, his most fruitful work has been done in the field of patrology.

After the war, Danielou, with the cooperation of Père de Lubac, continued the series *Sources chrétiennes* which they had begun in 1942, making available accurate translations of patristic works which at the same time reflected the best in up-to-date scholarship. Since the war, in addition to translations of Gregory of Nyssa for the *Sources chrétiennes*, a stream of works has flowed from his pen and at the present time there is no indication of any interruption in this outpouring. An inveterate writer, his work has appeared in almost every major theological journal throughout the world. He writes most frequently for the periodical *Etudes,* a Jesuit monthly which he has edited since 1944. His work, always of a strong patristic bent, has been of a historical nature as well as theological. His interest in patristics and interpreting the Fathers to the modern world has led him into the fields of missiology, liturgy and ecumenism, in the interests of which he has traveled widely.

At times it would seem that the themes that he treats, and for which he draws so deeply from the Fathers, are inexhaustible. Because of their great number, reference to his works here will be to English translations where they exist, and French editions will be cited only when no translation is available. It would be well to classify his works in the following working division: properly historical evaluations of early Christian history, typology in the Fathers, theology of the Fathers, and, finally, his small works on patristic themes or works of a popular spiritual and apostolic nature.

Père Danielou's contributions to early Christian history are to be found in *Platonisme et théologie mystique, Origen, The Dead Sea Scrolls and Primitive Christianity, Philon d'Alexandrie,* and *Théologie du judaeo-christianisme: Histoire des doctrines chrétiennes avant Nicée,* Vol. I.[146] His studies of typology used by the Fathers in exegeting Sacred Scripture are to be found in *Sacramentum Futuri,* and *The Bible and the Liturgy.*[147] Properly theological themes as they are found in the Fathers are treated in *God and the Ways of Knowing,* and *The Lord of History.*[148] Smaller works about Patristic themes are *Salvation of the Nations, Advent, The Angels and Their Mission According to the Fathers of the Church, Holy Pagans of the Old Testament,* and *The Presence of God.*[149] There are as well the short but important pamphlets: *Dialogue avec les Marxistes, les existentialistes, les protestants, les juifs, l'hindouisme* and *Sainteté et action temporelle.*[150] In all of these works Père

---

[146] *Platonisme et théologie mystique* (Paris: Aubier, 1944). *Origen* (New York: Sheed & Ward, 1955). *The Dead Sea Scrolls and Primitive Christianity* (Baltimore: Helicon, 1958). *Philon d'Alexandrie* (Paris: Fayard, 1958). *Théologie du judaeo-christianisme* (Tournai: Desclée, 1958).

[147] *Sacramentum Futuri* (Paris: Beauchesne, 1950). *The Bible and the Liturgy* (Notre Dame: University Press, 1956).

[148] *God and the Ways of Knowing* (New York: Meridian, 1958). *The Lord of History* (Chicago: Regnery, 1958).

[149] *Salvation of the Nations* (New York: Sheed & Ward, 1950). *Advent* (New York: Sheed & Ward, 1951). *The Angels and Their Mission* (Westminster, Md.: Newman, 1957). *Holy Pagans of the Old Testament* (Baltimore: Helicon, 1957). *The Presence of God* (Baltimore: Helicon, 1959).

[150] *Dialogue* (Paris: Le Portulan, 1948). *Sainteté et action temporelle* (Paris: Desclée, 1955).

Danielou has reflected his continuing interest in the theological treatments of the early Fathers, their aptness and application for the Christian in the modern world, and their necessary position in any adequate theology based upon the sources of the Christian faith.

We are not concerned with the personal theology of the Fathers; but what constitutes for us the supreme value of their work is that in them we meet apostolic tradition of which they are the witnesses and the depositories. Their sacramental theology is a Biblical theology, and it is this Biblical theology which we are to try to recover. We are to look for it in the Fathers of the Church inasmuch as they are the witnesses of the faith of primitive Christianity. In them, we see the Biblical theology as refracted through a Greek mentality, but this mentality affects only the method of presentation. The fact that the Good Sheperd appears dressed as Orpheus does not alter the fact that it is He whom Ezechial announced, and whom St. John showed us as actually having come in the Person of Christ.[151]

The Meaning of Patristics

As we have mentioned, the *Sources chrétiennes* series of translations from the Fathers had begun in 1942 under Danielou and de Lubac. After the war Danielou contributed the second volume to the Jesuit theology series from Fourvière, *Théologie*, on Platonism and mystical theology. Both the theology series and the insistence of Danielou upon theology based on the Fathers created a certain uneasiness among the more conservative of French theologians. Danielou's work was to occasion the airing of the long-felt opposition among the traditional Thomists.

In 1946 he authored an article for *Etudes* on the relationship of patristics to modern thought, and stated that the Fathers both in language and themes, were most adequate spokesmen to the modern world for the Christian position. The article, *"Les Orientations présentes de pensée religieuse,"* created a furore. On the basis of this article, and the work produced by both Danielou and de Lubac, the Dominican Thomist scholar Père Labourdette leaped into action in denouncing the "new theology" created by the "Jesuit theologians" Danielou and de Lubac.

[151] *Bible and Liturgy, op. cit.,* p. 8.

Actually Père Danielou's statements were to some degree apparently extreme in language, but nevertheless the substance of what he had to say remained unaffected by Labourdette's criticism. Danielou stated that in the Fathers were to be found the elements of a properly theological treatment of history—and the importance of this concept for the modern mind was to be seen in the modern philosophies from Hegel to Marx. The inevitability of historical progress has constituted no small part of the Marxist challenge. To these erroneous concepts, he stated, must be opposed that theology of history to be found in the early Christian writers. The job of the theologian, he went on, is to be open to what is of value in modern thought. It would not do simply to dismiss Marxism, Existentialism and scientific evolutionism, and to miss the dynamic appeal based upon some partial possession of truth that these philosophies represented. In conclusion, Danielou made favorable comment upon some of the achievements of Existentialism, and praised Teilhard de Chardin's attempts to forge a new synthesis between religion and science.

Labourdette's rebuttal in the *Révue thomiste* took particular note of these statements of Danielou. He accused Danielou of propounding patristics because in the Fathers' statements of Christian theology there was a certain fluidness of language to be found, as a strictly theological structure such as Thomism had not yet been erected. The sum and substance of Danielou's patristics was relativism, the desire to be "open" to these modern errors because of the unsettled theological conditions and language that marked the era of the Fathers. The attack upon both Danielou and the patristic revival he represented, and upon the other theologians was to mount in intensity from this time on.

In his masterful study of the third-century Christian philosopher and theologian, Origen, Père Danielou in 1948 once again repeated the theme of the importance of the Fathers. Origen's contribution, as he saw it, lay in his constant use of the sources:

. . . he created the critical study of the Old Testament text, and more important still, worked out the theology of the relationship between the Old Testament and the New. . . . The perishable elements in his theology of the Bible, the things he derived from the culture of his time—

the allegorical methods of interpretation he borrowed from Philo and the gnostics—in no way lessen the value of his work as a whole.[152]

Origen is put forward by Danielou as an apologist for and an archetype of contemporary theologians laboring with the problems created by the modern world for the theologian. In a sense the reference to Origen is his justification of the theologians attacked by Labourdette: "It can thus be said that the two things which make the real theologian are both found in him: on the one hand he attempts to systematize, and on the other he is determined not to distort revealed truth by forcing it into the framework of the system, and therefore he accepts a certain incoherence." [153]

Early Christian History and the Dead Sea Scrolls

In the twofold function Père Danielou fulfills, as professor of early Christian history and patristics scholar, much of his interest is necessarily taken up with the origins of Christian theology, with that dim and distant past in which Christianity began. Until modern times scholars have been deprived of the materials that are now available to the careful researcher. The great medieval theologians, even St. Thomas himself, had little or no access to the information currently available to the Christian historian. These significant advances in the understanding and penetration of an era formerly shrouded in mystery, because of lack of sources, are basically scientific and historical advances. Archeology, language study, manuscript families, philology, the critical tools and apparatus of modern science have been joined to the manuscript finds at Qumran to shed new light upon the earliest years of Christian development.

Utilizing these advances in 1958, Père Danielou presented a study of Philo, a contemporary of Christ.[154] Philo was a Jew, living at Alexandria, a theologian and philosopher whose great work consisted in his defense of the Old Testament Biblical revelation. His position in a pagan society and culture forced him to express much of the theology contemporary to his age in the philosophical terms and systems of that age. It is by studying Philo that much light is

---

[152] *Origen, op. cit.,* p. 311.
[153] *Ibid.,* p. 313.
[154] *Philon d'Alexandrie, op. cit.*

shed upon the common theological heritage that was immediate to both the Jews and Christians of that era.

Historians of the nineteenth and early twentieth centuries delighted to see in Philo the origin of the New Testament concepts found in the Fourth Gospel, and thus both Philo and his work became, as it were, a stick with which to beat the traditional Christian concept of the uniqueness of the Christian revelation. Père Danielou advances facts that, in the light of this limited historical research of the past, are simply startling. Philo, he maintains, did exercise an influence upon the early Christian theology of the Fathers, but he was himself influenced by the New Testament. The New Testament is not to be regarded as the product of his influence, but many of his themes were to find their origin in the New Testament and the traditional Jewish theology of that age. Those outstanding resemblances between Philo and the New Testament, especially evident in the Fourth Gospel, are to be found, according to Danielou, in a common source. The common source of both is the theology of the Old Testament, and the Jewish thought patterns of that theology current in the first century.

Turning to a more detailed inspection of this common source, Père Danielou has begun a series of works on the Judaeo-Christian theology that existed up until the Council of Nicea.[155] He chooses for particular examination and detailed analysis early Christian theology as it developed from dependence upon the theology of the Jews and their thought patterns in which that theology was expressed. The source is actually twofold, a general division of which would be the orthodox theological sources (the Apocrypha, Old and New Testaments, and the earliest documents and writings of the Fathers), and the heterodox theological sources (represented by the Ebionites, and various gnostic groups).

This theological heritage for Jews and Christians of the first century A.D. is represented in the Fourth Gospel and St. Paul. It has one constant strain, that of eschatology, of preoccupation with the last things. These eschatologists were constantly developing parallels with the Creation account to be found in Genesis, and were

---

[155] *Théologie du judaeo-christianisme, op. cit.*

dominated by the theme of the two creations. Thus, Danielou concludes, the earliest theology is basically a theology of history.

The postwar manuscript discoveries at Qumran have added not only to the knowledge of Scripture scholars, but have as well provided more accurate information about the mysterious background of eschatology and the heritage of theology in which early Christianity developed. In the hands of overhasty and supercilious historians the Dead Sea Scrolls, as they are called, have also provided a number of problems for the Catholic historian of the early Church. It has been stated by these historians, after only a cursory perusal of the finds, that the alleged "uniqueness" of the Person of Christ is destroyed by the appearance of the "Teacher of Righteousness" in these documents. It was primarily as a historian that Père Danielou turned toward these questions. "The immense interest aroused in this question and the freakish consideration it has sometimes occasioned in scholarly circles led me to make an attempt at establishing a basic orientation toward the question of the Scrolls. . . ." [156]

From a number of intrinsic and extrinsic considerations he is led to conclude that the figure of John the Baptist was strongly affected by the Community of Qumran. "It is possible that he may have been an Essene. But it is more probable that he was only deeply influenced by Essenism." [157] However, he goes on, "the distinctive message of John is not, like that of the men of Qumran, only, the announcing of the visitation of God, the coming of the Messiah, the effusion of the Spirit." His mission is to bear witness that the "visitation has taken place, that the Messiah is already here, and that the Spirit is abroad. His mission is to designate Jesus as being the realization of the expected event." [158]

The allegation by the more sensational of the critics, who saw in the figure of the Teacher of Righteousness a comparison with Christ, is handled by Danielou in a succinct manner. He relates the points of contact between Christ and the Essenes of Qumran: the joint usage of the Qumran calendar (Jaubert's theory), the ceremonial of the Last Supper, the analogy in number and hierarch-

---

[156] *The Dead Sea Scrolls, op. cit.,* p. 5.
[157] *Ibid.,* p. 23.
[158] *Ibid.,* pp. 23–24.

ical nature of the Apostolic College and the Qumran community, and also the similarity in attitude of Christ and the sectaries of Qumran toward the Pharisees. But the result of these points of contact, and of the more questionable exegesis of the critics, is not that with which they rushed into print.

Thus certain aspects of Christ's conduct are not without their analogies in the community of Qumran. Must we conclude, then, that Christ had been an Essene, at least for a certain period during His life? On this point the historians are unanimous in asserting the contrary. Nothing in either the origins of Jesus or in the social frame in which He regularly lived, compels us to such a conclusion. The similarities that we have pointed out are striking, but they are not decisive. And if the characteristics that we have disclosed are, as a matter of fact, to be found among the Essenes and the disciples of Christ, there is nothing to indicate that they were peculiar to the Essenes.[159]

As to the question of the Teacher of Righteousness, very little is known of his life from the Scrolls. He is, however, even from the documents, to be considered uniquely different from Christ. He considered the Messiah as imminent, but Christ declares He is the Messiah; it is almost certain that the Teacher did not suffer violent death, but the New Testament is fundamentally concerned with the Passion, Death and Resurrection of Christ; the Teacher is aware of his sinfulness, but Christ is devoid of sin in any sense; finally, it is only in the case of Christ that there is a cult offered to His personality.

In his treatment of the Scrolls and the problems they involve, Danielou is not so naïve as to think that there are no real problems left for the Christian scholars. Rather, he is most insistent that the exegete and the theologian take up this figure of the Teacher of Righteousness, and both evaluate and place his position in the scheme of Christian revelation.

Thus between the great prophets of the Old Testament and John the Baptist he (the Teacher of Righteousness) emerges as a new link in the preparation for the Advent of Christ . . . the question is put to Christians: how to contest the authenticity of such a message which they

[159] *Ibid.*, p. 34.

claim has been fulfilled? Why does not this message, then, form part of inspired Scripture? This is the true mystery of the Teacher of Righteousness.[160]

The real problem which "will require mature reflection from exegetes and theologians" is the nature of this link in the revelation of the coming of Christ; "but one falsifies the problem when one transposes it to the level that purports to establish an equivalence between the Teacher of Righteousness and Christ." [161]

The Theme of "Cosmic" Revelation

In a number of works Père Danielou has advanced with some regularity the concept of a "cosmic" revelation. The constant appearance of this idea has its origins in many of the writings of the Fathers, and from it Danielou draws meaningful implications for the modern Christian. In the *Salvation of the Nations* he remarks that all studies of man started from a fundamental consideration, "the universal character to the religious fact." [162] All men have a religion of some sort, and the reason for this must be sought in an unarguable and real revelation: "If all men have a religion, it is because . . . the Word of God makes Himself known to them." [163] At the heart of all religious forms lies a revelation: the philosophers choose to call it natural theology, or natural law, but this is primarily and essentially a form of revelation.

There are testimonies of God by which He manifests Himself to men; these testimonies are all the things which He has made; "the entire visible world . . . indicates to them that there are things besides what they see." [164] In another place Danielou comments: "the very regularity of the laws of nature is a sort of revelation through which man can recognize the existence of a provident God." [165] This evidence of God in the reality He created and sustains is to be conceived of as a real "revelation" to reason, the basic cause of the universal religious fact, and the "first" revelation. "By

[160] *Ibid.*, pp. 83–84.
[161] *Ibid.*, p. 87.
[162] *Salvation of the Nations, op. cit.*, p. 18.
[163] *Ibid.*, p. 20.
[164] *Ibid.*, p. 21.
[165] *The Angels and Their Mission, op. cit.*, p. 15.

first revelation I do not mean a primitive revelation, made to the first men and handed down . . . I am referring to God's revelation through nature. . . ." [166] Danielou prefers not to use the term "natural religion" in this context, because it is a term "which has been rendered so obscure by the discussions of modern theologians and is so full of ambiguities . . . [that] to avoid all equivocation we have preferred to talk of 'cosmic' religion. The word connotes, indeed, a clear reference to the world of nature and in particular to nature in its bearing on religion." [167]

Following the Fathers, Danielou sees this real revelation of the Creator through His creation as the "natural" and "first" covenant entered into by God with man, and testified to in Scripture. It "corresponds to the first covenant, the covenant with Noe, by which God bound Himself to observe the laws of the seasons, to make them rainy and dry at the proper times, so that man should get to know His Personal Providence by the fidelity with which He gave His gifts." [168]

Thus this first covenant, the cosmic revelation, makes the knowledge of God accessible to all men in the revelation that is creation. But it is not a covenant to be supplanted by the covenant that God entered into with the Jews, but it is like the relationship of Old and New Covenants. The succession must be seen as a fulfillment of the Old. It is to have enormous implications, particularly in the question of the salvation of pagans who have not known Christ:

Saint Thomas replies to this question in a notable text on "the growth of faith according to the succession of the ages" [IIa-IIae, I, 7]. He points out that the substance of faith is always the same and that it consists in belief in Christ. But he observes that this faith in Christ can be unfolded in the course of the ages. . . . This text is of prime importance. It lays down in effect that the essential object of faith is the existence of a God Who intervenes in the world. The Incarnation is the supreme point of these divine interventions, but they began with the creation of the world. Now belief in the intervention of God in creation and in the conduct of human life is accessible to the pagan; that is indeed the purpose of the cosmic revelation which is manifested, according to the

166 *Advent, op. cit.,* p. 153.
167 *Holy Pagans of the Old Testament, op. cit.,* pp. 2–3.
168 *Advent, op. cit.,* p. 53.

Epistle to the Romans, by the action of God in the cosmos and by His call to the conscience.[169]

In the first covenant between God and humanity, that of Noe prior to the Covenant with Abraham, God gives His angels a specific role to play. "It is in fact a common doctrine in the whole of ancient tradition that God has entrusted the nations to His Angels." [170] The mission of the Angels, and the Divine origin of the cosmic revelation have inference for the Christian today:

It is their mission to lead the pagan peoples to God. This is a very fertile doctrine from the missionary point of view. The heathens are not entirely deprived of aid: the angels of God assist them, trying to lead them to the true God, preparing the way of the Lord. . . . This is also important for judging the pagan religions. No matter how perverted they are, they retain some vestige of the natural revelation, and that vestige is due to the angels who have passed it on to them and who strive to keep it alive among them.[171]

Thus, Danielou can speak in another place of pagans: ". . . all pagan religions attain some knowledge of God. However, since they have not the revelation of God Himself, they focus on the wrong object and often turn out to be gross caricatures of religion. . . . All that is good in these religions comes from God, in respect to whatever intuition they can have of Him through the signs that He gives to them." [172] And he tells us again in *Holy Pagans of the Old Testament*: "There is no need for me to point out how great a bearing this has from a missionary point of view. The Church has always affirmed her respect for the religious values of the pagan world. Incomplete, often corrupted, these values remain real; and the saints discussed in this book are a striking witness to this. They typify the mysterious advent of Christ into the Pagan soul." [173]

Not only is there an obvious principle for missiology in the consideration of the cosmic revelation, but as well an approach to be

---

[169] *Holy Pagans of the Old Testament, op. cit.,* pp. 22–23.
[170] *The Angels and Their Mission, op. cit.,* p. 15.
[171] *Ibid.,* p. 17.
[172] *Salvation of the Nations, op. cit.,* p. 23.
[173] *Holy Pagans of the Old Testament, op. cit.,* p. 4.

made to contemporary Protestantism in defense of that natural theology which it has rejected. Because of the Fall of man, the renewed Protestant stress upon the transcendence of God has led these theologians, preeminently Karl Barth, to the insistence that outside the free Revelation of God to Abraham and through Jesus no religious truth can be attained by man. Danielou sharply observes that "in this criticism two different questions are involved. The first, which does not concern us here, is that of the possibility of a purely natural knowledge of God . . . but it is clear that, for Catholics, this natural knowledge does not suffice for salvation. . . . But the other question is that of the extension of belief in Christ to the cosmic covenant." [174] It is this latter point that Protestantism has ignored, and it is upon this that such a seemingly contradictory concept as a "pagan saint" is based:

It can be said, therefore, that Scripture and Tradition are at one in declaring that the living God has never ceased to manifest Himself to man, His creature. Before doing so fully in Jesus Christ, He manifested Himself to Abraham and to Moses by His intervention in their history. But before manifesting Himself to Abraham and Moses, He had manifested Himself to Henoch and Noe, that is to say to the nations of the earth. Granted this revelation was still obscure, nevertheless it had a bearing upon what is the very purpose of revelation, namely the redemptive action of God in the world. As to how many men in the pagan world gave their adherence to this revelation that is God's hidden secret. Scripture teaches us that certain of them gave their adherence to it in full; this suffices for our own purpose and warrants our calling them the saints of the cosmic covenant.[175]

Typology and Theology

In the presentation of the theology of the Fathers based upon the apostolic tradition immediately entrusted to them, Père Danielou presents to the modern Catholic a preeminently Biblical theology, closely linked to the symbols, types and facts of Sacred Scripture. In order to clarify for the modern mind the difficulties inherent in any representation of the thought of the Fathers, Père Danielou has

---

[174] *Ibid.*, pp. 25–26.
[175] *Ibid.*, pp. 26–27.

frequently touched upon the problem of typology. Typology, in brief, is that form of Biblical exegesis in which actual Biblical realities are seen in a historical dimension as foreshadowing later realities. Thus, the real, actual and historical David, psalmist and King of Israel, is—in addition to his actual place in the history of Israel—a "type" of the future Messianic king of Israel. "That the realities of the Old Testament are figures of those of the New is one of the principles of Biblical theology. This science of the similitudes between the two Testaments is called Typology." [176]

Again, such a method of Biblical exegesis is common to the Fathers, and is justified by an appeal to the Biblical authors themselves. Its foundation is in both Old and New Testaments, thus, "At the time of the Captivity, the prophets announced to the people of Israel that in the future God would perform for their benefit deeds analogous to, and even greater than those He had performed in the past. So there would be a new Deluge . . . a new Exodus . . . a new Paradise." [177] And, in another place, relating typology as a real sense of Scripture to real historical events, he says:

. . . typology is an intrinsic element of Christian doctrine. It stems from the basis of all sound scriptural interpretation in Patristic times; and it is fully used in the Christian liturgy. . . . But this use of figure, this strictly historical kind of symbolism, is something altogether different from the use of allegory by such as Philo, and some of the Fathers after him. The latter is a recrudesence of nature-symbolism, from which the element of historicity is absent. . . . Typology, being historical in character, is a new thing, depending on the occurrence, at given moments of time, of particular divine events in the historical process of redemption. . . .[178]

In his detailed examinations, Père Danielou sees typology closely related to the basic element of the theology of the Bible and the Fathers: history. This theology is essentially a theology of history, of the entrance of God into the line of human history giving reason, meaning, intelligibility and goal to human history. Related to this

[176] *The Bible and the Liturgy, op. cit.,* p. 4.
[177] *Ibid.,* p. 4.
[178] *The Lord of History, op. cit.,* p. 141.

concept, then, typology "gives expression to the specific intelligibility that belongs to history as such." [179] Without the typological approach "the events recorded would convey no assimilable meaning to our bewildered comprehension; the key is in the possibility of reference back to earlier manifestations of the same ways." [180]

This theology of history has for Danielou a primary element, namely, that it is eschatological; that is, it is related to the last things. This as well is found in the Biblical usage of typology:

The real source and foundation of typology has sometimes been obscured in the course of theoretical discussions about methods of Scriptural exegesis. Aquinas defined it accurately when he showed that it is not a meaning of words but a meaning of things—not a sense of Scripture but a sense of history. It begins in the Old Testament, where episodes in the past history of Israel are presented as a figure of what shall come to pass in the end of time. It is thus *originally and essentially eschatological.* In the New Testament, Christ is shown as inaugurating the regime of the last days: it is in this eschatological view that he was prefigured in the Old Testament.[181]

Typology is an excellent means of introducing modern man to the theology of history. Père Danielou, following the brilliant outlines of the work of the Protestant Oscar Cullmann, is insistent upon the importance of this theme for the contemporary Christian. Not only is Christianity essentially historical in character, but it gives purpose to human history itself. The accent upon a theology of history is not, for Danielou, simply the product of modern Christian thought, but it is a basic constitutive element in the Biblical Revelation itself. The challenge of existential preoccupation with historicity, and of the Marxist appeal to history have forced the modern Christian to return to the source of theology and its theme of meaning in history.

This Christian theology of history must be viewed as eschatological—concerned with the "last things." Not that the early end of the world was the whole message of Jesus, but that the end of human history was realized in himself. The end lay not in the future, but

[179] *Ibid.,* p. 6.
[180] *Ibid.,* p. 6.
[181] *Ibid.,* p. 140.

in Christ himself. The foremost exponent of this view, the Anglican critic C. H. Dodd, has given this theology the name of "realized eschatology." Père Danielou comments that in Dodd's view "history since Jesus is a sort of remainder, and theologically insignificant. From this position it is but a step to that of Bultmann, who regards all ideas of a future judgment as nothing but apocalyptic myth: holding that the only judgment is each man's momentaneous relation to God, and the only end, the ineluctable consequence of each decision in this kind." [182]

There is much of value in realized eschatology, and Danielou is aware of this but nevertheless finds that Dodd and Bultmann "are both wrong in trying to reduce the whole of the Gospel to this message." [183] He prefers to follow Oscar Cullmann here, seeing in the Resurrection of Christ the essential event in the end of human history, "there can never happen anything of comparable importance in the future." [184] However, even Cullmann "is perhaps too exclusively concerned with the beginning and the end of the 'last days' to the neglect of the interim in which our lives are spent." [185]

In making a still further exact outline of a theology of history, Père Danielou finds himself in agreement with Father Mollat in expressing this theology:

Between the inauguration of Judgment at the time of Christ's first coming, and its fulfillment at His coming again, Christian life in its entirety is thus continual judgment. . . . It will be seen that this conception subsumes and reconciles the historical and the existential interpretations. Judgment does indeed consist now from moment to moment in the relation of man to God; but that is because mankind is historically going through the time of judgment. And this process has only begun; it looks forward to the Last Judgment for the final ratification.[186]

Père Danielou's study of Christian antiquity, his use of the Fathers, and his reconsideration of Biblical typology has opened up to the contemporary Catholic theologian the entire question of the

[182] *Ibid.*, p. 271.
[183] *Ibid.*, p. 271.
[184] *Ibid.*, p. 271.
[185] *Ibid.*, p. 272.
[186] *Ibid.*, pp. 272–273.

theology of history. It is this theme of the theology of history that today exercises a continual fascination upon the theologians in France, and to which many have committed themselves along specific lines of orientation.

History and the Theologians

One of the most remarkable elements in the theological revival of the twentieth century, particularly in France and particularly at the present time, is the growing interest in a theology of history. Philosophers, theologians and historians within the Church seem almost obsessed, so to speak, with the idea of history and its relationship to theology.

Basically what lies at the bottom of their considerations of history in the light of the Christian Revelation is the unique value brought by that Revelation to man. In the entire line of human history it is only in the Judaeo-Christian religion that meaning is given to human history itself. The point of the human race, the term for which it was made and is striving, the destiny of mankind and of each man is brought to man only in this Christian Revelation. The Greeks before Christianity, and all other non-Christian civilizations and cultures, no matter to what degree they are developed, either fail to consider the meaning of the history of man, or if they do they conclude to some fatalistic or determined conception which in no less a manner empties human existence of ultimate meaning.

The most philosophically developed of the ancient peoples, the Greeks, bring to man a purely cyclic conception of human history. Time is a matter of ever-recurring cycles, and time like eternity are terms empty of true meaning. There are no absolute beginnings, no real ends, for because of cycles there are always the "ends" and the "beginnings," each terminating in the other. In line with this, the Greeks, as did all pagan philosophers, arrived at a fatalistic concept of human history. Everything is decided, nothing is decisive. There is no real term, end, and consequently no real meaning to historical development. Passivity in the face of such a philosophic outlook becomes inevitable, and Greek philosophy without a real concept of what "creation" could possibly mean is left only with pessimism. "Nothing ever comes to term, nothing is of any real utility, and the supreme happiness consists in an escape from this fiction which is time to the contemplation, through knowledge, of the eternal laws. Salvation lies in flight—flight achieved through knowledge." [187]

In contrast to this universal picture we have the Biblical Revelation of the God-who-acts. A God who speaks and acts in human history, who gives meaning and destiny to man. Time becomes in the Christian conception a linear rather than cyclic conception, there is a real beginning in Creation, a real end in the Parousia. The concept of Providence becomes evident, of a Divine direction of human history. And more than this, the transcendent God enters into history; He who made it and holds it in the hollow of His Hand, deigns to share the nature of His creatures. God gives meaning to history, and in His act and revelation makes that same history intelligible for man. "It is easy to understand, therefore, why this religion that is so eminently historical substitutes for the pessimism and individualism of philosophy an atmosphere of optimism and an acute sense of social and traditional values along with the primacy of free choice and, in the last analysis, of grace." [188]

The examination of this phenomenon has led then in our day a number of moderns either to the construction of theologies of history or at least toward Christian conceptions of history. Among those specifically considering the problem we have the distinguished historian of Primitive Christianity at the Sorbonne, Henri Marrou, and the philosopher Jean Guitton. Others include the Jesuits Malevez, and Fessard, the Dominicans Feret and Montuclard, as well as Jules Monchanin and Roger Aubert. However, the great Catholic contributions to the formation of theologies of history have come from Teilhard de Chardin, Jean Danielou, Louis Bouyer and Gustave Thils.[189] There is now no end in sight to the works pouring from historians, philosophers and theologians all over the world devoted to this problem.

The knowledge of the specific contribution of the Christian Revelation toward an understanding of human history is not, of course, a new element suddenly introduced upon the stage of theological thought. Consequently for what reason have theologians suddenly

[187] Paul Henry, S.J., "Christian Philosophy of History," *Theological Studies*, Vol. 13 (Sept., 1952), p. 423.

[188] *Ibid.*, p. 427.

[189] Gustave Thils, *Théologie des réalites terrestres* (Paris: Desclée de Brouwer, 1948–1949), 2 vols.

become engrossed in this conception? There are, as we see it, a number of reasons, influences and factors that have served in our time to converge upon this problem and call forth from the Christian intellectual new appreciations of Christianity and history.

Outside the Church there is the influence of the Protestant theologians, and the effect of the challenge of Marxism. Contemporary Protestant theologians, especially Barth, Brunner and Oscar Cullmann have developed theologies of history; Barth and Brunner because of the existential exigencies of their dogmatic constructs, Cullmann as a result of the positive achievements of Biblical study within Protestantism. These in turn, most especially Cullmann, have provoked Catholic studies along the same line. The inherent dynamism of the Marxist lies in the historical inevitability of the dialectic; the attractiveness of such a philosophy and the challenge it presents to the contemporary Christian forced Catholics, especially in France where the Marxist intellectual problem is acute, to consider more attentively the problem of history.

The progress in science, the seeming inevitability of evolution, and the attempts of Teilhard de Chardin not merely to harness the evolutionary drive to Christianity but to synthesize both, contributed to the growing preoccupation with history. Within the Church the developing ecclesiology, the constant examination of the Mystery of the Church as the extension of the Incarnation and the working out of the Divine plan in human history focused consideration upon the relationship of the Church to history itself. Again the scriptural revival, the acquaintance with the Biblical imagery and thought, the fresh and accurate contact with the sources of Revelation fixed the eyes of the Biblical theologians upon the enormous importance of both the beginning and end of human history, Creation and Parousia. As we shall see, an entire approach to the theology of history has grown up among Biblicists preoccupied with the concept of the Parousia as presented in the New Testament. It is in these elements, challenges and influences then that we can see the reason for the growth in modern times of the concept of a theology of history.

As we have mentioned, these theologians of history are well aware of the unique contribution to thought inherent in the Christian conception of reality. The theologians of history center their gaze about the Christian fact—the Person and work of Jesus. For them the decisive event of history is Jesus Christ. Christ grants to each man and to mankind victory over sin and over death; the Paschal event—the Passion, Death and Resurrection of Jesus—is the central moment that gives meaning to all of human history. The Incarnate God, Jesus Christ, is the key to human history—He is the Revelation of history.

However, this Mystery of Christ and the meaning it brings to human history may be approached in two possible ways, and thus among the theologians a diversity of opinion has grown up. There are two schools, roughly corresponding to what we may call for want of labels the "Incarnational" and the "eschatological." Each accepts, of course, the total Christian Revelation, but each is prone to view the entire question of the theology of history from a differing point of view. The Incarnationalists, stressing the Person of Christ and His Mission and His Church, include among their ranks de Lubac, Teilhard de Chardin, and Père Paul Henry, S.J. The eschatologists, stressing the Parousia, the last days of Scripture in which the human race is now present, fix their gaze upon Christ who is to come. These latter number Père Feret, Louis Bouyer and, preeminently, Jean Danielou.

The commitment of the Christian theologian to either of these views leads to certain "attitudes" with regard to the world and the necessities of daily life. The Incarnationalist is more inclined toward a favorable attitude with regard to humanism, human values, culture, the progress of the human race. As a Christian he is to build the Body of the Church which is both human and divine, he shares the transforming mission inherent in the Incarnation. The eschatologist leans toward accentuating the radical disassociation of the Christian and the world that lies in the Christian Revelation. His vision is not limited to the present but goes forward, joyfully awaiting the "day of the Lord," the Parousia, the final consummation and term of all things. The practical difference of both general schools of the theologians of history is one that manifests the general tendency or outlook of the individual upon the problem of man here and now.

Père Paul Henry, S.J., among the world's foremost Plotinian scholars, and a Professor at the Institut Catholique in Paris, expresses succinctly the Incarnationalist attitude:

[Incarnationalists]—and I range myself among them—think that the Christian cannot be indifferent to natural values, to human progress; they believe that the Christian has not only the right but also the duty, and therefore the possibility, of working with all his forces for the construction of a better world, the natural substructure of a world spiritualized by grace. He has confidence in reason, in thought, in human action, inserted in Christ, and the prolongation of His action in the unfolding of time and in the extension of space. I believe that in the New Testament there are elements which support this conception of a theology of the Incarnation prolonged by the action of the Christian in the bosom of the Church of Christ. Before all else the appeal addressed to Christians is to build the Body of Christ, the Church, a society not only divine but human. By the incarnation Christ has reconciled us with our "human condition" and invites us to make of this world a real anticipation, a beginning of the world to come.[190]

It is in the work of Père Jean Danielou that the eschatologists have found their most eloquent spokesman. Danielou brings to his support of the eschatological theologians of history his fine sense of Scripture as well as his immense learning in patristics, both being abilities that in themselves would incline their possessor toward the eschatological position. Danielou's great work, *The Lord of History*, in which he makes his position quite evident, is not a full-scale exposition of the theology of history from this point of view, but rather a series or collection of studies and observations closely linked to the problem of history for the Christian. His consideration of the Christ as the decisive event of human history leads him to reject the Incarnational interpretation found in such Incarnationalists as Teilhard de Chardin:

Christ's resurrection being the decisive event in all history, nothing that will ever happen will equal it in importance. This disposes at once of all the errors of evolutionism. No progress now can ever bring about for us what we have already got in Christ; that which is beyond all progress is here and now in Him; the last state exists already in the Christian mysteries. Consequently no indentification is permissible between the Christian hope and a belief in progress: they are radically different things.[191]

190 Paul Henry, *op. cit.*, p. 431.
191 *The Lord of History, op. cit.*, p. 7.

The Incarnationalist view, as seen by Danielou, is to a degree essentially his own. However, the Incarnation—the central meaningful event of history—has the quality of finality, of end-in-itself that the proponents of the Incarnational view frequently forget.

Granted that the Person of Christ is the point of intersection of the two Old Testament themes, there is a further stage to make good, namely to grasp that this is not simply a point among others, a term of reference for a continuous line, but an absolute termination, in the sense that there can be nothing beyond: the possibilities of development are exhausted. Here we face a characteristic paradox of Christianity. Although the time process continues, and the last day, or chronological end of the world, is in the future, yet the ultimate reality is already present, in the Person of the Incarnate Word; there is not, because there cannot be, anything beyond this.[192]

Theologically and historically, according to Danielou, it was the Council of Chalcedon that made this fact most evident. For that Council, by defining that the humanity of Christ preserves its own proper quality forever, albeit transfigured, thus affirmed that "the Incarnation, the union of the two distinct natures without confusion, belongs with the 'last things,' to eschatology, being the goal and conclusion of God's plan, subsisting forever in its own unique reality." [193]

Père Louis Bouyer has reaffirmed the eschatological "vision" of Père Danielou, and faced squarely the problem such an approach brings:

The sacramental world is characteristic of the Faith, and of these "last times" of history in which we are to live, in that the sacramental world effects a paradoxical meeting point between this world of everyday life and the world to come, the world of the resurrection into which Christ has led the way. . . . How are we to conceive the relation between the world to come which is brought into contact with us here and now in the liturgy and in the sacramental order, and the world of everyday affairs? . . . It is to this world that we are to give witness of the divine *agape*, in order to snatch out of its power the children of God who are there enslaved and bring them to liberty. But this task can only be ac-

192 *Ibid.*, p. 190.
193 *Ibid.*, p. 195.

complished by means of our cross and theirs, borne patiently and even joyfully as being Christ's own Cross. And thus we shall come to the resurrection, where everything which we had to lose in order to follow Christ will be found once more in the new cosmos, the new order of things and of being, where He is King, having overcome Satan and thrust his power down to hell.[194]

Like his colleague in the Institut Catholique and the ranks of eschatologists, Danielou, Père Bouyer does not hesitate openly and frankly to confront the Incarnationalist attitude in the strongest of terms:

Today we meet many people, and often they are in the ranks of the most zealous apostles, who live only for the conversion of the world to the Gospel, but who do not realize that the methods they are using to accomplish this purpose might much better be called an attempt to convert the Gospel to the world. Under the name of "incarnation," such people attempt in all good faith to incorporate all the ideals held by men today into the total ideal of Christianity. But such a Christianity becomes something quite different from the authentic Christianity of the "divinization" of man through the Cross. It becomes instead an unconscious but desperate struggle to avoid the Cross in an effort to "divinize" the world as it is. That is to say, it becomes in fact, under all sorts of Christian phraseology, a purely pagan apotheosis of the created things. . . . One would cease to believe at all in the Christian Mystery if one held that God in Christ is not the only author of man's salvation, but that man, even if he does not wholly accomplish that salvation himself, still contributes something toward it which has saving value of itself, apart from any root dependence on God's own work on the Cross.[195]

These spokesmen then represent the two trends among Catholic theologians of history today. It is worth examining their backgrounds to see if there are among Incarnationalists and eschatologists any common strains of thought or influence that predispose them to the acceptance of the one or the other view. It seems as though those Christian intellectuals most taken up with the meaning of the Church, ecclesiologists, as for example de Lubac, lean toward an Incarnational view. Others, more impressed with the evolution-

[194] Louis Bouyer, *Liturgical Piety, op. cit.,* pp. 257–258.
[195] *Ibid.,* pp. 265–266.

ary tendencies of the world, with progress and human values, also incline toward this position. Eschatologists seem to have one thing in common: they are drawn primarily from the ranks of Scripturists and patrologists; both Bouyer and Danielou are eminent patristic scholars, Père Feret is a Scripturist. These general fields of study and reference seem, therefore, to shape or incline a theologian toward one school of Christian history rather than another.

It does not seem to the observer that a strict theological either/or proposition must be advanced. Cannot one have the best of both? Why one and not the other? A synthesis of both Incarnational and eschatological views certainly seems to be possible. Despite his eschatological orientation in these discussions it does seem that Père Danielou offers the eventual settlement of these outlooks within the eschatological viewpoint: the supreme moment in the history of the world is, of course, the Incarnation, but this moment must also be perceived as the inauguration of the last days, the Incarnation itself is the absolute termination of history.

V

❀

THEOLOGY IN MOTION:
ADAPTATION

1. THE MORAL THEOLOGIANS

Introduction

In moral theology as in all the general divisions of theological thought we cannot say that the influences bearing upon its development are simple and clear-cut.[1] There are always the general influences of development in the other theological disciplines, dogma, Scripture, liturgy, *et al.* Today scientific studies such as psychology lead to new insights and solutions of old problems. The complicating factors of modern life, technology, economics, social relationships and obligations face the theologian with new problems demanding immediate answers. The instruction and direction of the Church, never absent to the theologian working with problems, have never been more helpful and as full as during modern times. The pontificate of the late Pius XII produced an enormous corpus of documents dealing directly with the problems of our age. The late Holy Father spoke frequently on marriage, sex, technocracy, warfare and numberless other subjects. The documents of his

---

[1] A summary of the work being done in contemporary moral theology may be found in the work of the American Jesuits John Ford and Gerald Kelly, *Contemporary Moral Theology. 1. Questions in Fundamental Moral Theology* (Westminster, Md.: Newman, 1958).

154

pontificate touch upon every moral problem facing modern man, and are yet to be thoroughly investigated, collated and evaluated.

The Critique of Modern Moral Theology

The traditional concept of the structure and framework of moral theology has been the object of study for many modern theologians. The undeniable drive of the return to the sources of Christianity and the Christian life in the scriptural, liturgical and patristic revivals has created enormous dissatisfaction with the traditional casuistic approach to morality. A number of scholars have adopted a questioning attitude toward the negative concepts of the manuals, and expressed a desire for a more positive expression of the moral life of the Christian.

The German movement of kerygmatic theology, that is the preparation and presentation of theology for preaching, and the positive work of the German theologians Schilling, Tillmann, and Ermecke, have created a response among the French theologians. At the present time this strong German-Austrian influence upon the French is exercised by Rahner, Haring and Schmaus. In the late 1930's the Jesuit Émile Mersch attempted to present a positive synthesis of morality built around the concept of the Mystical Body of Christ,[2] and in 1940 Gustave Thils raised the question of the excessively negative attitude toward morality on the part of the manual theologians.[3] Thils in his slim volume accused the professional moral theologians of reducing morality to abstractions presented with the solid precision of mathematics, and of a dated and closed vocabulary. In short, according to Thils, the moralists seem to have lost sight of the reality of Jesus.

After the war, serious French criticism of the traditional moralist presentation became much stronger, and steps were taken by some to bring moral theology into line with the progress made in positive theology by the return to the sources. Primary among these postwar critics were Canon Jacques Leclercq and the Jesuits Gilleman and Delhaye.

[2] Emile Mersch, S.J., *Morality and the Mystical Body* (New York: Kenedy, 1939).

[3] Gustave Thils, *Tendances actuelles en théologie morale* (Paris: Gembloux, 1940).

This critical movement began to gain strength in the postwar era with the publication of Leclercq's *L'Enseignement de la morale chrétienne* in 1949.[4] The traditional view and presentation of moral theology had in Leclercq's mind two major faults: first, a formalism based on excessive legalism and casuitry; and secondly, a too exclusive Aristotelian framework. He said that the mission of the modern moralist must be to bring Christ back as the center of the theological system; stress is to be placed upon themes compatible to modern man: personality, love, and the search for the Absolute. Against the traditional moralist, Leclercq made the telling objection that moral theology of the traditional manuals was not positively presented, was concerned only with sin, and therefore was more preoccupied with nonmorality than morality.

Leclercq's work was followed by a flurry of controversy as the moralists moved to defend their theological position and traditional approach. In 1956, according to the *Osservatore Romano*, the work was withdrawn from circulation because of what were regarded as its destructive tendencies. It must be remembered that a "withdrawal" is not a condemnation so much as a judgment that publication of the work at the moment is not expedient because of other conditions. By this time the controversy had been complicated by the growth of an existential morality called "situation ethics."

The withdrawal of Leclercq's work, then, was because of the inability of many to distinguish between the absolutist basis of Leclercq's criticism and the relativistic basis for morality proposed by the existentialists. Because of the withdrawal the work achieved a questionable reputation. Unfortunately, only recently two American commentators have left a bad impression of Leclercq's work by stating: ". . . his criticisms have a certain resemblance to the tenets of the new morality which has come to be known as situation ethics."[5] Actually it is unfair to Leclercq to state his position in such a manner, for though the critique of Leclercq and that of the existentialists might be the same, it remains to be proved that Leclercq's thought bears any resemblance to the "tenets" of the existentialists, or to imply that because of his critique he might in any way be a proponent of situation ethics.

[4] Jacques Leclercq, *L'Enseignement de la morale chrétienne* (Paris: Editions du Vitrail, 1949).

[5] Ford and Kelly, *Contemporary Moral Theology, op. cit.*, p. 59.

In 1952 Gerard Gilleman published *Le Primat de la charité en théologie morale*, a work which has remained as a more lasting and important achievement than the critique of Leclercq.[6] Gilleman, like Leclercq, reflects the view of the necessity of a positive point of view in moral theology; unlike Leclercq, he did not maintain his thesis on a pure criticism of the traditional approach, but advanced and worked with a central theme for moral theology, the theme of charity. The point of Gilleman's work is that charity—the love of God—is the basic meaning and form of moral theology.

In a discussion of the various new approaches to moral theology, the American theologians, Fathers John Ford and Gerald Kelly, in an otherwise excellent survey, make the astonishing statement: "The French can now write about a 'mystique of the non-obligatory'! People can speak beautifully of the law of love casting out fear. But sometimes it leaves one with the uneasy feeling that they are casting out the restraints of objective morality along with the fear. . . ." [7] This is a serious charge, and those guilty of it seem to be identified only as "the French." The argument continues and Fathers Ford and Kelly explicate their point with reference to "the modern critics, especially in France," and speak of French criticisms of the traditional moralists: ". . . their objections have much deeper philosophical and theological roots and are concerned with an alleged incompatibility between the ethics of love and the ethics of obligation, the palm being awarded, of course, to the ethics of love." [8]

The attitude toward the French reflected in this criticism is a rather common one, and should be carefully examined. Are the critical approaches of Leclercq the object of this severe judgment? Or perhaps the more positive proposals of Gilleman? Or for that matter, of any major French theologian? It seems not, for in a footnote to this statement we find references to the criticisms of two Italian Jesuits, Bortolaso and Boschi, whose articles in 1952 and 1956 took up and refuted "certain propositions of Yves de Montcheuil" in his *Mélanges théologiques*. As far as one can judge, therefore, it would seem that the charge against the French remains, if

[6] Gerard Gilleman, *The Primacy of Charity in Moral Theology* (Westminster, Md.: Newman, 1959).

[7] Ford and Kelly, *Contemporary Moral Theology, op. cit.*, p. 87.

[8] *Ibid.*, pp. 89–90.

not unsubstantiated, at least unproved. Fathers Ford and Kelly have constructed the "French" as such along the lines of one minor (in the sense of contributions) theologian who died in 1944. The French are not, we hasten to add, equivalent to Père de Montcheuil, nor are they, properly speaking, a single-minded and monolithic unit in their theological opinions.

Existentialism and Christian Morality

The moral theologians have not escaped the pervading influence of the existentialists. The impact of Existentialism and consequent "situation ethics" upon the study of morality produces a problem. The modern existentialist who faces Christianity faces what he considers to be *a priori* dogmatism, absolute law, and these, he thinks, are concepts that dehumanize man, providing barriers to his deepest longings rather than completion. Dondeyne accurately summarizes the problem the theologian faces in his dialogue with those outside the faith:

Christianity, which urges us to look for the things that are above us, and gives us a revealed and unchangeable morality, is supposed to make us less apt to face our tasks as men. Such is the reproach that modern unbelief makes against the Christian religion, and in particular against Catholic morality. . . . It is a plain fact that modern man is not impressed by a morality that is mainly negative, presented as a complicated code of prohibitions imposed from outside by an outside authority. He wants an "open" and creative morality, springing from the necessities of life itself and experienced not as a lessening or denial of life, but as the affirmation of an existence going forward to master all opportunities that lie before it. Many believe, though of course wrongly, that Christian morality, because of its revealed, dogmatic and immutable character, is a closed and negative one. They conclude that Catholics are in a position of inferiority. They are supposed to be less than others, poorly equipped to meet the problems of modern life, condemned to be always behind times. [9]

Dondeyne later links up the primacy of charity to these conceptions and points toward the way of Father Gilleman as a positive approach to moral theology:

[9] Albert Dondeyne, *Contemporary European Thought, op. cit.,* p. 186.

. . . no reason to question the free character of faith. It is the same with faith as with all our judgments of value. Every value judgment is a call to make ourselves freely receptive to the value, to accept it in our everyday existence and to promote it for ourselves and for others. Because it is a theological life, faith develops an attitude of confidence and fidelity. This is the sense of the phrase "believe in," in the statement of "I believe in God." To "believe in" someone is to have confidence in him, to entrust oneself to him, to place oneself at his disposal. By faith, we adhere to God and to his love for man. For this reason, faith is in practise inseparable from charity, which in one undivided impulse goes out both to God and to our neighbor." [10]

Nor does the morality of a Christian deprive him of a social consciousness toward others, for as he remarks, "no society can be authentically human unless it has a moral basis, unless it rests on 'truth, justice and love.'" Finally, Dondeyne faces the question of the dehumanizing effect of morality as envisioned by the existentialist:

The Christian Faith, by proposing to us an unchangeable revealed moral doctrine, is supposed to make us less able to face the world as men. Is it true that belief in a supernatural revelation lessens in us the sense of man and of history? The question is important, not only because it is still the source of innumerable misunderstandings between believers and unbelievers, but also because an answer to it is for the Christian a positive task whose significance he cannot safely deny. If Christian faith is a light for man, and gives to human life its deepest and ultimate meaning, then Christianity has an earthly vocation. A Christianity divorced from the realities of this world is untrue to itself. The more Christians withdraw from the world, the more easily the world becomes an obstacle for the Church. "The greatest fault of Christians in the 20th century," as Cardinal Suhard once remarked, "would be to leave the world to shape itself and bring itself to unity without them." [11]

Laboring with the problems created by the existentialist approach to morality, some theologians during the early 1950's fell into the pitfall of an "open morality" or situation ethic. This error lay basically in its deprival of absolute binding force to the moral law

[10] *Ibid.*, p. 186.
[11] *Ibid.*, p. 189.

of God. Morality, the good or evil of a human act, according to this error is to be derived from the situation and the conditions that surrounded it and in which the act is performed. Thus, for these men, what may have traditionally been considered sinful may in some concrete instance not only be not sinful but even a moral good. This situation ethic, although it had proponents—few in number, and these more among the philosophers than the theologians—was something quickly recognized and equally as quickly condemned. We shall in the next chapter deal with the papal condemnation and events in France surrounding it. A situation ethic would completely empty Christian morality of its absolute character based upon the eternal law of God.

Psychology and the Moralists

Perhaps because of an exaggerated watchfulness for situation ethics, Catholic commentators often erroneously label other modern and extreme positions as situation ethics. Thus, the work of Abbé Marc Oraison, *Vie chrétienne et sexualité* has been frequently mislabeled a product of this heresy.[12] In this controversial work, Abbé Oraison, basing himself upon the findings of modern psychology, argued for the existence of what he terms "immaturity of the sexual instinct." Because this frequently is found in men he concludes that in many cases of sins against chastity there is no real guilt in the commission of the act. The consideration of man's unconscious at times rendering him freedomless in principle, coupled with the traditional distinction of material and formal sin, led Oraison to the conclusion that although frequently sins were found to be material, they were not formally sinful, having been committed without the complete freedom demanded for a human act.

In January, 1955, the work was condemned, placed on the Index, and Abbé Oraison immediately consented to the action of the Holy See.[13] The work was quite unlike situation ethics, and its consequent condemnation was not based upon such considerations. The con-

---

[12] Marc Oraison, *Vie chrétienne et sexualité* (Paris: Lethielleux, 1952).

[13] Actually the Decree of condemnation was dated March 18, 1953, and was published in the *Acta Apostolicae Sedis*, Vol. 47 (1955), p. 46. Oraison's submission was announced in the same volume, p. 89.

demnation, foreseen by many, was based on the fact that Oraison had so accentuated the lack of freedom implied in "sexual infantilism" that he had overstated his case by denying the possibility of freedom in the commission of such sins. However, the view of Fathers Ford and Kelly mirrors the hope of most theologians: "We may express the hope that this condemnation will not discourage other serious, but more conservative efforts to solve what Vermeersch referred to, almost thirty years ago, as one of the great challenges to the modern moralist, the 'grave and thorny problem . . . of subjective imputability.' " [14]

Turning his talents toward the pressing problem of the lapsed Catholic, Abbé Oraison produced "*Amour ou contrainte?*" in 1957.[15] He skillfully applied psychology and theology to the problem of the religious education of Catholics, and accented the deficiencies in both fields which leave the Catholic actually weakened in his faith.

It would be proper to mention here the theological approaches of the French toward the work being done by moderns in the field of psychology and research among the mentally and emotionally disturbed. The great strides made in psychology, psychiatry and allied fields bring with them many problems relating to moral theology, and to the object of theology, the human act. The French Dominican, Albert Plé, and his fellow Dominican in Belgium, Augustin Léonard, the Jesuit Louis Beirnaert, and the Carmelite Bruno Jésus-Marie have all contributed significantly toward the reconciliation of modern psychology and Thomistic philosophy. They are attempting to forge a synthesis between the moderns (Freud, Jung, Adler) and the traditional Thomistic system.

To meet the moral implications of the new science the medical-moral quarterly *Cahiers Laënnec* was founded.[16] In addition, many of the individual works published under Père Bruno Jésus-Marie's collection *Etudes carmelitaines* deal with specific problems suggested by psychology. Ascetical and moral theologians have also

---

[14] Ford and Kelly, *op. cit.*, p. 179.

[15] Marc Oraison, *Love or Constraint?* (New York: Kenedy, 1959).

[16] Many recent opinions on psychiatry and Catholicism, on Freudian therapy and Catholic principles have been presented in the *Cahiers Laënnec*. Of these, a great number are available in English in the collections of Dom Peter Flood, *New Problems in Medical Ethics* (Westminster, Md.: Newman, 1957).

been influenced by the psychologists, and in 1953 Père Henri Snoeck, S.J., published his findings in *L'Hygiène mentale et les principes chrétiens*.[17] Père Rondet has also been active in utilizing the findings of the psychologists, and in 1955 the monumental work of Père Schaller on the sacraments, *Secours de la grâce et secours de la médicine*,[18] was published. Schaller considered the sacraments and grace, not only in their properly theological aspects but also from the point of view of their therapeutical value. He skillfully related the findings of modern psychology with the traditional theology of the sacraments.

Thus, in moral theology as in all the fields of theological endeavor among the French, we find an enormous amount of work being carried out, influenced by the theology of the sources, the Teaching Church, and also by those fields of secular research most challenging to the Catholic concept of man.

2. CHURCH HISTORY

The boundaries of Church history are extremely wide and difficult to distinguish from allied spheres of interest. The Church historian faces not only the simple chronological catalogue of dates and facts, but the meaning, the causes and the results that lie behind those facts. No field of the Church's endeavor and mission, her teaching, her internal development or external contact with the world is, properly speaking, beyond the ken of the Church historian. Many facets of the Church, in themselves properly historical, belong to other fields as, for example, Scripture and patrology. Even such a fundamental problem as the nature of history itself may be found under a doctrinal discussion. Therefore we limit our investigation here to the traditionally accepted concept of a Church historian.

The modern theological revival owes a debt of gratitude to the historians and the tradition of historical scholarship of the French at the turn of the century. This tradition is firmly based on the work of the very able Père Duchesne both during the modernist crisis and after. During the modernist period the Church historians

---

[17] Paris: Lethielleux, 1953.
[18] Bruges: Desclée, 1955.

Duchesne, de Broglie, Baudrillant, Battifol and Denifle were invaluable to the Church.

Père Louis Duchesne (1843-1922) was a Breton, a Doctor of Letters and the Professor of Church History at the Institut Catholique in Paris from 1877 to 1885. A personal friend of Alfred Loisy, it was Duchesne who introduced Loisy to the critical historical method. In the late nineteenth century he suffered the penalty of being a scholar in an extremely touchy era and lost his teaching post. This occurred after he was rash enough to conclude from his researches that Mary Magdalene did not eventually make her way to Provence. Such was the attitude of pious beliefs, unfounded traditions and lack of scholarship at the time Duchesne began his work.

In 1885 he became a lecturer at the Ecole Pratique des Hautes Etudes, and in 1888 a member of the Academie des Inscriptions et Belles Lettres and the director of the French School of Archeology at Rome. His monumental *Culte chrétien* appeared in 1889, as well as his *Mémoire sur l'origine des dioceses épiscopaux dans l'ancienne Gaule*. Rapidly establishing himself as one of the most gifted of living Church historians he was made a Monsignor and Protonotary Apostolic in 1900, and a Consultor to the Congregation of Indulgences and Relics in 1901. His greatest work, the *L'Histoire ancienne de l'église*, was published in 1908. This crowning work of his life was widely praised, and earned a commendation from the Pope, and in time became known as a masterpiece of the critical method. In 1912, after its appearance in Italian translation, it was placed on the Index because of what was regarded as its too critical tendencies, because of the suspicion of modernism that hung above the head of its author, and, no doubt, because of the enemies his bitter and caustic wit had earned him.

Although today the tradition of scholarship he established in the field of Church history has surpassed many of his conclusions, Duchesne's works remain an outstanding production of his time as well as the first critical work in Church history in the modern age. When he died in 1922 the Abbot Cabrol could say: "He was a first-class scholar . . . he left an admirable example of serious work, and scientific loyalty . . . he was [as well] a pious priest."

As the modernist period ebbed away, the work of the Franciscan

Piette and the Benedictine Gougand kept alive the tradition of historical scholarship. During the 1920's and 1930's two major names stand out in the French tradition: the Jesuit Delehaye, and the Abbé Henri Bremond. Père Hippolyte Delehaye, an indefatigable hagiographer, spent most of his life working as a Bollandist. Eventually he succeeded to the presidency of the Bollandist group. Bremond's enormous contributions to Church history were crowned by his monumental six-volume work, *The History of Religious Experience*. In addition to the work of these men, we have left for us the books of Abbé Constant of the Institut Catholique in Paris, and the hagiographer Père Trochu, and layman Pierre Janelle.

Today, among the projects undertaken by French historians of the Church, must be mentioned two: The History of the Councils, and the Fliche-Martin series. In the nineteenth century the German Hefle began the great work of a complete history of the Councils of the Church. His work was continued by Hergenroether, and was completed as far as the Council of Trent by the French scholars Richard and Michel. This work was translated into French by Henri Leclercq. By 1952, Charles de Clercq had actually completed the eleventh section of the work begun by Hefle and Hergenroether, by publishing in two volumes a *History of the Councils of the Oriental Catholics* from 1875 to 1850, and from 1850 to 1949.[19]

An immediate and lasting contribution began with the Fliche-Martin series in 1942. At that time a twenty-six-volume history of the Church was projected and undertaken under the leadership of Augustin Fliche, Dean of the University of Letters at Montpelier, and Msgr. Victor Martin, the Dean of the Faculty of Catholic Theology at Strasbourg. The earlier volumes on the history of Primitive Christianity and the Early Church were done by the Abbé Jules Lebreton, the layman Jacques Zeiler, as well as by de Labriolle, Bardy, Planque, de Plinval and others.[20] Some of these volumes still have not appeared, but those that were published met a wide and enthusiastic reception. The entire series has today passed over to the editorship of J. B. Duroselle and Eugène Jarry.

[19] Paris: Letouzey et Ané, 1952. 2 vols.
[20] The first set of English translations available are: *The History of the Primitive Church* (New York: Macmillan, 1942–1944), 2 vols.; and *The Church in the Christian Roman Empire* (New York: Macmillan, 1952), 2 vols.

Of the volumes that have appeared in the Fliche-Martin series, that on the pontificate of Pius IX is worth special comment. It has been extremely well thought of in historical circles and is an excellent example of the work of the Abbé Roger Aubert. Aubert is a professor at the University of Louvain, and among his works is the slim volume, referred to in other places, *La Théologie catholique au milieu du XXe siècle*.[21] Here Aubert states his thesis that modern theological development is dominated by two major preoccupations: first, a desire to contact the sources of tradition, that is, the Word of God as proclaimed and explained in the Church (therefore, leading to the threefold renewal of Biblical, liturgical and patristic movements); second, a willingness to turn to the modern world, thus producing for the theologian the themes of a theology of the laity, a theology of history, of ecumenicism and an approach to the existentialists. Because of Aubert's thinly veiled toleration of the Germans, and his cool indifference to the Italian, Spanish and Roman theologians, it is alleged that he has been requested to withdraw the book from circulation. Whether this be true or false, and it is impossible to say which, the criticism implied remains valid. However, Aubert, for all his shortcomings, remains an extremely capable historian, and a man marked by his love for the Church, as well as a capable theologian in his own right. Aubert, like his predecessor, Duchesne, is an example and inspiration for the historian of the Church in France today.

3. MISCELLANEOUS

Theology in modern France faces not only the traditional problems of the theologian, but as well those specifically created by the age. This has brought to the theologian in contemporary France not only the collection of human experience and wisdom passed on to him along with God's Revelation, but also the specifically new, and there have been created in France new lines of theological endeavor, such as missiology, religious psychology, religious sociology and even such a movement as catechetics has blossomed to a full scientific and theological status.

The modern progress in psychology has not only created, as we

---

[21] Roger Aubert, *Théologie catholique au milieu du XXe siècle, op. cit.*

have said, specific problems for moralists, but places extremely valuable material in the hands of those concerned with the welfare of the Church and the formation of the Christian mind among the faithful. Quite obviously this new science has implications for the apologist, catechist and ascetical theologian. Religious psychology may date itself from the work of the Jesuit Pierre Rousselou during the first decade of the twentieth century. The field is at present dominated by the Germans; however, a considerable contribution has been made by Père Augustin Léonard. At forty-nine, Father Léonard is Professor of Fundamental Theology at the Dominican house of studies at La Sarte in Belgium. He helps to edit for Casterman the *Cahiers de l'actualité religieuse*, which has become the periodical of the religious psychology movement. Léonard has also published *Récherches phénomenologiques autour de l'expérience mystique*, and contributed the article on ascetics, *Procédés ascétiques en usage dans l'église*, to the *L'Ascèse chrétienne et l'homme contemporain*.[22] Père Léonard is known to English-speaking readers for frequent contributions to the *Lumen Vitae*, and at the same time he contributes regularly to *La Vie spirituelle: supplément* on psychological questions. In 1957 the *Lumen Vitae* gave an entire issue over to discussions of this comparatively new study of theologians.[23]

The traditional field of ascetical theology is, of course, for the most part strongly influenced by the other fields. The concentration on the sources of the Christian life; the Biblical, liturgical and patristic movements reflect this influence upon the ascetical theologians continually in such a periodical as *La Vie spirituelle*.

As Scripture scholars have explored the depths of the Gospel message and as organized presentations of the Joannine and Pauline writings appear, the ascetical writers are turning toward a more positive system, more closely related to Biblical concepts. The doctrine of the Mystical Body of Christ has come to dominate the

[22] Augustin Léonard, O.P., *Récherches phénoménologiques autour de l'expérience mystique* (Paris: Editions du Cerf, 1952). The interesting collection of essays in *L'Ascèse chrétienne* has been translated as *Christian Asceticism and Modern Man* (New York: Philosophical Library, 1955). A collection of essays on mysticism by Plé, Bouyer, Cerfaux and Léonard can be found in *Mystery and Mysticism* (New York: Philosophical Library, 1956).

[23] *Lumen Vitae*, Vol. 12 (April, 1957).

thoughts and work of these theologians. The salvific power of the Resurrection of Jesus as co-joined to His Passion, the meaning of the Ascension, and an appreciation of Pentecost and the Parousia also strongly mark modern ascetical theologians. The mystery of grace, formerly considered almost exclusively with regard to actual grace, has received a shift of emphasis, leading to a renewed appreciation of the true foundation of Christian living in habitual or sanctifying grace. Studies of Old Testament spirituality by Gelin and Tresmontant, and by Dupont, Spicq and Bonsirven in the New Testament have provided materials for this new approach.

Within the Church, the growth of ecclesiology and the Catholic Action movements have caused an accentuation of the place of the laity within the Church. A Church-centered spirituality, a spirituality of the Mystical Body of Christ has therefore developed. In addition, the scientific advancements of psychologists and sociologists have brought to the ascetical theologian a more acute awareness and specific knowledge of the human individual. Allied to these is the field of religious psychology, and the combination and synthesis of the elements of traditional teaching and religious psychology are to be observed in the works of Canon Jean Mouroux and the approach that he adopts.[24]

A *Dictionnaire de spiritualité* has been established for the ascetical theologian, and is published by Beauchesne in Paris, under the editorship of the Jesuit, Père Charles Baumgartner. Three volumes have been completed and favorably received. The finished project will be a complete treatment of ascetical theology on the historical as well as theological level.

The influence of theological awareness of the Church and the place of the laity in Catholic Action have created two auxiliary sciences to apply the fruits of theological speculation. The first of these is missiology, a specifically French contribution to the theological sciences. To the great Belgian Jesuit, Pierre Charles, this new science owes its beginnings.[25] Since his death his position as

[24] Jean Mouroux, *The Christian Experience* (New York: Sheed & Ward, 1954).

[25] Pierre Charles, S.J., *Missiologie* (Paris: Desclée, 1959). See also Père Masson's collection of Père Charles's works in *Etudes missiologiques* (Paris: Desclée de Brouwer, 1956). Père Vincent Lebbe, a Belgian, founded a congregation of mission priests, the Société des Auxiliaires des Missions, who

evident leader of the movement has been taken by Père Masson, S.J. Important studies of the Church's missionary effort have been published,[26] concentrating on the theological problem involved in the confrontation of an alien civilization and culture by Christians, admittedly products of the Western mind.[27] As we have mentioned, Père Danielou has been a moving spirit in creating and sustaining interest in the missionary vocation of the Church. Others such as the Abbés Godin, Boulard and Michonneau have translated missionary theology and orientation to the problem of the paganized section of France.

In addition to the valuable work accomplished by Godin and Michonneau in translating the missionary effort to the parish level, the importance of the parish unit has been stressed as well by the liturgical revival, and by the new science of religious sociology, born between the wars in the pioneering efforts of Gabriel Le Bras. Today the acknowledged leader among the French in religious sociology is Abbé François Houtart of Malines.[28] This new science puts the statistical findings of professional sociologists working in a religious framework at the disposal of the parish priest. The importance of this for the establishment of an effective religious program is obvious, for it is in the truthful and accurate knowledge of a situation that a workable and realistic program can be established.

The effective translation of theological truth in a vital way to the modern Christian has long been the object of many a contemporary theologian. The Biblical and liturgical revivals have terminated with religious sociology and religious psychology in a strong and influential catechetical movement. The heart of the movement lies in the International Center for Religious Education at Brussels. In

---

serve under the Ordinaries of the mission dioceses in which they are assigned. Lebbe's insistence upon native clergy and hierarchy became a *cause célèbre* in the Belgian Church. He was killed by the Chinese Communists during the Second World War, and was himself a Chinese citizen. The Société publishes the highly respected bimonthly *Eglise vivante*. See the life of Père Lebbe by Jacques Leclercq, *Thunder in the Distance* (New York: Sheed & Ward, 1958).

[26] Henri de Lubac, S.J., *Le Fondement théologique des missions, op. cit.*

[27] *L'Eglise et les civilisations* (Paris: Editions de Floré, 1956).

[28] A brief but excellent treatment of religious sociology may be found in the English translation and abridgement of an article by François Houtart in "Religious Sociology," *Theology Digest*, Vol. 4 (Spring, 1956), pp. 116–119.

1946 it began to publish the distinguished periodical *Lumen Vitae*, which is now available in four languages. There are few major theologians in France or Belgium who have not at some time or other in the past twelve years appeared in the pages of *Lumen Vitae*.

In France there have been the National Congresses of Religious Education and a continued interest in the catechetical movement by the Episcopate. The work of the Jesuit Rimaud and the Dominican Tremeau have had far-reaching influence. The Jesuits under the leadership of Père Georges Delcuve dominate the work of the International Center at Brussels. Père Delcuve has had able assistance in his work with his Jesuit confreres, Godin, Ranwez and Van Caster.

The French catechetical school is led by the enormously capable Canon Joseph Colomb. Canon Colomb's great modern catechetical achievement, the *Catechisme progressif* was published in 1956.[29] The Catechism was arranged in three parts: *Parlez, Seigneur; Dieu, parmi nous;* and *Avec le Christ Jésus,* and was designed to be "progressive." This meant that the teachings of the faith were to be adapted to the ages of psychological growth in the development of the child. "Reason," said Canon Colomb, "and its processes and logic wish to be in the service of the faith."

Shortly after the appearance of the *Catechisme progressif* a series of articles by Msgr. Lusseau, Dean of the Faculty of Theology at Angers, appeared in the periodical of that institution, *Revue de cercles d'études d'Angers.*[30] The gist of Msgr. Lusseau's articles was highly critical of the catechism and the principles that inspired it. The catechism was not traditional, and the avoidance of complicated dogmatic truth because it was opposed to the slow growth of the child was labeled clearly erroneous. Msgr. Lusseau's criticisms prevailed and later that year (1957) the Holy Office ordered the catechism withdrawn.

Thus began the so-called "catechism affair." A commission of the French Episcopate assented to certain insertions into the catechism, to the dropping of "Progressive" from the title, and to the condemnation of certain educational methods that were clearly excessive. Rome, pacified, withdrew the condemnation.

---

[29] Paris: Vitte, 1956.
[30] Msgr. Lusseau, "Littérature catechistique," *Revue de cercles d'études d'Angers* (Jan.-Mar., 1957), pp. 92–96, 115–116, 116–119.

Père Georges Delcuve, editor of *Lumen Vitae*, reviewed the affair in an excellent article in that periodical.[31] In interpreting the changes demanded by the Holy Office Père Delcuve brought the affair into a proper light. In his evaluation of Lusseau's articles, Delcuve recognized many arguments of merit, arguments that had not gone unnoticed by the authorities in Rome. However, this appreciation of Msgr. Lusseau did not hinder Delcuve from being critical of Msgr. Lusseau's excessive "traditionalism," a traditionalism allegedly restricted to the nineteenth century.

The catechetical movement, and the organizations devoted to the religious education of adults as well as children, have been aided by the publication of Abbé Marc Oraison's previously mentioned book, *Amour ou contrainte?* To the traditional concepts of religious education Oraison has brought the findings of modern psychology, and attempts to explore the possibilities of their adaptation to traditional catechetics. We might conclude with the observation that the catechetical movement in France and Belgium has produced in addition to worth-while studies of the problems of religious education many noteworthy aids: pamphlets, recordings, filmstrips and movies, aids which have greatly enhanced the job of translating theology to the layman.

4. FRANCE IN THEORY vs. FRANCE IN FACT

We might recall here the frequent criticism voiced by some that the actual state of the Church in France is far removed and in sharp contrast to the intellectual appreciations of the theologians. And while to some degree this is true these impatient critics frequently forget that the actual state of Catholicism in France had for its first critics the French themselves, nor do they give these men credit for being honestly aware of their own situation. Abbé Godin's *France, pays de mission* was quite as severe in its judgments as the title indicates.[32] The Episcopal Pastorals on the Church indicate an acute awareness on the part of authority in the French Church of the perilous situation of Catholicism in France.

It is not enough to be aware of this occasionally valid criticism of the Church; one must, like the historian, be aware of the reasons for

---

[31] Georges Delcuve, S.J., "The Catechetical Movement in France," *Lumen Vitae*, Vol. 12 (Oct., 1957), pp. 671–702.

[32] Maisie Ward, *France Pagan* (New York: Sheed & Ward, 1950).

it. The causes of this weakened state of the Church are too frequently forgotten by the non-French critic who has suffered few, if any, of them: the initial estrangement of the Church and the Revolution of 1789, the intransigence and mistakes of members of the hierarchy, the efficiency and political dominance of the anticlericals and the despoilation of the Church.

Valid criticisms of the state of the Church should give attention and proper evaluation to the powerful and inspirational steps the Church in France has taken to bridge the chasm between the Church and the people. Among these are the growth of Catholic Action, the missionary movement and spirit extended to the parochial level, the ill-fated movement of the worker-priests, and the growth of a theology of the laity. These steps reflect an awareness of the Church and her mission, and of the place each baptized Christian possesses in the Kingdom of God.

There is as well one basic fact that must be subjected to examination, that is, the actual state of the Church in France as presented by the critics. While acutely aware that there are sections of France which are virtually pagan, and for which the French have attempted new forms of the apostolate, nevertheless it must be asked if such a picture as Godin's *France Pagan* paints accurately reflects the French nation as a whole?

Accentuation of the negative aspects of French Catholicism, concentration upon those instances in which the French Church has flagrantly failed can of course make it easy ". . . to conclude that France, the eldest daughter of the Church is today a harlot just as it is easy to conclude that her inability to form a stable government, her disasters in Algeria and Indo-China, her inflation and near bankruptcy, are indications of a social disease. It is, indeed, all too easy to dismiss France as a debilitated tramp." [33]

Adrien Dansette in his *Destin du catholicisme française, 1926–1956* presents an interesting collection and collation of statistics gathered by Gabriel Lebras of the Sorbonne and Canon Boulard.[34] These figures reveal an interesting pattern: 75 per cent of the

---

[33] D. P. O'Connell, "France Catholic," *The Catholic World*, Vol. 187 (Oct., 1958), pp. 34–42, 36.

[34] Adrien Dansette, *Destin du catholicisme français, 1926–1956* (Paris: Flammarion, 1957). See also Canon Boulard's earlier works: *Problèmes missionaires de la France rurale* (Paris: Editions du Cerf, 1945), 2 vols.; *Essor ou declin du clergé français* (Paris: Editions du Cerf, 1950).

French population are baptized, make first communion, and marry in the Church; 50 per cent make their Easter duty, and 40 per cent attend Mass and receive the sacraments regularly; only 5 per cent of the entire population profess atheism. In addition to these figures it must also be noted that according to one commentator Catholicism varies in strength from province to province. It is extremely strong in the north (Brittany, Normandy, Beauvais), as well as in Alsace, the Basque region about Lourdes, and in upper Savoy. The center and south of France, Languedoc, Provence, and the working-class areas in the cities present a dismal picture. The commentator reflects meaningfully: "France is a bewildering country, and those who know her best are most bewildered. No stream of French attitude or culture may be said to be the essential France. . . . In part, the failure of the French to follow the direction of the Church is one of temperament. There is no French opinion; there is only a Frenchman's opinion." [35]

Frequently one hears the critic who with a meaningful sweep of the hand dismisses the contemporary theological movement in France. He discards the real intuitions and substantial contributions of that movement, simply because, for him, the phenomenon of a Catholic France does not agree with his construction of reality. The sociological facts and figures available describe for us an essentially Catholic France, and the man who bases his criticisms of contemporary French theology upon the statement that this movement is far removed from the real situation of the Church errs seriously in two ways. First, granting the rectitude of his presumption, nevertheless the dismissal of the theologians for that reason is a *non sequitur*, neither logical nor reasonable. Second, the criticism is based on a false assumption that substantially all of France is pagan, or non-Catholic.

There may be and there should be and there is, among the French, a true evaluation of those areas in which the Church has failed to fulfill her mission. But this in no way obscures France's real achievements both in theology and in the apostolate.

35 D. P. O'Connell, "France Catholic," *op. cit.*, p. 36.

VI

❃

CONTEMPORARY FRENCH
THEOLOGY AND THE
TEACHING CHURCH

No question is more perplexing, complicated, and at times puzzling than the relationship of the French theologians to the Holy See. It is our contention that what is called the French theological revival has for its basic formative influence the Magisterium of the Church. Nor, furthermore, has any like period of theological thought in the history of the Church manifested such loyalty and constancy toward the Holy See.

It would be an oversimplification to see in this deep-seated loyalty to the Pope the simple reappearance of Mennasian ultramontanism, for today there is no comparative servitude toward the State such as the Gallicanism of the Lamennais era. The immediate relationship of Roman influence upon the sweep of contemporary French theological thought is based upon the *"Action française"* decision of Pope Pius XI. Roman influence and direction is particularly evident during the war years in the encyclicals of the early Pontificate of Pius XII, and after the war, in the monumental *Mediator Dei*. The crisis in Roman-French relationships came with *Humani Generis* in 1950, and throughout this period of the early fifties, in the condemnation of the worker-priests and situation ethics; the French in the main obediently followed the Vicar of Christ on earth.

It is the habit of many of the critics of contemporary French thought to identify the Church with their own conservative position. This is evident in the United States in the attitude taken by some theologians. For them there is no proper area of theological debate outside their own positions, and frequently no sympathy or understanding for thoughtful men of a different intellectual milieu and training than their own. It is our contention that this theological movement among the French is based upon the best meaning of "*sentire cum ecclesia*" and a deep-seated faith and loyalty to the living voice of the Teaching Church.

Action française—1926

The continual efforts of the Church toward *ralliement*, the policy of Catholic acceptance of the Republic, had been frequently frustrated in France both by the intransigence of the Royalist Catholics and the anticlerical attitudes of the Republicans. Through the years the advocates of *ralliement*, the "left," steadily grew in numbers until the issue was fully met and settled in 1926. Charles Maurras and his paper, *L'Action française* had become the spokesman of the right wing. The conservative sentiment that clustered about Maurras had been alienated from the Republic because of the laicizing laws and extreme anticlericalism.

However, as time went on, the *Action française* displayed a complete unwillingness to follow papal direction toward a *rapprochement* with the government. After they refused to heed the condemnation of Cardinal Andrieu, Archbishop of Bordeaux, the question went beyond one of simple politics or political expediency to become the root difficulty of the question of the survival of the Church herself. Pope Pius XI did not hesitate to move against the *Action française*.

In 1926 Maurras, his journal and his movement were placed under papal condemnation. The future now lay with the Republicans, and on the whole, with the liberal Catholics. "The more radical element in French Catholicism, amongst whom the Dominicans were prominent, were to inherit the Twentieth Century at the expense of the authoritarians of the school of *Action française*." [1] The action of

---

[1] Hales, *op. cit.*, p. 236.

the Holy Father was not popular with the right wing of the Church, and even such a distinguished personage as Cardinal Billot expressed his dissatisfaction by resigning the cardinalate. The Right, the traditionalists, were rejected in the political order, and many of them in ecclesiastical positions were soon replaced. Indeed, the future lay with the radicals.

As we have remarked, the result of the furore following the papal directive was the dismissal of opponents of papal action from positions of power and influence. The implications are evident. Into the vacuum came the moderns, the radicals, men in authority who, if they were not "progressive" were at least in sympathy with the modern *rapprochement* of the Church and the Republic, and of the Church with the world around her. Within twenty years the results of the *Action française* affair became clear, for the religious movement in France, theological and otherwise, had few conservative authorities to hold it in check. The French, many of whom possess the particular intellectual quality of being continually *avant garde*, had by the 1940's few conservatives to check or even retard the undeniable force of the movement. The removal of these possible stumbling blocks for the French was basically the work of the papal decision to enforce the *ralliement*.

The Early Pontificate of Pope Pius XII

In 1943 Pope Pius XII issued the monumental encyclicals that contributed force, direction and encouragement to the religious movement in France: the theological *Mystici Corporis Christi* and the scriptural *Divino Afflante Spiritu*. French theological preoccupation with the meaning and Mystery of the Church and its implications for the modern world received a vindication, a stimulus and an encouragement, while the French scriptural critics looked upon *Divino Afflante spiritu* as a "breath of fresh air."

In his encyclical on the Church, the Mystical Body of Christ, the Holy Father pointed to the Church as the extension of the Incarnation. As Christ had used human nature to redeem man, so also He continues to use the Church to make the Redemption present to every man, remaining himself as the Head of that Body of the saved and the source of all grace. The papal treatment extended to the sacraments and the organization of that Mystical Body, and especially of Christ present in His members. This latter point led to a long treatment of the place and function of its members. The lay apostolate, the apostolic work entrusted to each member of Christ, was stressed, and this was a theme the French were to develop completely in the postwar years. Finally, the Holy Father spoke of the unity of the Church and of love for the Church, another note which the French took seriously to heart. As we have seen, this love of the Church and reflection upon her mission would become a hallmark of the theological revival. At the same time, we shall see that throughout the trials of the theologians this love of the Church would be adequately witnessed to and vindicated.

In his encyclical on Holy Scripture the Biblical revival received its strongest encouragement and most useful direction. The movement, begun in reaction to Modernism and controlled by the earlier papal directives, was now directed to the field of "literary genres," —the study of the literary forms used by the sacred writers. On this question alone the Holy Father made a lasting contribution to the solid steps taken by the Biblical movement.

During these early years of the pontificate of Pope Pius XII, France was a conquered and defeated nation. As these encyclicals set the tone of the French theological movement, so also with them came the influences proper to the wartime era. In the wartime experience of the French, many, such as de Montcheuil of the Institut Catholique, were in contact with the Underground; others, priests and students, were in prison camps, and throughout this time Frenchmen grew closer together working in common for the day of liberation. Throughout these years a new influence was acting upon the French Church, that of personal meeting with existentialists, Marxists and atheists. A feeling of reaching out to these comrades-in-arms, of bringing to them the message of the Church, the Body of Christ, occupied the minds and work of many of the clergy.

The Postwar Era—The "New Theology"

The best description of the French Church after the war would be to state that she was seized by the missionary spirit. As the onus of the occupation was lifted, the French Church stood marked by certain qualities: a theological movement rooted in the sources of theology, and preoccupied with those notes sounded by the Magisterium; a dynamic Catholic Action movement, many of whose members had shared the wartime horrors with non-Catholics; some extremely capable and enlightened members of the Episcopate, Léonard of Lille, Gerlier of Lyon, Weber of Strasbourg and Suhard of Paris; men in authority of a fairly liberal turn of mind; and, finally, thinkers and writers of great intellectual caliber, open to the intellectual currents of the modern world.

This era has been succinctly categorized and summed up as the era of the "new theology," and indeed a "new" theology was obviously emerging. The term took on an opprobrious meaning in 1950 with the *Humani Generis*. Specifically, though, exactly what was this "new theology"? We may state that it possessed the following elements:

First, this new theology was rather a mood than a specific set of principles. Most of its theologians were Thomists; however, they abandoned the rigidity frequently connoted by that term and listened to and appreciated the modern intellectual milieu, and then they set about utilizing what was of value in it.

Secondly, the new theology was certainly marked by a dissatisfaction with the traditional elements which they referred to as "Thomistic rigidity," "scholastic abstractions" and "the divorce from the real." These expressions marked their impatience with the conservative minds. Much of it was no doubt attributable to the serious inadequacies of some theologians, as well as to the juvenile interest that intellectual novelties create.

This leads us to a personal judgment that marks the third characteristic: there were many excessive elements, as well as the balanced, experienced and trained theologians. Young students and priests frequently and without much basis struck the "radical note" more as a pose than a conviction. The new reflections of the maturer minds were frequently seized upon for no other reason than their "newness."

Finally, the movement of the "new theology" was characterized in the external order by its attachment to the "worker-priest" movement. The *Mission de France* and *Mission de Paris*, the commitment of the priesthood to new forms of action, were closely linked to their intellectual patrons in the "new theology." Thus, for example, many of the worker-priests looked upon Yves Congar as "their" theologian.

Who were the leaders of the "new theology"? For the most part they were looked upon as the Jesuits and Dominicans: de Lubac, Danielou, Bouillard, Teilhard de Chardin in the Society of Jesus; Congar, Braun, and Dubarle in the Order of Preachers. However, it would be unfair to say that those characteristics that detracted, and eventually imperiled the movement, were ever present in these extremely capable and scholarly theologians.

1947—Mediator Dei

On November 20, 1947, the Holy Father issued the encyclical letter *Mediator Dei*, devoted to a consideration of the sacred liturgy. The liturgical movement, which had become an integral part of the theological revival's interest in the sources, came in for considerable praise by the Pope. The extraordinary length of the encyclical, its universal character and the importance attached to it at Rome assured its warm reception in France.

The Holy Father dwelt upon the nature of the sacred liturgy, and the entire spirit of the encyclical was aimed at fostering and directing the liturgical movement. No doubt France was one of those countries that he praised for serious, scholarly and practical contributions. However, the Holy Father also criticized certain "unbalanced" elements: the derogation of the traditional practices of piety, the independent changing of rubrics and an excessive archaism. These abuses were no doubt to be found among the French as well as others, and the Pope gently but firmly corrected such false courses of action.

It would be unfair to the entire spirit and tenor of *Mediator Dei* to look upon it simply as a critical document obsessed with the shortcomings of certain liturgists. It was, basically, a letter of encouragement and direction, and more especially of papal teaching on the nature and implications of the worship of the Church. And it was as such that the French received it, be it noted, with great enthusiasm.

Thus in the postwar years the intellectually thriving Church of Belgium and France, with her theological-Bibilical-liturgical movement resting upon episcopal encouragement and three major papal documents, enjoyed its heyday of international prestige. There were, however, even then critical rumblings from conservative quarters. And in 1947 Henri de Lubac became the center of a full-scale theological debate, and his case became the bellwether of the "new theology."

The Critics

The forceful drive of the Franco-Belgian theological revival, sweeping to eminence as it did in the era immediately after the war, was not accomplished without some objections from the conservative forces. The postwar outpouring of books, articles and pamphlets of the "new theologians" soon provoked a highly critical movement.

This movement that attempted to check the "new theology" was initiated because of three factors. First, the Jesuit theological faculty at Lyon-Fourvière, in cooperation with the publishing house of Aubier in Paris, began publication in 1941 of a series of works on theology entitled simply *Théologie*. To this the Jesuits Bouillard, Danielou and de Lubac contributed controversial works. The second factor was the joint direction of the *Sources chrétiennes* by Danielou and de Lubac. The third and most immediate factor that brought the opposition out into the open was an article by Danielou in *Etudes* on contemporary theology. This article, calling for "openness" to the modern world, served to trigger the smoldering conservative impatience into action.

Père Labourdette opened the first critical barrage in the respected *Revue thomiste*.[2] In an article on the "new theology" he was highly critical of the tendencies of the "new theologians," especially of Bouillard, de Lubac and Danielou's contributions to the *Théologie* series. Labourdette, concentrating his fire upon the Jesuit theologians, made de Lubac, long a critic of the excessive rationalism of the traditional theologians, his first victim. In addition to attacking de Lubac's criticism of rationalism Labourdette accused de Lubac of being entirely too relativistic and too inattentive to the absolute and objective value of the traditional presentation of Thomism.

Continuing his criticism, Labourdette turned upon Danielou. He

[2] Aubert synopsizes and evaluates Labourdette's criticism in *La Théologie catholique au milieu du XXe siècle, op. cit.,* pp. 84–86.

attacked Danielou's relativistic tendencies in the field of patristics. Furthermore, he suggested, that perhaps Danielou's preoccupation with the Fathers was a deliberate attempt to diminish the importance of the conceptual constructions of the theologians. He went on to state that the patristic revival itself received its motivating force in the new theology as an evident movement against scholastic theology. Patristics and scholasticism, he alleged, were not ancillary but advanced to the position of being opponents—and this was the work of the new theologians.

Labourdette's criticism of the Jesuit theologians, their tendencies, of Danielou and de Lubac, concluded with the judgment that the entire movement of the new theology was shot through with historical and subjective relativism. It is the charge of "relativism," of the denigration and diminution of the absolute character of Christian theology, that would be repeated again and again against the new theology, and eventually find its way into papal judgment. While many of Labourdette's criticisms were of value, and in some instances valid, and while his charges of relativism had some substance, nevertheless it must be noted that his charges against de Lubac and Danielou were substantially unproved. Msgr. Bruno de Solages entered the dispute by defending the Jesuit theologians. However, if it was Labourdette's intention to apply a brake to the dynamism of the new theologians and their influence upon the young clergy and students of France, he certainly succeeded.[3]

Within the year, de Lubac's *Corpus Mysticum*, the third volume of the *Théologie* series, was under attack for relativism by the Dominican Père Nicolas. The towering figure of Garrigou-Lagrange entered the scene with an article on the new theology directed preeminently against Bouillard and Teilhard de Chardin. The importance of this opposition is to be found in the fact that Garrigou-Lagrange was the best known of the French Thomists, and, as a resident theologian in Rome, was alleged to have enjoyed the personal favor of the Pope. In 1947 he published *La Synthèse thomiste*, and in an appendix to that book he reprinted most of his article of 1946 in another consideration of the new theology, *La Nouvelle*

[3] See the "Current Theology" sections of *Theological Studies*, 1948–1951. These provide an account of the debate as it developed. The opinions of many theologians are given, and apt summaries of their positions presented.

théologie, où va-t-elle? In that appendix Garrigou-Lagrange revealed that there had existed in France since 1934 what we might loosely term a theological "Underground" among the theologians. Mimeographed articles, notes and other works had been distributed throughout France to priests, seminarians and lay intellectuals. These articles, he asserted, contained "fantastic" opinions, ranging the full theological line from apologetics through extreme opinions on evolution. The story has frequently been told of how these mimeographed articles, obviously intended for private circulation, had been sent to Garrigou-Lagrange at Rome. His charges in the book certainly bear out the factual substance of the story, although its details remain unclear.

This much must certainly be admitted: that such mimeographed articles did as a matter of fact exist. However, it must be remembered that their existence in such a state bears witness to the fact that they were intended for private circulation. It must also be remembered that their alleged radical nature, "fantastic opinions" as Garrigou-Lagrange describes them, remain for the most part not a proved public fact but the personal judgment of Garrigou-Lagrange himself. If, negatively stated, one were to argue from the later (1950) strictures of *Humani Generis* as accurately mirroring the content of these papers then it would seem that they actually did go to extreme lengths, if not to actual heresy.

It seems fairly certain that among these papers were the unpublished mimeographed notes of Teilhard de Chardin on the *Phenomenon of Man*. This seems evident from the later development of the argument; in fact, de Solages published an article defending these unpublished but widely circulated notes of Teilhard de Chardin. De Solanges comments:

It [the thought of Teilhard de Chardin] is known from his scattered articles, and—what is much worse—from his unpublished studies. These deal only with partial phases of the subject, and were written primarily for non-Catholics; competent authority has not judged their publication opportune. But they have circulated among his friends (not all of whom have been prudent) and indiscreet admirers *a great deal more than could have been foreseen by their author. . . .* They have nothing about them of the anonymous or the clandestine; their author has never set out to disseminate his opinions. His fault, if it is a fault, is rather that of a too-confident straightforwardness. I have protested against the indiscreet use made of these documents in public controversies, but I notice that more and more, as if it were inevitable, people are talking about them . . . on the other hand, they are read with more enthusiasm than insight by young people who are insufficiently formed, or who have never known them except very partially, and have therefore often been completely misunderstood.[4]

Beyond these questions of fact and interpretation, however, there is one fact of great importance, the fact that unalterably shaped relationships between the new theologians and Rome. This lay in the revelation of the fact that there did exist some type of theological substratum, and this did irreparable harm to the French theological movement at Rome and throughout the world. The Church was still quite aware of the recent modernist crisis and of the deception, delusion and fraud that frequently masked the true meaning of that insidious heresy. If there were such notes and articles that could not be published in the light of day they must to some degree be extremely dangerous to the Church. Thus at Rome and among the Roman theologians the new theology had fallen under a cloud. Religious thought in France would bear close watching, and the prolific work of the French theologians underwent a careful scrutiny. The memory of Modernism coupled with the criticism of very able theologians brought the new theology from its moment of eminence to a highly suspect position.

At this critical moment a theological debate of fantastic proportions swirled around one of the greatest of the French theologians, Père Henri de Lubac, the alleged leader of the new theologians. The subject matter was the extremely delicate and highly involved problem of the necessity or gratuity of the supernatural order. The occasion of the debate was the 1946 publication of de Lubac's *Surnaturel*. This book became the center of the argument that marked the closing years of the 1940's.

Shortly after the publication of *Surnaturel* de Lubac came under sharp attack. Labourdette, of course, immediately opposed de Lubac's presentation of the supernatural order as a destruction of

---

[4] Msgr. Bruno de Solages, "Christianity and Evolution," *Crosscurrents,* Vol. 1 (Summer, 1951), pp. 26–37.

the traditional concept of the gratuity of the supernatural order. Soon other theologians—all Jesuits and all French—leaped into the fray, each highly critical of de Lubac's presentation: de Blic, Malevez, and the distinguished Charles Boyer at Rome. In 1948 the Jesuit, Père Guy de Broglie in his manual on the ultimate end of human life went out of his way to reject explicitly de Lubac's presentation. From Rome Garrigou-Lagrange announced his opposition, and in France the Dominican Plé declared that de Lubac had misread St. Thomas. Père Danielou spoke in de Lubac's favor as did the influential Bruno de Solages. In 1949 the Jesuit Père Henri Bouillard, in a lengthy study of Blondel's shifting views of the supernatural, committed himself to the same position as de Lubac. Throughout the world there were few theologians who did not enter the debate, and fewer still who had support for de Lubac. The lines were drawn: de Lubac and Bouillard versus almost every major French and Roman theologian.

Some judgments of this debate and its meaning are in order. First, the preponderance of adverse criticism should give any attempted apologist for de Lubac pause. However, it is rarely pointed out that de Lubac was engaged in a theological debate as a Thomist with other Thomists. For many of the critics of de Lubac his most galling allegation was that he called to witness for his theory no other authority than that of St. Thomas. Clearly then this was not the new theology versus the old theology, it was not a simple case of radicals versus conservatives, but rather a true theological debate among Thomists. It is therefore unfortunate to see how many regarded this delicate intellectual question as a simple example of old versus new. For many, the *Surnaturel* was lifted from the realm of theology to become the symbol of the radical and dangerous new theology and, consequently, lesser commentators saw not the question of real theological difficulty, but rather a gigantic, though nebulous, struggle against a "new modernism."

The theological revival in France was now suffering a number of reverses: the criticisms of reputable, though conservative theologians, the revelation of unpublished views, the weakness of their most eminent member in an open debate, and added to these came the crushing blow of the death of Cardinal Suhard, long the spokesman and able representative at the Vatican for the French. By the end of the 1940's the attitude of Rome was changing significantly: the worker-priest movement was not living up to its expectations, and the religious movement in France was "suspect" of a contamination reminiscent of Modernism. Nor did the excessive statements in print of many lesser lights on the French theological and literary scene improve the position of the French Church in the eyes of Rome.

August 12, 1950—Humani Generis

The growing dissatisfaction at Rome with the excessive elements of the "new theology" culminated on August 12, 1950, when Pope Pius XII issued the encyclical *Humani Generis*. In the main it was of a corrective nature and reaffirmed the traditional teaching of the Church against certain extreme opinions in France and Germany. In some cases the condemnations were leveled against propositions accepted outside the Church, but which, in the judgment of the Pope, were of possible danger to Catholics. The *Humani Generis* marks the critical moment of the French theological revival, and consequently it is relevant here to summarize briefly the statements of the Pope. We may do this by dividing them into separate classifications: general errors to be avoided, the position of scholasticism within the Church, the Magisterium, Sacred Scripture and modern science.

In the first part of the encyclical, among the propositions enunciated by the Holy Father are those concerning the moral necessity of Revelation, and the credibility of the Christian faith. He also warned against that form of "scientific" evolution which, by destroying absolutes, prepares the way for an existential philosophy which would completely neglect the problem of immutable essences.

These new forms of thought, however, must be studied and understood by Christian philosophers and theologians. This is not to be done out of a purely negative attitude, that is, simply to defend the truth, but for two positively important reasons: first, in order to disengage that portion of truth upon which they are based, and secondly, to provoke discussions leading to a deeper grasp of philosophical and theological truth.

The Holy Father goes on to condemn a "false irenicism" which may be distinguished by a definite relativism toward dogmatic truth.

The Pope then takes up the problem of the widespread dissatisfaction with the traditional forms of scholasticism, of Thomism as it is encouraged and approved by the Church.

It is also manifest that the Church cannot be bound to every system of philosophy that has existed for a short space of time. Nevertheless, the things that have been composed through common effort by Catholic teachers over the course of the centuries to bring about some understanding of dogma are not based on any such weak foundation. . . . Hence to neglect or to reject or to devalue these resources . . . is supreme imprudence and something that would make dogma itself a reed shaken by the wind. The contempt for terms and notions habitually used by scholastic theologians leads of itself to the weakening of what they call speculative theology, a discipline which these men consider devoid of true certitude because it is based on theological reasoning.[5]

In a later consideration of this problem in the light of the continuing approval granted the Thomist method in the Church by the various Popes throughout history, the Holy Father succinctly placed the position of Thomism thus:

If one considers all this well, he will easily see why the Church demands that future priests be instructed in philosophy "according to the method, doctrine and principles of the Angelic Doctor," since as we well know from the experience of centuries, the method of Aquinas is singularly preeminent both for teaching students and for bringing truth to light; his doctrine is in harmony with Divine Revelation, and is most effective for the safeguarding of the foundation of the faith, and for reaping, safely and usefully, the fruits of sound progress.[6]

The problem of the place of scholasticism, since it has papal approval, also is related to the attitude of the critics toward the Magisterium of the Church. The Holy Father stated:

Unfortunately these advocates of novelty easily pass from despising scholastic theology to the neglect of and even contempt for the Teaching Authority of the Church itself, which gives such authoritative approval to scholastic theology. This Teaching Authority is represented

---

[5] Pope Pius XII, *Humani Generis*, N.C.W.C. translation, paragraphs 16, 17.
[6] *Ibid.*, para. 31.

by them as a hindrance to progress and an obstacle in the way of Science. . . . What is expounded in the Encyclical Letters of the Roman Pontiffs concerning the nature and constitution of the Church, is deliberately and habitually neglected by some. . . .[7]

The Holy Father recalled the importance of the Teaching Authority of the Church and the Divine warrant that lies within this Ordinary Magisterium as it is expressed in its normal manner: letters, responses and decrees of the Roman pontiffs.

The Holy Father devoted time and consideration to the problems brought forward by the progress in science. With some emphasis the question of evolution was considered and a number of norms were laid down by the Pope. The question of the corporal evolution of the human body, he stated, is still open to investigation, and any discussion of this question must be carried on only by experts in the respective fields of science and theology. One rule binds both in the legitimate exercise of this investigation—that all must be prepared to submit to the final judgment of the Church. The facts of Revelation, he stated, demand reserve and caution, and the liberty of this discussion is violated by those who assume that the evolution of the human body from preexistent living matter is treated as if it had been fully demonstrated.

However, he went on to say, there is no free discussion with regard to the question of polygenism. The reason he gave is the traditional Christian understanding of the problem of the Original Sin of the first parents. Therefore the faithful cannot embrace the opinion that a number of first parents existed, that is, polygenism. Thus far "it is in no way apparent how such an opinion can be reconciled with that which the sources of revealed truth and the documents of the Teaching Authority of the Church propose with regard to original sin." [8]

Finally, in *Humani Generis*, certain specific statements were made with regard to Sacred Scripture. The old error of limiting inerrancy simply to matters of faith and morals, to what directly concerns God, is reprobated. This error is based, according to the Holy Father, upon the error of denying one literal sense to Scripture.

[7] *Ibid.*, para. 18.
[8] *Ibid.*, para. 37.

Thus, those who say there are two meanings involved, that of God and that of man which is merely utilitarian and made to bear God's message, these, the Pope states, surely fall into the first error of limiting inerrancy.

The Holy Father also struck out against those proponents of what is called the "independent method of exegesis" in which the Sacred Text is submitted to a purely rational literary criticism and according to textual laws, without any recourse whatsoever to the teaching of the Church. An excessive "spiritual" interpretation is also rejected, in which typology and the "fuller sense" (*sensus plenior*) is used to the disregard of the literal meaning of the Sacred Text.

The problems that are unique to the Book of Genesis, dealing as it does with the origins of the human race, were also treated by the Holy Father. He did not settle the many questions that perplex the scholars but laid down certain norms: that these early chapters have a true "historical" meaning, they "pertain to history in a true sense." [9] He went on to state that if the ancient writers took anything from popular narrations of their day, "and this must be conceded . . . they must in no way be considered on a par with myths or other such things which are the product of an extravagant imagination." [10]

The encyclical of the Holy Father made no mention of any particular author by name, but its censures were leveled at the new theology which held such opinions. If there were theologians not holding such opinions, they were obviously not involved in the censures of the Holy Father. Substantially this is the burden of the encyclical as it was received in France. Many of its propositions affected the "new theologians," but there were as many again that it did not directly affect. The encyclical was received with total acceptance throughout the Catholic world, and in the months that followed, the eyes of most turned toward France. The ugly memory of Modernism caused many to see in *Humani Generis* a new *Pascendi* aimed at the radicals. Few at first realized the reasonableness, and in many cases the deliberately moderate tone adopted by the Holy Father.

[9] *Ibid.*, para. 38.
[10] *Ibid.*, para. 39.

The Crisis of French Catholicism

The publication of *Humani Generis* fell like a bombshell upon the French theologians. The great unspoken fear of many was that there would be on the part of the theologians some defections from the Church. To the everlasting credit of the French Church, and as a vindication of the solid depths of the theological movement, there were no Loisys forthcoming, no theologians preferring their own opinions to the voice of the Teaching Church. Theologian after theologian, de Lubac, Congar, others, all announced their adherence to the propositions of the papal encyclical.

The encyclical was not liked in France. More extreme circles said that it had been strongly influenced by the conservative Spanish Church; others looked upon it as an obstacle to progress and to scientific advancement. There were those for whom the encyclical could only be termed "reactionary." But these extreme opinions were not those of the alleged leaders of the "new theology," or any reputable theologian. For de Lubac, Congar, Danielou, there could be no question of dispute or criticism; the Church had spoken and there could be no recriminations. The extremist position, which now received the label "progressive" rather than "new theology," represented lesser minds in the French Church, and more frequently figures in the literary and intellectual world rather than the theologians.

It has been alleged by many commentators that the strictures of *Humani Generis* were aimed at the excessive claims of de Lubac's *Surnaturel*, Danielou's patristic theology and Teilhard de Chardin's theories of evolution, among others. However, in the absence of any *nominatim* condemnation of these men and their work, it would be presumptuous, to say the least, to accept this interpretation. The specification of definite theologians as the object of censure has been in many cases most unfair to these men. It is interesting to note, for example, that many commentators have alleged that de Lubac's *Surnaturel* was the object of the papal censure based on the gratuity of the supernatural order, and yet de Lubac himself says that he does not fall under this specific criticism, and that the critics have misunderstood his position.

Since the *Humani Generis* one observer of the French scene has

pictured the shifting intellectual emphasis in this manner: "The issues of the present disputes are infinitely more clouded and intricate.
The main trouble is a phenomenon, not peculiar to France alone
but rampant there at present: the strong Leftist, even Marxist, tendencies of an important section of French Catholic intellectuals." [11]
The periodicals *Témoignage chrétien* and *Esprit*, the followers of
Mounier for the most part, represent this "left" orientation of a
segment of French Catholicism.

That there is a continuing resentment among the political left
toward *Humani Generis* is stated by the same commentator on the
personal information of Père Danielou himself:

Père Danielou . . . told me how early papers on this theory [of Teilhard de Chardin] were widely circulated in mimeographed form in
clerical circles . . . many progressives were still harboring these ideas,
he said, after they had been refuted. . . . Yet, it was not the warnings
about the evolutionary theory, or any other passage in the *Humani
Generis* which caused the feelings of guilt and resentment among some
progressive Catholics. It was the insistence of the Church on certain
unchanging principles reaffirmed throughout the encyclical. . . . They
seem to think that principles are subject to change, subject to constant
revision, readjustment, adaption, in accord with the varying exigencies
of historical developments. They are obsessed by the Hegelian and
Marxist notion of the inevitable, blind progress of history and the
continual evolution of all reality.[12]

Thus *Humani Generis*, while accepted by the French as a whole, and
especially by the alleged leaders of the "new theology," is still
resented by the left segment of French Catholicism.

In May of 1951 an interesting evaluation of *Humani Generis*,
by the eminent expert in anthropology, Count Begouen, appeared
in *La Vie intellectuelle*. In the article entitled "*Testament d'un
anthropoloque*" Count Begouen admits that at first reading *Humani
Generis* seemed to "declare war on scientific research," and to be a
purely negative document. However, the more thoroughly he
studied it and had it explained to him the more impressed he became

[11] Borisz de Balla, "The Marxist Influence in Catholic France," *The Catholic World*, Vol. 186 (March, 1953), p. 411.
[12] *Ibid.*, pp. 414–415.

by its reasonableness and moderate tone. In fact he notes that in *Humani Generis* the Holy See gave its first recognition to the advance of science in the last fifty years. It was quite clear in the document that Rome, instead of coolly ignoring scientific progress, was now most anxious to recognize what was of value and to give positive encouragement to Catholics laboring in scientific fields.

We may see in the first reaction and later appreciation of Count Begouen toward *Humani Generis* a fairly accurate symbol of the widespread assent that the Teaching Church received in France after the authoritative proclamation of *Humani Generis*.

The Worker-Priests

The delicate relationships of the French Church with Rome were further troubled by the 1953 revision of the worker-priest movement. As we have remarked, the theological drive in postwar France was marked by a firm apostolic alliance, a realization of necessary commitment in the everyday life of the Church. Thus Catholic Action, the various groups of young Christian workers and students, and other lay groups followed upon the papal allocutions of the place of the layman in the Church and on studies of the theological position of the baptized. This apostolic alliance of the theologians, however, affected the clergy as well. The implications of the Christian message, and the Mystery of the Church along with major sociological studies of the state of the Church in France led to the realization of the loss of the proletariat to the Church. The worker-priest movement was the clerical experiment in new methods of apostolic activity.[13]

The movement began in the early 1940's, and its aim was to Christianize the proletarian masses, which for all intents and purposes were pagan. The movement as such was threefold: The

[13] Little of lasting value has been written on the worker-priest movement. Among better works see Adrien Dansette, "Les Origines de la Mission de France et de la Mission de Paris," *Etudes*, Vol. 292 (Feb., 1957), pp. 186–201, and the novelized presentation by Dariel, *Chez les Prêtres-ouvriers* (Paris: Chambriand, 1950). In English, see the book by Claire Bishop, *France Alive* (New York: Macmillan, 1947), and the articles by Friedrich Heer, "The Priest-Workers in France," *Cross Currents*, Vol. 4 (Summer, 1954), pp. 262–274, and Robert Barrat, "Heroes of the French Church," *Commonweal*, Vol. 59 (January 8, 1954), pp. 348–350.

Mission of France, the Mission of Paris, and the small Mission of the Sea. The priests involved in this work had one major line of activity, namely, to live and work with the proletariat, to witness there to the Church's concern for them, to evangelize and ultimately, it was hoped, to return them to the Church.[14]

At the urging of the Sulpician Père Augros and the Abbé Perrot the bishops of France began the worker-priest movement in 1942 with the founding of a religious center at Lisieux called "The Mission of France." A seminary for priests entering the work and for seminarians was established there, and was later moved to Limoges. The entire work was placed under the jurisdiction of the bishops of France and Abbé Perrot became the episcopal delegate to the Mission of France.

Abbé Hollande was later commissioned in 1943 by Cardinal Suhard to duplicate the work for the diocese of Paris. Suhard had been strongly influenced by the findings of the Abbé Godin, and wished to launch this program for the recovery of the masses in his own diocese. The scope and aims of the Mission of Paris were substantially those of The Mission of France.

By the late 1940's a number of dissatisfactions with the worker-priest movement were voiced. As we have commented, after *Humani Generis* many of the worker-priests were known to be in disagreement with this document of papal teaching, and some had become strongly Marxist. The fear was expressed that the worker-priests has been converted by the proletariat, and not vice versa.

The events of 1952 and 1953 did not serve to allay these criticisms. The anti-NATO riots in Paris on the occasion of General Ridgeway's arrival in France involved two worker-priests who had been arrested with others for demonstrating. The international publicity that followed upon these arrests did severe harm to the prestige of the worker-priest movement. It should be noted honestly that Abbé Hollande has been quoted as saying that the priests were there not to partake in the riots, but purely to give aid to any victims of police brutality. The publicity that followed was deliberate by

[14] The pre-World War period was marked by the emergence of an attempt to form a "spirituality" of the proletariat. Thus see the work of Canon Glorieux, *Notre Chef le Christ* (Paris: Editions Ouvrières, 1938), and Père Doncoeur, "*L'Evangile du travail* (Paris: Editions de l'Orante, 1940).

". . . the reactionary press, representing circles that resented the very idea of priests as workers, [and they] had intentionally maintained the misrepresentation in their columns. . . . The ecclesiastical authorities were fully informed of this situation, I was told, and the Cardinal of Paris was deeply shocked by the attitude of the '*bien pensants*,' a term coined to describe the smug and the reactionary." [15]

Far greater harm, however, was done to the movement by well meaning writers. Gilbert Cesbron, the novelist, published his *Les Saints vont en enfer* in 1952. While quite sympathetic to the movement, the novel was a highly sensational account of the life of a worker-priest in a Paris suburb. Taken as a fairly accurate picture of these men, a storm of criticism rose within the Church against the worker-priests.

In July of 1953 a confidential letter of Cardinal Pizzardo, Dean of the Congregation of the Seminaries, was sent to all the bishops of France. In this letter he advised the bishops that all seminarians were to refrain from any manual labor on their vacations. The letter became public knowledge in September, and the opening of the seminary at Limoges was also delayed. During this summer, the papal nuncio, Msgr. Marella, had visited many of the dioceses of France. It was obvious that some official displeasure existed against the movement of the worker-priests. The resultant publicity throughout the length and breadth of France forced the three French cardinals to go to Rome for some definite expression of official thought. Amid a growing controversy Cardinals Lienart, Gerlier and Feltin journeyed to Rome.

Upon their return, they made a public statement confirming the fears of many: "After ten years of existence the experiment of the worker-priests, as it has developed up to now, cannot be continued in its present form." The cardinals pointed out that this was not a condemnation of the movement that they were bringing home, but rather a well thought-out restriction upon the movement, a restriction deemed necessary by the Church because of the manner "in which it has developed up to now." The consequent cries of anguish from "progressive" circles, from the journals of the Left, and

[15] H. A. Reinhold, "The Worker Priests," *Commonweal*, Vol. 63 (March 1, 1956), p. 561.

from some eminent French Catholic literary figures frequently sounded the note of regret for a deceased Gallicanism.

On January 19, 1954, the bishops of France met in Paris and issued the restrictive rules for the worker-priest movement,[16] in which five points were stressed: first, the parish was to be the basic unit for the work of the penetration of the milieu of the proletariat; second, the restrictions requested by Rome (for example, priests must live in the parishes, must hold no temporal elective or union office and so on) were to be the norm of action for all priests engaged in the work; third, the work of the priesthood (mass, office, preaching and other duties) must come first; fourth, there would be a severe limitation of the amount of manual labor that might be done by priests; fifth, there was a request for prayers for these priests to accede to the wishes of the Church and the bishops. However, on March 1, the deadline for the worker-priests to accept these restrictions, 70 per cent continued to carry on their work against the rulings of the bishops. These men then published a collection of essays in the fall, explaining their position.[17]

Although many romantic notions may serve to cloud an objective consideration of the Roman action disciplining the worker-priests, some facts cannot be questioned. Many of these men were poorly trained, ill equipped—both intellectually and spiritually—for the job they took upon themselves. The suspicion of their motives after their opposition to *Humani Generis* was proved by their disobedience in 1954. The movement, idealized on paper, did not work out in reality. It seems for the historian to have been the translation of "angelic intellects" and "metaphysical politicians" to the ecclesiastical scene. When confronted by an untenable situation the French Church accepted a plan in the abstract, a plan too neglectful of experience and tradition, and nevertheless put it into action.

The position of the Church vis-à-vis the French worker-priests has been aptly summarized:

The intrigues of the *bien pensants*, the denunciations of the calumniators, the gossip of the small minds perhaps did nothing but dramatize the

[16] "Déclaration episcopale sur les prêtres-ouvriers," *L'Actualité réligieuse dans le monde*, No. 21, Feb., 1954, p. 8.

[17] Since translated as *The Worker Priests* (New York: Macmillan, 1957).

fate of the movement and highlight its dangers. Basically the Holy See had nothing to do with these actions; instead it weighed the whole affair and judged it to be both immature and premature. . . . It is obvious that the solution the worker-priests offer is in its execution untimely; in its assumptions unrealistic; in its outcome destructive of ecclesiastical tradition; and in its doctrinal grounds, to say the least, dangerous now. A later age may profit from the daring and generosity of these brave and zealous men and distil out of their venture the wine of a new apostolate. But to the present era this was an experiment "born out of due time." [18]

The official termination of the priest-worker movement came in 1959. The decision to suspend the experiment as it had existed was revealed in a private letter to Cardinal Feltin, the Archbishop of Paris, by Cardinal Pizzardo, the Secretary of the Sacred Congregation of the Holy Office. The letter was dated July 3, 1959, and the substance of it appeared in the journal *Le Monde* on September 11. The result of this leak to the Parisian daily led to publication of the entire letter. The most relevant sections read:

After listening to the advice of all their consultors, the Cardinals of the Supreme Congregation have attentively examined the important and delicate question of the priest-workers. Here are the conclusions which they arrived at in their plenary sessions of June 10th and 24th, 1959: The Holy See shares the conviction of the French Bishops on the subject of the necessity for an intense and active apostolate in working-class circles . . . [however] the Holy See believes that it is not indispensable to send priests as workers into the workers' world for the evangelization of the working-class. It believes that it is not possible to sacrifice the traditional conception of the priesthood to this aim, which the Church nevertheless regards as one of its dearest missions. In fact, it is essentially to exercise sacred functions that a priest is ordained— to offer the Holy Sacrifice of the Mass and the public prayer of the Church to God, to administer the sacraments to the faithful and preach the word of God. . . . The Holy See believes, in addition, that work in a factory or in an outdoor laborer's job is incompatible with a priestly life and obligations. In effect, daily work would make it nearly impossible for a priest to fulfill all the duties of prayer that the Church demands of him each day. . . . On the other hand, work in factories or even in smaller enterprises exposes a priest little by little to the

[18] H. A. Reinhold, "The Worker Priests," *op. cit.*, p. 562.

influence of that milieu. The priest-worker not only finds himself plunged into a materialist atmosphere, which is harmful to his spiritual life and often dangerous to his chastity, he is also led in spite of himself to think as his comrades at work in regard to social and trade union matters, and to take part in their claims. This formidable combination of circumstances rapidly involves him in the class struggle. And that is inadmissible for a priest. These are the reasons which have led the Holy Office to decide on the cessation of jobs for priests as workers or employees in factories and other enterprises or as sailors on fishing or merchant vessels, and on the replacement of priest-workers by groups of laymen specially consecrated to an apostolate to the working-class world. At the audience on June 11th, 1959, the Holy Father deigned to approve these decisions. . . . It is now for the Bishops of France to prepare the different forms that the apostolate to the working-class will take. . . . The Holy See asks the French Bishops to consider if the moment has not now arrived to add to these excellent initiatives the creation of one or more Secular Institutes composed of priest and lay members. . . . In this new form of the mission to workers, priests will play an important and effective role. To their lay co-workers they will give religious instruction and a profound spiritual training adapted to their conditions of life and their status as workers. . . . Thanks to the contacts made by the lay members of this Secular Institute, they can begin to exercise a priestly ministry among workers outside the factory and among their families and children. . . . The Holy See asks your Eminence to study this new form of the Apostolate, which seems to fulfill all the special demands of evangelization of the working masses. . . . Needless to say, this substitution for the priest-workers means that they should not undertake any new activities, and that on their return [to the normal priestly life] they should cease those activities in which they have been engaged. . . . The Holy See knows that it is imposing a real sacrifice on priest-workers in asking them to renounce their jobs. But it also knows that it can count on their filial submission to these decisions, which were taken in their own interests and in the interests of their apostolate to the workers. That they may have confidence in the fruitfulness of their obedience for their priestly lives and their ministry and that they may know that the Holy Father has a most benevolent solicitude for them, His Holiness sends them His Apostolic Benediction.[19]

A week after the publication of the letter, the hierarchy of France announced on September 18, 1959, that ". . . contrary to certain

[19] The English translation of Cardinal Pizzardo's letter may be found in *The Tablet*, Sept. 26, 1959, pp. 819–820.

information that appeared in the press the priest-workers have been carrying on their apostolate in conformity with the mission entrusted to them by their Bishops . . . [who] are resolved to pursue, with their priests and faithful . . . the efforts undertaken to solve the grave problem of the evangelization of the working-class world." [20]

The premature and unauthorized publication of Cardinal Pizzardo's letter by *Le Monde* stirred up a public furore. Both the information conveyed by *Le Monde* and the consequent press treatment of the situation was a further attempt at embarrassing ecclesiastical authority. Cardinal Feltin himself protested the publication maintaining that such premature revelations had done immense harm. It had been the plan of the hierarchy to put forward the decision of Rome along with actual and concrete proposals for developing the approaches to the workers along the lines of a new Secular Institute. "The suggestion for this also came from Cardinal Pizzardo, but the negative, condemning part of the letter has inevitably attracted far more attention that the constructive part." [21]

The letter of Cardinal Pizzardo revealing the decisions of the Holy Father and the Congregations in Rome marks the close of one attempt by the French to meet the challenge of a pagan world. But the Church is well aware of the intent and spirit that brought this apostolate into being, and at the same time that she keeps a lively care for her priests she fully realizes the sacrifice she demands from the worker-priests. Archbishop Guerry of Cambrai states the case for the worker-priests and the end of their mission:

The dominating theme of the letter is the preoccupation—how moving this is for every priest and believer—with protecting the purity and integrity of the priestly functions. . . . This does not detract at all from the merits or the often heroic generosity, or the courage of those priests who, suffering in their hearts because of the separation of the working world from Christ and the Church, sought to share it's life to bring it the message of salvation. Some persons are heaping sarcasm on them and speaking of condemnations. The Holy Father himself thought of them and of the "real sacrifice" which he was going to impose on them, as is indicated in the letter, closing with these words:

[20] *The Tablet*, October 3, 1959.
[21] *The Tablet*, October 10, 1959.

"May they know that the Holy Father has a most benevolent solicitude for them." [22]

Situation Ethics

As has been mentioned, the existentialist orientation of modern thought has made a great impact upon contemporary French intellectual life. This philosophical movement, because of its novelty, its dynamism and its apparently up-to-date approach to the modern mind, and finally, because of its attention to certain neglected truths about man has created a definite current of thought among modern theologians.

The existentialist approach toward moral values has led to the construction of what is called a "situation ethics," or "situational morality." [23] For the existentialist moralist the fundamental moral problem of a human act is determined by the full, concrete, and singular instances of the situation in relationship to the general will of God. Consequently, there can be no *a priori* absolute law of God; no abstract, necessary, universal or systematic law independent of man's situation in the here and now.

Christian existentialists in situation ethics reject what they regard to be the "rationalistic" morality for one that they claim is living and dynamic, dependent upon the given situation in which the subject finds himself. Some base this upon what they consider to be the existentialist "nature" of man, and others upon the absolute transcendence of God, which would be imperiled should God, as it were, chain himself to an absolute law.

Atheist existentialists are also faced with the ethical problem: the question of a man's determination of value. These, notably Sartre and de Beauvoir, using man as the measure of being for whom life and existence itself is absurd, declare that a man's values are constructed by himself. Man becomes the architect of the good and the bad. No matter what its source, a situation ethic or morality has made great inroads upon Protestant theology, and is accepted by many contemporary Protestant theologians.

[22] *Ibid.*

[23] On situation ethics see Dietrich von Hildebrand, *True Morality and Its Counterfeits* (New York: Sheed & Ward, 1955); also the articles abridged in *Theology Digest*, Vol. 2 (Winter, 1954), pp. 24–32.

This attractive and growing movement of situation ethics was quickly recognized by the Holy See, and Pope Pius XII saw fit to issue a number of condemnations throughout the early 1950's. On March 3, 1952, he spoke by radio to Catholic Action groups throughout Italy, and severely condemned this "new morality." He repeated his condemnation in an allocution on April 18, 1952, to the International Congress of the World Federation of Catholic Young Women in Rome. Again, in 1953, to the Fifth International Congress on Psychotherapy the Holy Father explicitly rejected the existentialist construction of man and its consequent personalist ethics. On February 2, 1956, the Holy Office issued a specific instruction and condemnation of situation ethics.

This "new morality," however, must be clearly delineated from what is called the "new approach to moral theology," although they are related as we shall see. The "new approach" to moral theology, as we have previously pointed out, is not the rejection of the traditional Christian teaching on the absolute character of the law of God, but rather primarily a dissatisfaction with the systematic "theology of sin" which it is claimed moral theology has fallen into.

Men such as Gilleman, Leclercq and others are by no means situationalist theologians, but rather traditional theologians seeking a new and more positive expression of the revealed and absolute law of God. Although the theologians of "the new approach" may at times be intemperate in language and a trifle excessive in their criticisms of contemporary Catholic moral theology manuals, they nevertheless represent a sincere attempt to present the more positive and dynamic aspects of the revealed law of God. They are concerned in their study of a new approach, not with the changing of law, but with its traditional method of presentation that often ignores the vital and meaningful area of motivation.

There is no area of relationship that exists between this new approach and the new morality of situation ethics. The dissatisfaction of the new approach, when coupled with the impact existentialist thought has made, provides a dangerous tendency, or "wide possibility" toward the new morality. It was this accumulation of circumstances: the spread of Existentialism, the growth of situation ethics, and the dissatisfaction of many for traditional moral theology presentations that prompted the Holy Father to take severe and continued stands against any possible encroachment of the new morality.

Among the contemporary French theologians it seems that only the Jesuit Yves de Montcheuil showed any inclination to what may be called a situation ethic. In his *Mélanges théologiques* published in 1946 (Paris) de Montcheuil demonstrated a preference for the intuitive rather than the rational approach to morality. Intuition, for de Montcheuil, is based on the love of value, that is, the immediate perception of moral value, and also upon the ultimate absolute value—God. Nevertheless, de Montcheuil's critics have pointed out that, first, there exist differences of opinion among men, and secondly, if intelligibility is removed, morality by feeling will soon follow.

The apostles of situation ethics, if absent from Catholic theological circles, are extremely active in French literary circles. Postwar French literature, of which the works of Sartre, de Beauvoir, Camus and Malraux are representative, has been influenced by situation ethics. These authors, however, have not been without their perceptive Catholic critics. Yet in 1951, the French translation of a novel by the Italian, Carlo Coccioli, *Le Ciel et la terre* was widely praised in Catholic circles. The hero of the book, an existentialist priest, is understanding, sympathetic, and above all uses a unique morality of the heart to settle his numerous problems and crises. Coccioli published a second novel in French in 1953, *Fabrizio Lupo*, implying a moral defense for homosexuality. The ethical implications of his first novel now became obvious when translated into another life situation. It took *Fabrizio Lupo* to make the French Catholic existentialists aware of the rejection of Christian morality implied in situation ethics. Indeed, Coccioli himself told his admirers that they had completely missed the point of *Le Ciel et la terre*.

This problem of situation ethics reveals another aspect of the relationship of the modern French theologian and the Teaching Church. Few, if any, had deliberately adopted this new morality. Yet, their obvious fascination with the philosophy upon which it is based coupled with their impatience with manual-moralists were among the causes of the continued warnings against situation ethics by the Pope. It would be terribly unjust in the light of the recurring papal condemnations to see an implication of any widespread commitment by the French to situation ethics.

France Today: The Challenge of Marxism

In contemporary France today the arena most dominated by tension between ecclesiastical authority and the French intellectuals has shifted from the theological to the political. In this are to be found the *chrétiens progressistes*. These men are marked by an unreasonable attachment to the extremist ideas reprobated in the *Humani Generis*, by their public hue and cry over the termination of the worker-priest movement, and by their memory of Père Teilhard de Chardin by which they attempt to envelop themselves in the mantle of his reconciliation of evolution and the Christian revelation. But lurking beneath these many faces turned to the world lies their basic spirit and belief—an acceptance of Marxism and the inevitability of history. They play the role of Lamennais foreseeing their eventual vindication in an age yet to come; they see themselves as the prophets of an inevitable Christian-Marxist axis and the reconciliation of both.

Many factors have contributed to their growth: the experiences of the wartime resistance, the growth of the apostolic spirit, and the "openness" to the ideologies of the modern world. Père Rouquette wisely distinguishes in their numbers the various elements that contribute to the phenomenon of the *progressistes:*

The few Catholics who have for various reasons been attracted by communism are very limited in number. But they are often authentic believers, inspired by an unquestionable apostolic fervor. Here we must distinguish different degrees of pro-Communist sympathy on the part of sincere Catholics: some completely reject Marxist ideology in itself, but are impressed by the efficacy of communism as a revolutionary movement; others try to do for Marxist ideology what St. Thomas achieved for Aristotle's paganism, that is, to Christianize the Marxist synthesis; still others, finally, going even further and taking up a position actually on the border of Catholicism, welcome Marxism as a means of healthful revival for an institutional Christianity they consider has become sterile.[24]

[24] Robert Rouquette, S.J., "French Catholicism Confronts Communism," *Thought*, Vol. 28 (Autumn, 1953), p. 362.

The principal leaders in the approach to Marxism have been the Dominican priests, Père Desroches (who left the Church) and Père Montuclard. Desroches attempted to incorporate Marxism into Christianity, seeing in its atheistic teaching a purely accidental consideration. He proposed this theory in the publication in 1949 of his *Signification du marxisme*, which was immediately placed on the Index by Church authority. "The real danger of such a position is that it insists on commanding immediate action. If Marxism can be Christianized, then one contributes to this possible Christianization by grasping the hand extended by the Communists and by collaborating with the revolutionary action of the party as it exists concretely today." [25]

A small group, the *Jeunesse de l'église*, have united around the figure of Père Montuclard. Earlier the publication *La Quinzaine* represented their thought and feeling, but it ceased publication when it was condemned by the Church. Montuclard's *Les Evénements de la foi*, published in 1952, and placed on the Index a year later, expressed the thoughts and aspirations of both Montuclard and the *Jeunesse de l'église*. For them Marxism is a valid social critique and an exact science of society, Communism is basically a creative movement which must be baptized by the Christian in the world and society. Shortly after his book was Indexed Montuclard sought and obtained from the Holy See a reduction to the lay state.

Perhaps, Père Rouquette remarks, "one should not attach too great an importance to a movement which consists of only a few intellectuals and which expresses itself in texts badly lacking in balance and formulated in disturbing language which must often exceed the intended thought of their authors." [26] However, the existence of these groups testifies to the strong attraction that Marxism exerts in certain intellectual circles in modern France. The willingness of some, and a very few at that, to forego obedience to the Teaching Authority of the Church because of what they consider to be historical inevitability should not lead us into the error of identifying the French intellectual scene with the *progressistes*. The experience of *Humani Generis* and the obedience rendered by most French theologians then and since symbolizes more

[25] *Ibid.,* p. 371.
[26] *Ibid.,* p. 372.

effectively the attitude of the overwhelming number of intellectuals toward the Teaching Church.

Conclusion

Some Americans have frequently misunderstood the meaning and depth of the contemporary theological revival in France. What is more, a few publicists in the United States have seriously libeled the French when they leave in the minds of their readers the idea that the theologians at work in modern France are at worst neo-modernists, and at best deluded fools. Among the theologians writing today there are few who write as well or as perceptively on the meaning and Mystery of the Church as the French.

Nor are these expressions of the minds of the French theologians simple words committed to paper. They have undergone in recent times the gamut of theological emotions from acceptance and encouragement in the early pontificate of Pius XII to the disciplinary and purifying action of the *Humani Generis*. It is unfortunate that in the line of events, the worker-priest restriction and the catechism controversy followed so soon upon the heels of the *Humani Generis*.

Radicals, hidden heretics, dangerous innovators—these are the thoughts of many about modern France. But it is these alleged radicals and innovators who stood fast in their loyalty to the Church in the face of the strictures of *Humani Generis*. They watched many of their projects, notably the worker-priest experiment, end in failure. And yet these men continue to produce extremely capable, and deeply penetrating studies of the Church.

If there is a relationship between contemporary French theology and the Teaching Church, and it is difficult to see how it may be denied, it is one of which the French have every right to be proud. It is a relationship in which study, respect and, above all, obedience have marked the French attitude toward Rome. They have taken their themes from the teachings of the Popes; they have made the Church itself the vital center to which all their work is related; and, finally, contemporary French theologians have lived, in Congar's words about Lacordaire, ". . . punctuated by acts of docility, often of a very meritorious nature . . . they will to be in harmony with the ordinary life of the Church."

VII

❊

CONCLUSIONS

In surveying contemporary France and the theological revival in which so many Catholic scholars are actively engaged, one cannot record their contributions without passing some personal judgments and appreciations upon so vast an undertaking. Conclusions are based upon the consideration of historical facts and at the same time to a large degree are the result of personal evaluations. The man who approaches the French scene with some knowledge of the tragic history of the Church in France, and with some sympathy for the attempt of the French to revitalize Catholic life in their country will no doubt reach conclusions strongly approving many modern French contributions. But likewise the man who approaches modern France with a prejudice, based perhaps upon the lack of historical understanding, will also reach conclusions at variance with the judgments of the man who looks upon the French attempt with favorable dispositions. Thus the nonsympathetic observer and the sympathetic observer will reach two sets of conclusions based upon the same facts.

We should therefore in honesty, call attention to the fact that we have approached the phenomenon of the theological revival in France with some sympathy, and that the reader must be aware that many of our conclusions have to a degree been predetermined by a willingess to find the best in France. Nevertheless this does not preclude strict application of the historical method. Although we approach the French with this favorable predisposition, nevertheless, we have based that predisposition upon certain facts too frequently ignored by the hypercritical approach.

These facts have been frequently referred to throughout the book. They are basically historical, offering the observer the depth and dimension that only history can bring. The French Church does not live in a vacuum which we may enter at will, and make our judgments; rather, she is the heir to those momentous events of history that have contributed to make her what she is today.

The Revolution and the rejection of the Church that followed, the restoration and the attempt to tie the Church to the cause of the Bourbons have had their tragic importance. The petty conservative minds of the nineteenth century in France, who lacked the vision of Christ's Church existing unhampered by ties to any specific political system, did the Church irreparable harm. If they wanted the Church attached to a governmental system, then they had also to accept the popular rejection of the Church with the rejection of that system. It was not until the *Action française* was finally suppressed in the 1920's that the Church could really settle down to adjusting to the ideas and ideals of a democratic republic.

The historical events that are the heritage of the Church in France, the revolution, the ill-fated restoration, the estrangement of the Church and the republican tradition, the despoilation of the Church's material wealth at the turn of the century and the internal discord sown by the modernists have all served to alienate the Church from great masses of the French people. For the urban proletariat the Church has been relegated to the ineffectual confines of the sacristy. In recognizing and meeting the challenge of France pagan, the theologians and bishops of the Church bravely embarked upon a rugged path with unshakeable faith in the presence of Christ in His Church.

In addition to a firm grasp on the historical tradition of modern France and of the Church, there should be for the observer who wishes to portray the real situation of French Catholicism accurately an appreciation of the intellectual approach of the French toward Catholicism. The American Jesuit, Father Ong, has said:

Aspects of French Catholicity itself puzzle Americans. American Catholics can become enthusiastic when they are told of the growing number of university students (some ten thousand in 1953) making the annual pilgrimage—the last twenty miles or so on foot—to our Lady of Chartres. But they cannot understand how this evident devotion can be nurtured in the twentieth century world without courses in apologetics of the sort which American Catholic colleges and universities feature but which are quite unknown at the Institut Catholique in Paris, Toulouse, or elsewhere. American Catholics are lost when they find that the French apologetic tends to train the youthful mind to think through modern problems in Catholic ways, as these problems are being thought through for the first time, and this with a strong stress on familiarity with the Scriptures and with Sacramental symbolism rather than by means of an exclusive training in epitomes of theses, which the French regard as part of Catholic intellectual training, not as its quasi totality.[1]

Dispute may be made with Father Ong's creation of an "American" attitude. There exist among American Catholic intellectuals and theologians significant understanding and support for the progressive steps taken by the French, just as there exists a conservative as well as "liberal" attitude among the French. But the point Father Ong makes remains valid, that is, the French have developed an intellectual approach to theology peculiar to themselves.

The combination of these elements: the historical tradition and a psychological appreciation of the French approach, these are the legitimate facts upon which we base a sympathetic consideration of the phenomenon of Catholic France and its theologians.

The Unfortunate Qualities of the French Theologians

In the evaluation of the contributions of the theological revival in modern France and Belgium, it would be both unwise and unhistorical to ignore what is obviously to be reprobated. There have been some Francophiles so dazzled by the real achievements of the French theological revival that they feel that to admit the existence of unbalanced elements within the Church in France would be to open the door to hypercritical elements. But they, in no less a manner, err in the opposite direction. Each of these extremes is to be avoided as presenting a distortion of the French phenomenon, and

[1] Walter J. Ong, S.J., "Contrasts in Catholicism," *Commonweal*, Vol. 62 (Dec. 2, 1955), p. 215.

a nonobjective judgment of the meaning of the theological movement.

The most significant tendency among the French theologians that ecclesiastical authorities have found uncomfortable is the French approach to the question of the individual and authority. The trend of the Church since the Reformation has been one of authoritative centralization in administrative affairs. But even the comparatively recent ultramontane influence in French Catholicism has never completely obliterated the traditional French accent on the importance of the individual, nor has it completely overshadowed the Gallican tendency to be distrustful of Rome. Without doubt, the French Catholic does not question the infallible Teaching Authority of the Church, nor question the divine authority of the Church's Magisterium, yet the traditional French proclivity toward maintaining the rights and privileges of the individual has in recent times led to some severe disagreements on ecclesiastical policy. On the part of authority there is the all too painful memory of Lamennais and Loisy, as well as the more recent widespread worker-priest resistance to an established policy.

For many critics this proclivity of the French toward individualism is assumed to be typical rather than exceptional, and those rare instances of actual disobedience are proffered as evidence, critically assumed to be representative. A more balanced view would be that taken by the French themselves, who, regarding these individual instances as unfortunate, nevertheless maintain that they are to be simply accepted as the results of a conflict that is innate to any institution of hierarchical nature.

The conflict of the individual and authority exists for the French in both the abstract arena of ideas, as well as in the practical order. In the abstract, the attempt to define and limit the bounds of the legitimate exercise of authority is a continual exercise for the theologians, and also a continuing intellectual difficulty. It is unfortunate that there has existed among some of the "progressives" and the literary class, rather than among the theologians, the weakness of a defective attitude toward the Magisterium, viewed not as the divinely established guarantee of freedom from error, but as an obstacle to and at times unwarranted intrusion in the processes of free inquiry and action.

In the practical order, there are those who do not look upon the authority of the Church with a spirit of obedience. History teaches us that many such personalities, while beginning their programs of action with the best of intentions and in perfectly good faith, nevertheless at the critical moment when they conflicted with ecclesiastical authority were unable to assent to their "faith" in the Church over what in the confines of their vision, they believe to be absolutely necessary. Thus, there is the attitude of Lamennais, who publically assented to the propositions of *Mirari Vos* but when he returned to his circle at La Chesnaie continued to propound that which he had ostensibly foresworn.

This attitude of practical disobedience is of course not singular to the French Church. Throughout history schisms and heresies have borne witness to the fact that no one culture or people has a monopoly on disobedience. Yet this attitude, based upon too great a concern for the individual, has returned to haunt the Church in France. It is most certainly not characteristic of those magnificent men who are the acknowledged leaders of theological thought, but rather of those lesser groups for whom the meaning of the theological revival, the Church itself, has been lost.

There are in addition to this major drawback two further criticisms which may be mentioned as unfortunate disadvantages where they do exist. These are the recurring tendencies toward intellectual pride and love of novelty.

For many, intellectual pride lies at the root of the problem of disobedience. However, here we are not referring to such a deep-seated warping of the spirit or of the mind that indeed does lie at the basis of most alleged intellectual defections. We rather refer here to the spirit that is prevalent not only among the theologians of lesser note but also among the most competent which at times shadows and colors their judgments and appreciations of others. Perhaps "intellectual pride" is too serious a misnomer of this attitude. The expression "intellectual haughtiness" would be a better concept.

French theologians frequently adopt this attitude because of pride in the very real attainments of their revival, and tend toward a superior attitude against other national groups within the Church. Aubert's *La Théologie catholique au milieu du XXe siècle*, an excellent survey in many respects, would, for example, carry this haughty attitude in a negative way.

Aubert professedly surveyed twentieth century theology, and concentrated upon Franco-Belgian contributions, and the contributions of the Germans to theology in the twentieth century were minimized. He ignored German works which, while solid enough, were not highly scientific, and yet he referred to many French works of the same category. Any "Roman" contributions seemed to be studiously ignored. Whether this is because Aubert sincerely believes no contribution has been made to theology outside of those in the French and Belgian schools, or whether it is based upon a contempt for what he considers conservative theologians and their schools, which are for the most part settled in Rome, we may certainly say that in the first case he is outrageously in error, and in the second case, guilty of intellectual haughtiness. In either case this remains the very real weakness of Aubert's survey; namely, that it is historically incomplete, and a selective choice of what the author believes to be theology.

It is to be regretted that the attitude of contempt toward "Iberian [Spanish] Catholicism," a favorite French epithet for the conservatives, has created a certain reaction, on the part of the conservatives, of opposition to any and all theological reflection other than their own. In honesty to the French, it should be noted that this tendency toward haughtiness, which has created an intense conservative distrust, has at times been evoked by an unreasonable theological intransigence on the part of the conservatives. The frightening spectacle of a vicious circle has been the fruit such haughtiness has borne.

The Holy Father, Pope Pius XII, in *Humani Generis* referred to the desire for novelty that frequently lay at the basis of extreme tendencies among the "new theologians." There is no doubt that the adherence of many of the younger French clergy to theological radicalism has been based, not upon any true knowledge of what they were rejecting or what they were accepting, but simply upon youthful reaction to the traditional and conservative. As we previously remarked when discussing the new theology, young members of the clergy frequently struck the pose of radicalism for radicalism's sake rather than basing it upon sincere intellectual appreciation and genuine conviction.

It is not strange to find this attitude among the younger clergy; in fact it would be strange not to find it. Being young seems to bring out the rebellious attitude toward their elders to whom they are continually subject. Frequently, rebellion arising from idealism, from their picture of the world as it should be, leads to dissatisfaction with their immediate superiors whom they judge to have failed in their commission to convert the world. However, actual disobedience has been rare among the French clergy because they do recognize in idea and in fact the demands of the hierarchical nature of the Church. Thus, they express their rebellion, their dissatisfaction with the state of Christ's Church, by adhering to the newest and latest opinions. This adherence is frequently not based on understanding, but upon the emotional ground that these opinions, since new, are not therefore the opinions of the men who have gone before them and are now in the positions of authority. The love of novelty is rarely found among the elderly or in the disciplined and mature mind. When the Holy Father reprobated its existence in the Church, he was trying to expose the actual evil of error by stripping from it its attractive aura of newness.

It would be a real injustice to the competent French theologians to say that their continual interest, scholarship and work in the theological revival is based on novelty, or the love of newness for newness' sake. But at the same time it is most accurate to say that some of the clerical support received by these men, especially the support of the younger clergy, was based upon such a fascination with their work as an intellectual expression of their dissatisfaction with the state of the Church.

An Appreciation of the Contributions of the French Theologians

If there are these serious drawbacks which exist to a greater or lesser degree among the French, one must agree that they are far outweighed by the serious contributions that the French have made to theology today. The theological revival has manifested many highly desirable traits in the Franco-Belgian complex: the seizing of the theological initiative, the existence of theological controversy, the revival of interest in the sources of Christian theology, an open-ness to the modern world, and an effective translation of theological truth on the level of the ordinary Catholic. In addition, the glory and wonder of the theological revival has been its enormous appre-ciation of the Church and the attractive picture of her which the theologians have presented to modern man.

As must be evident, the French have not remained serene in the possession of theological truth. Not for them the intellectual pas-sivity of simple acceptance and letting it go at that, but rather the sincere drive of all true theology to explore, examine, discuss and evaluate theological truth as God has proposed it to man; and then to draw from this scrutiny the implications that effectuate its ful-fillment in reality.

There is a certain compatibility between the lucidity of the French mind, its willingness to explore, and the true traditions of theology. For some, reflection must be so abstract that there are no really disturbing conclusions to be reached which might upset the comfortable *status quo;* there are others for whom there must be little or no thought, as if the Church's teaching power absolved one from the very processes of thought. The theological movement in France has scorned these attitudes of mind, and adopted the attitude that God has given His message to man, not for simple assent to something unknown and uncertain, but to be examined and searched out and explored so that the Mystery of Christianity, while remain-ing shrouded in the glory of God, is at the same time quite evidently demonstrated as inexhaustible to the mind of man.

The apostolic endeavors of the French Church have been the reflection in action of its exploration of Christian truth and of its application in the world, so that theology does not remain a sterile, lifeless study of an anachronistic theory, but rather is translated into necessary and effective measures for the extension of the Kingdom of God among men. Emile Mersch, S.J., in speaking of this in-itiative in theology, gives a vivid picture of the meaning of the theological revival not frequently considered:

The theologians who keep silent for fear of attracting notice and are content merely to criticize or to treat of subjects that are safe and lacking in vital interest, are not those of the strongest faith; Christians who leave to ecclesiastical superiors the task of thinking out their religion for them, resigning themselves to a passive faith, are not the most fervent. As though the internal act of thinking were the exclusive prerogative of the external magisterium as such or as though God had not fortified His Church with an unfailing authority for the express purpose of enabling men to think without fear.[2]

To seize the theological initiative, to think out and examine the content of Christian faith, has not been the only contribution of the French theological revival, it has also led to and inexorably called forth theological controversy. The evocation of theological controversy in France, without heresy, schism, or disregard of the Magisterium is an evident good for the Church. There are those who would state that the controversy that has attended the revival in France ought to be placed on the debit side of the ledger in calculating the evaluation of the revival itself.

To speak of theological controversy as a good, it is first necessary for us to examine the attitude of mind of those who see in its existence something to be feared and avoided, and who consequently are highly critical of the French on this very point. The regret displayed by some toward such controversy is frequently based on a natural tendency to regret any unpleasantness, theological or otherwise. Serenity and a placid life are all that they wish, and they find those who disturb and disrupt their settled ways unbearable. Such controversialists, they believe, must of necessity be wrong, be disturbers, be "radical" in the most pejorative sense.

There are still others for whom the existence of theological controversy in some way discredits the Revelation of God. The existence of controversy seems to imply that God hadn't been clear enough in His Revelation, and obviously, for these men, He has. Therefore, the controversialist is, in their opinion, simply "creating" difficulties. At the basis of this lies an excessive rationalism, a purely rationalistic approach to the faith. Faith and its truths become in some strange way the object of reason, and in the place of reasonable faith is substituted a faith emptied of the intellectual mystery that lies at the heart of faith itself.

[2] Emile Mersch, S.J., *The Theology of the Mystical Body* (St. Louis: Herder, 1951), p. 531.

Theological controversy is not, however, a value in itself; rather, it is the means toward a greater end, namely, the illumination of God's truth. To reduce theological controversy to an argument from which one expects a winner and a loser is to misunderstand the part that controversy has always played in the history of the Church. Properly speaking, such controversy is not the opposition of opponents but rather a common struggle for one object, the acquisition of truth. Thus controversy serves to fulfill its purpose, and does not become an end in itself.

The critics of French contributions to these fruitful debates ought to be aware that Cardinal Newman, patron of the contemporary French, pointed out that controversies where they existed without disregard for the Teaching Church have led to deeper and better understanding of Christian truth. It is extremely gratifying to note that the present Holy Father, Pope John XXIII, in the first encyclical of his reign, *Ad Petri Cathedram*, himself pointed out this august purpose served by theological controversy. Such papal approbation was also sweetened for the French by his gracious reference to Cardinal Newman.[3]

The theological revival has for its most distinguishing feature a return to the sources of theology: Sacred Scripture and the Fathers. This use of the positive proclamation of the Christian message is not simply a method of frequent quotations, but a scientific exploration into the mechanics of Revelation and inspiration, into the critical determination of documents and the circumstances that produced them. Historical research, language and document study, archeology, all the scientific advancements of the past century have been utilized in the establishment of the Revelation of God insofar as it is scientifically possible. From this intense and protracted study of the Old and New Testaments has come not simply history and the record of events, but a theology of the Word of God as well, a theology based upon the singular fact of the God-who-acts.

This evolving Biblical theology, the great fruit of fifty years of research, has fixed definite norms and laws for a proper use of the Bible. A certain kind of exegesis in which Biblical texts were some-

[3] Some long-time critics of the French theological revival have taken to setting right what they have come to regard as a "Newman legend." This seems to be a preoccupation of extremely conservative theologians.

times used to prop up the theses of manual theologians, is waning. For Biblical scholars, Biblical theology and exegesis have their own proper norms and rules: a complete study of the human element involved in Revelation, a Biblical exegesis rather than philosophical because Divine Revelation is a whole, and finally, a view of the Bible as the history of God's saving action toward man.

In addition to a preoccupation with the sources of Christian theology, the French theological revival has also been marked by an openness to the world in which the Church has found herself. Although many of the institutions of Western culture are no doubt the contributions of the Judaeo-Christian heritage, it would be deceptive for any Christian to believe that the Church exercises any significant influence in the secular community of today. The theologians have not adopted an ostrichlike attitude toward the world and its problems, but rather the result of their continual reflection on the Mystery of God and His Church has been an outgoing force of undeniable propulsion. The "openness" of the theologians as expressed by the French extends to a renewed consideration of the place of the laity within the Church; to the establishment of a relationship between the Church's preference for Thomistic philosophy and the modes of thought in current vogue; and, finally, it has extended into a study of the religious intuitions of those outside the Church and an estimation of their value in the light of the Church's possession of the total Revelation of God. Thus the theologians have gone out to the scientists and secularists, to the atheists and Marxists who compose the pluralistic society which is the modern world.

This openness has given theologians entirely new lines of investigation into the many-faceted Revelation of God, and thus they have developed theologies of history, of science and of technocracy, not as it were new theological facts, but rather new insights into the facts of the Christian Mystery, and their very practical relationship to the everyday life of man in today's world.

The theologians have maintained this open relationship with the secular world as a tradition since the secularist control of the universities placed the representatives of the Church in the field of higher learning in direct contact with the representatives of the modern world. This demand of the world to the Church for living witness to Christ in the intellectual arena has become ever more insistent with the rapid advancements made in all fields of human knowledge. The war years, the companionships of the resistance and the prison camps, accentuated this demand for witness. Marxists and Jesuits, existentialists and Dominicans rubbed shoulders, became co-workers, and established friendships in the common struggle against the Germans. In facing these questions of their companions, French Catholic intellectuals became more than ever aware of the differences that separated them from their immediate wartime allies.

The French attitude toward, and the representation of, the Church that the theologians of today have demonstrated has been an enormous contribution. The theological crisis at the time of *Humani Generis*, and during the various difficulties with ecclesiastical authority that followed aptly demonstrates the unswerving loyalty of these men to the Church. They have more than adequately explored the Mystery of the Church—they have made it the touchstone of their work and the keystone of the intellectual arch they have erected to bridge the chasm that yawns between Christianity and the modern world.

The image of the Church these men have created equals the contributions they have made to the Church. A false notion of Christ's Church has been propagated by those inimical to it: they picture the Church as a crushing monolith, in which there is an absence of freedom of thought and action, and which at the most is a unified and isolated anachronism. To this popular concept the theologians have presented the challenge of a living Church, the dynamic and active body of Christ working in the world. Even through their disputes and disagreements, witness was paid to a true image of the Church, for the popular concept of a monolith was destroyed by the obvious existence of the Church as a dynamic, vigorous and animate organization.

Conclusion

In concluding this survey of contemporary French theology we have made it plain that our sympathies and admiration lie with these men who have done so much to base the Church in the modern world on a firm intellectual substratum. We have surveyed those historical events and traditions that contribute to the total framework in which these men have found themselves, and which have created the present concrete situation in which they work. Throughout we have appealed to the history of the French Church, to its intellectual traditions and to the psychological predispositions of the Gallic mind as some parts of the total explanation for the current theological phenomenon as we find it.

When we sketch the themes of the theologians, and the concrete work that has and is being done, we are well aware that we have not exhausted—and at the most have highlighted—the extraordinary breadth and depth of their exploration of the Christian message. But perhaps we have succeeded in indicating the axiom that "nothing is alien to theology" has achieved an undreamed-of meaning. For these theologians, by dint of research, scholarship and arduous labor have harnessed the sciences and achievements of the modern world to the service of the Christian message. If throughout this book we have been critical at times and pointed out their all too human failures, we have done so in a spirit of honest evaluation.

For weal or woe the French theologians have had the vices of their virtues. And in this light may be understood their occasional failures and sometime mishaps. The French, more than any other national section of the Church, have been forced to face the modern world. They have lived in the universities under constant pressure, unable to adopt an attitude of "watchful waiting" toward the intellectual difficulties of their contemporaries. The traditional Cartesian dualism which has afflicted the French character gave them two alternatives: to retreat within the confines of traditional theological endeavor, or, on the other hand, to meet the moderns on their own grounds, to attempt to work out Christian theology within the intellectual framework erected by the secular scholars of their own age. Unfortunately, in following this latter path many stumbled in their haste to force a "new theology" for their modern world. Deprived by the Gallican severance from the traditional and yet evolving Thomism, the theologians found themselves outside a tradition of working within an institution.

The critic can see the difficulty, but can he ever really appreciate the intense belief and personal conviction of Christianity that impelled these men into the contemporary forum of thought? Can he ever totally explore the motivation by which these men became *"engagés"*—totally enmeshed, utterly embroiled, completely committed to a Christian witness in a pagan society?

BIBLIOGRAPHY

THE SOURCES

In surveying the theology of any period, especially in the fluctuating modern scene, one must of necessity turn to the printed word. An added difficulty faces the contemporary reporter, for from the great mass of printed material, books, journals, periodicals, he must choose not only those which in his judgment represent the trends of theological thought, but also those which he considers to be of permanent value and importance. Thus, one man's survey of what will be of importance will most probably disagree with another's. Such a wide field as theology, however, does provide guides in the eminent theologians, their own works and their evaluation of the works of other lesser men as expressed in reviews in periodicals.

Librarians will certainly be aware of the difficulty created for their particular field of endeavor by the vast number of excellent French works of reference and periodicals. Those who have done research during this shifting period of intellectual development will also no doubt be aware of the great lack of biographical information available about the men who have shaped theology in France and Belgium.

Reference Works

During the past fifty years many important theological contributions in France and Belgium have been enshrined in "dictionaries" of theology and its related fields. The *dictionnaire* is not the American or English equivalent of a dictionary: although arranged in alphabetical order, its articles are, comparatively speaking, longer, fewer in number and all related to a central theme. The *dictionnaire* achieves an encyclopedic treatment of one particular field.

The outstanding example of this work is the *Dictionnaire de théologie chrétienne* (1903–1951) frequently referred to as the DTC. Others exist in more specific fields: the *Dictionnaire d'archéologie chrétienne et de liturgie* begun by the Abbot Cabrol in 1907; the *Dictionnaire apologétique de la foi chrétienne*; and, the *Dictionnaire de la Bible* begun under the Abbé Vigouroux.

These works are kept up to date by the issuance of supplements. The monumental *Dictionnaire de la Bible*, for example, is kept topical by a more recent publication, the *Dictionnaire de la Bible: supplément*. This supplement, undertaken by Pirot and Robert, is now continuing under the direction of Henri Cazelles, the Professor of Exegesis at the Institut Catholique in Paris, and is published by Letouzey et Ané.

Contemporary works that have not as yet been completed include the *Dictionnaire de spiritualité* directed by the Jesuit Père Charles Baumgartner, and published by Beauchesne. The *Dictionnaire d'histoire et de géographie ecclésiastique* is directed by Aubert and Van Cauwenbergh of Louvain and is published by Letouzey et Ané. The encyclopedic *Catholicisme: hier, aujourd'hui, demain* is under the editorial direction of G. Jacquemet.

Christological doctrine has been gathered by Bardy, Tricot and others and published in the older encyclopedia *Le Christ* (1936) which underwent a new edition in 1946 by Bloud and Gay in Paris. A similar encyclopedia on Marian doctrine, *Maria*, has been edited by du Manoir and published in 1949 by Beauchesne in Paris. A projected history of Mariology by Joussard, Barre and Laurentin has not as yet been published.

On the more popular level, an excellent six-volume series on theology was edited by the Dominican Père Henry for the Editions du Cerf, and has been translated into English as *The Theological Library* (Chicago: Fides, 1954–1958). A one-hundred-and-fifty-volume work covering all phases of Catholic theology, worship, history and discipline is the well prepared, theologically capable and popularly written *Je sais, je crois* series. This is undergoing publication in the United States as the *Twentieth Century Encyclopedia of Catholicism*, and in England as the *Faith and Fact* series. It is published by Hawthorn in the United States and by Burns and Oates in England. Some of the volumes, more specifically written for a French audience, are being replaced in the translated series by works of more interest to a non-French audience. Finally, a word should be said about the monumental history of the Church, a series begun under Fliche and Martin, who have left their names to the whole series, now supervised by Duroselle and Jarry.

French publishers present the public with many fine works of contemporary theological thought through series of books on a general theme or subject, and which are called *Collections.* Among the more important of these may be listed: *Etudes bibliques* by Gabalda; *Lex Orandi, Lectio Divina,* and *L'Esprit liturgique,* all published by Editions du Cerf; *Bible et vie chrétienne, Eglise vivante* by Casterman; *Connaisance de la Bible* by l'Orante; *Verbum Salutis* by Beauchesne; *l'Eglise et temps présent* by Grosset; the historical *Bibliothèque ecclesia* by Fayard; *Visages de l'église* by Le Centurion; *Lumière et vie* from the Abbey of St. André in Belgium; *Maîtres spirituels, études carmélitaines, Etudes religieuses,* and *Textes et études théoligiques.*

Periodicals

The periodical sources for contemporary French theology may be divided into the journals of the diocesan and religious clergy. The French and the Belgians have maintained a great theological tradition among the secular clergy. It is unfortunate that the priest in the English-speaking world so quickly equivocates theology and religious orders (the Jesuits and Dominicans preeminently), and has lost the tradition of great scholarship so frequently found in Europe among the diocesan clergy. The University of Louvain, whose theological faculty is strictly limited to the secular clergy, names among its professors and lecturers such outstanding men as Cerfaux, Coppens, Massau, Moëller, Aubert, Philips, Thils and Dondeyne. The periodicals of Louvain include the *Revue philosophique de Louvain,* the quarterly journal of the philosophy department, and the *Ephemerides Theologicae Louvaniensis,* the quarterly of the theology department.

Most of the Belgian dioceses have their own periodicals, all of them outstanding and aimed at a clerical audience. These are the bimonthly reviews: *Collectanea Mechliniensia* of Malines, the *Revue diocésaine de Tournai,* the *Collationes Brugenses* of Bruges and the *Revue diocésaine de Namur.*

The French secular clergy produce the *Ami du clergé,* a generally useful weekly review edited by Abbé A. Michel, who is also director of the DTC. Many critical articles on contemporary theology, of value to the historian as well as the theologian appear in the *Ami du clergé.* The Catholic faculty of the University of Strasbourg publishes the highly respected *Revue des sciences religieuses.* Twice a year the Catholic faculties of the Institut Catholique at Lyons publish the *Mélanges de science religieuse,* while the Institut Catholique at Paris publishes the quarterly *Bulletin de littérature ecclésiastique.* The various *instituts catholiques* are the equivalent of Catholic universities with postgraduate faculties, and are staffed by some of the finest theological and scientific minds in France, seculars, religious and lay professors.

The French and Belgian Jesuits constitute a definite and formative influence upon modern theology. In Belgium the Jesuit College at Namur, and the College of St. Albert at Louvain can name among their faculty members Snoeck, Carpentier, Fransen and others. St. Albert's is responsible for probably the finest and most extensive review of theology in French, the monthly *Nouvelle revue théologique*, frequently referred to simply as NRT. Aside from their excellent faculties at many Jesuit colleges and seminaries throughout Belgium and France, many Jesuits teach at Roman institutions: Lyonnet is Dean of the Pontifical Biblical Institute, and in non-Jesuit institutions, Danielou, Paul Henry and de Broglie teach at the Institut Catholique. The International Center for Religious Education at Brussels, the publishers of the quarterly *Lumen Vitae*, is dominated by the Jesuits Godin, Ranwez, van Caster and Delcuve. In France the Jesuits edit the excellent monthly *Etudes* under Père Rouquette, and the scholarly quarterly of the Parisian Jesuits *Recherches de science religieuse* under Père Henri Rondet. Other Jesuit publications include *Christus*, a quarterly on ascetical theology, and the *Revue d'ascétique et mystique*.

The Dominicans with faculties at Leyesse and Le Saulchoir in France, St. Maximin and Le Sarte in Belgium, the Ecole Biblique in Jerusalem, and many members at the University of Fribourg in Switzerland and the Angelicum in Rome have also had a profound influence on contemporary French theology. Among their periodicals are the influential *Revue thomiste* from Belgium, and the monumental quarterly *Revue biblique*. Others include the bimonthlies *Lumière et vie* and *Evangliser;* and in the field of spiritual theology the Dominicans are illustrious for *La Vie spirituelle*, edited by Plé, and for *La Vie spirituelle: supplément*.

The French Dominicans have also successfully entered the publishing field with their publishing house, Editions du Cerf, located in Paris. The Dominican quarterly *La Vie intellectuelle*, long an intellectual staple of Europe, ceased publishing in December of 1956. It has since been succeeded in January of 1959 by a new monthly, *Signes du temps*, organized along the style of *Etudes* and which aims to relate theology to modern problems.

The work of the Order of St. Benedict must certainly be catalogued in any chronicle of the contributions to contemporary theology. The Benedictines have exerted great influence in the liturgical movement, and since Guéranger's nineteenth restoration of Solesmes, other abbeys have contributed to the growing theology of liturgy. The Belgian abbeys of Maredsous, Mont César and St. André have played a prominent part. Maredsous edits the quarterly *Bible et vie chrétienne*, and the Abbey of St. Pierre in Steenbruge publishes *Sacris Erudiri*. The Abbey of St. André produces the bimonthly *Paroisse et liturgie*. The great Benedictine scholars of Mont César, Abbot Capelle and Dom Botte, contribute to a wide variety of theological publications of a popular as well as a scholarly orientation. The periodical *Irenikon* is issued quarterly by the Abbey of Chevetogne, and is ecumenical in content and purpose.

Twice a year the French Capuchins publish *Etudes franciscaines*, a review of theology; and the Augustinians of the Assumption publish the quarterly *L'Anée théoligique augustinienne*. *Dieu vivant* is no longer published; however, among other influential publications may be cited the *Maison-Dieu* of the Centre Pastorale Liturgique in Paris, and the bimonthly review of social and religious problems, the *Cahiers d'action religieuse et sociale*. The *Documentation catholique* is a biweekly report on ecclesiastical documents, and the field of missiology is well covered by the quarterly *Eglise vivant*. The Lethielleux Press publishes a quarterly devoted to medical-moral problems, accenting the psychological, in the outstanding *Cahiers Laënnec*. In 1958 Jean Carmignac began to edit the new periodical *Révue de Qumran* dealing exclusively with discoveries and commentaries related to the Dead Sea manuscripts. The French "left" in the Church, the *"progressistes,"* have two principal organs of opinion, which unfortunately frequently transgress either the norms or the civilities of theology: *Esprit*, founded by Mounier, and *Témoinage chrétien*.

Periodicals for the English-Speaking Reader

There will, of course, be many who, while unable to read French, are most anxious not only to follow the fortunes of the French Church but also to be as informed as possible about the Franco-Belgian contributions to theology. For these we have provided a number of sources, all periodicals, all English, in which the French contribution may be continually surveyed.

The weeklies *America* and the *Commonweal* are excellent guides to the perplexing currents of French Catholicism. *Commonweal* is extremely sympathetic to the French intellectual revival, while *America* adopts a more careful and balanced view. The *Tablet* of England, however, provides the most complete coverage of the French Church, frequently adding to their perceptive reporting the translation of documents.

England and Ireland publish monthly *The Clergy Review*, *Blackfriars*,

The Irish Ecclesiastical Record and *The Life of the Spirit*. All contain capable book reviews of recent French works. The American liturgical review, *Worship*, at times prints translations from French and Belgian liturgical and scriptural scholars, and *The American Ecclesiastical Review* keeps a critical eye upon many tendencies of the French. Extremely useful reviews are *The Catholic Mind* and *The Catholic World*, the former for translations of articles of a general or historical interest, and the latter for a continual stream of articles sympathetic to the French intellectual revival.

Fides Press of Chicago publishes bimonthly *Perspectives*, with long translations of modern French theologians, and generally excellent surveys of the field. Of the theological quarterlies, *Theological Studies* consistently publishes excellent surveys and extremely capable book reviews. *Lumen Vitae* appears in English as a quarterly. *Thought*, *The Thomist*, the *Downside Review* and the *Dublin Review* are quarterlies marked by competent book reviewers devoting some care to modern French works. *The Heythorp Quarterly*, the theological publication of the English Jesuits, gives promise of the same. The *Catholic Biblical Quarterly* provides expert opinion on the developing Biblical movement in France and elsewhere, and the lay-edited *Cross Currents* provides many translations from the French periodicals cited above.

The thrice-yearly *New Testament Abstracts* is a complete guide to work being done in the New Testament by scriptural scholars throughout the world as well as in France. Also thrice yearly, the *Theology Digest* provides long abstracts, digests and translations in the whole field of theology, with particular attention to French and Belgian contributions. For the intelligent reader, and especially for the priest with little time to spare, the *Theology Digest* will more than adequately repay its modest subscription.

WORKS IN ENGLISH

Books

Benoit, J.-D., *Liturgical Renewal*. London: S.C.M., 1958. 112 pp.

Brogan, D. W., *The French Nation from Napoleon to Pétain*. New York: Harpers, 1957. 328 pp.

Coppens, Joseph, *The Old Testament and the Critics*. Paterson, N. J.: St. Anthony Guild, 1942. 167 pp.

Cristiani, Léon, *Why We Believe*. New York: Hawthorn, 1959. 124 pp.

D'Arcy, Martin, S.J., *The Meaning and Matter of History*. New York: Farrar, Straus & Cudahy, 1959. 309 pp.

Dondeyne, Albert, *Contemporary European Thought and Christian Faith*. Pittsburgh: Duquesne University Press, 1958. 211 pp.

Ford, John, S.J., and Gerald Kelly, S.J., *Contemporary Moral Theology*. Westminster, Md.: Newman Press, 1958. 368 pp.

Gautier, Jean (ed.), *Some Schools of Catholic Spirituality*. Paris-New York: Desclée, 1959. 384 pp.

Guerard, Albert, *France*. Ann Arbor: University of Michigan Press, 1959. 563 pp.

Hales, E. E., *The Catholic Church in the Modern World*. Garden City: Hanover House, 1958. 312 pp.

Latourette, Kenneth Scott, *Christianity in a Revolutionary Age*. New York: Harper, 1958–1959. Vols. I and II.

Loew, M. R., *Mission to the Poorest*. New York: Sheed & Ward, 1950. 184 pp.

McAvoy, Thomas, C.S.C., *The Great Crisis in American Church History*. Chicago: Regnery, 1957. 391 pp.

Moody, Joseph (ed.), *Church and Society*. New York: Arts, 1953. 914 pp.

Murphy, Richard T., O.P. (ed.), *Père Lagrange and the Scriptures*. Milwaukee: Bruce, 1946. 216 pp.

Phillips, C. S., *The Church in France 1789–1848*. London: Mowbray, 1929. 315 pp.

Phillips, C. S., *The Church in France 1848–1907*. London: SPCK: 1936. 341 pp.

Premoli, Orazio, *Contemporary Church History*. London: Burns, Oates, 1932. 407 pp.

Spencer, Phillip, *Politics of Belief*. New York: Grove, 1953. 284 pp.

Steinmann, Jean, *Biblical Criticism*. New York: Hawthorn, 1959. 124 pp.

Todd, John, *Catholicism and the Ecumenical Movement*. London: Longmans, 1956. 111 pp.

Tresmontant, Claude, *Pierre Teilhard de Chardin, His Thought*. Baltimore: Helicon, 1959. 128 pp.

Vidler, Alec, *Prophecy and Papacy*. New York: Scribner, 1954. 300 pp.

Ward, Maisie, *Insurrection Versus Resurrection*. London: Sheed & Ward, 1937. 588 pp.

———, *France Pagan*. New York: Sheed & Ward, 1949. 243 pp.

Watmough, David, *A Church Renascent*. London: SPCK, 1951. 125 pp.

Articles

de Balla, Borisz, "The Marxist Influence in Catholic France," *Catholic World*, Vol. 176 (March, 1953), pp. 411–416.

Bourke, Vernon, "Philosophy," *The Catholic Encyclopedia, Supplement II* (New York: Encyclopedia Press, 1950).

Brueggeman, Edward, S.J., "A Modern School of Thought on the Supernatural," *Theological Studies*, Vol. 6 (March, 1945), pp. 3–34.

Connell, Francis J., C.Ss.R., "Recent Dogmatic Theology," *American Ecclesiastical Review*, Vol. 122 (Feb., 1950), pp. 97–106.

———, "Theological Content of *Humani Generis*," *American Ecclesiastical Review*, Vol. 123 (Nov., 1950), pp. 321–330.

Connery, John, "Theology, Moral," *The Catholic Encyclopedia, Supplement II* (New York: Encyclopedia Press, 1950).

Cotter, A. C., S.J., "Alfred Loisy," *Theological Studies*, Vol. 2 (June, 1946), pp. 242–251.

———, "Abbé Migne and the Catholic Tradition," *Theological Studies*, Vol. 7 (March, 1946), pp. 46–71.

Courtade, George, S.J., "The Theological Movement in France," *Theology Digest*, Vol. 3 (Winter, 1955), pp. 55–60.

Delcuve, George, S.J., "The Catechetical Movement in France," *Lumen Vitae*, Vol. 12 (Oct., 1957), pp. 671–702.

Donnelly, P. J., S.J., "Recent Theological Opinion on the Supernatural," *Theological Studies*, Vol. 8 (Sept., 1947), pp. 471–491.

———, "Discussions on the Supernatural Order," *Theological Studies*, Vol. 9 (1948), pp. 213–249, 554–566.

The Dublin Review, "France Since the War," Vol. 231 (1957), entire issue, pp. 1–191.

Fenton, Joseph C., "*Humani Generis* and Its Predecessors," *American Ecclesiastical Review*, Vol. 123 (Dec., 1950), pp. 452–458.

———, "Lesson of the *Humani Generis*," *American Ecclesiastical Review*, Vol. 123 (Nov., 1950), pp. 359–378.

———, "Recent Works in Fundamental Dogmatic Theology," *American Ecclesiastical Review*, Vol. 126 (May, 1953), pp. 374–380.

———, "Appraisal in Sacred Theology," *American Ecclesiastical Review*, Vol. 134 (Jan., 1956), pp. 24–36.

Gleason, Robert, S.J., "New Directions in Catholic Thought," *Catholic World*, Vol. 188 (April, 1959), pp. 22–25.

Graham, Robert, S.J., "Rebellious Eldest Daughter," *America*, Vol. 97 (June 22, 1957), p. 336.

Greenstock, David L., O.P., "Thomism and the New Theology," *The Thomist*, Vol. 13 (Oct., 1950), pp. 567–596.

Heer, Friedrich, "The Priest Workers in France," *Cross Currents*, Vol. 4 (Summer, 1954), pp. 262–274.

Henry, Paul, S.J., "Christian Philosophy of History," *Theological Studies*, Vol. 13 (Sept., 1952), pp. 419–432.

Jarry, Eugene, "Belgium," *Catholic Encyclopedia, Supplement II* (New York: Encyclopedia Press, 1950).

———, "France," *Catholic Encyclopedia, Supplement II* (New York: Encyclopedia Press, 1950).

McNamara, Kevin, "Catholic Theology Today," *Irish Theological Quarterly*, Vol. 21 (June, 1954), pp. 243–258.

O'Connell, D. P., "France Catholic?" *Catholic World*, Vol. 187 (Oct., 1958), pp. 34–42.

Ong, Walter, S.J., "Contrasts in Catholicism," *Commonweal*, Vol. 62 (Dec. 2, 1955), pp. 215–219.

Rouquette, Robert, S.J., "The Evolution of the French Church," *Catholic Mind*, Vol. 51 (Aug., 1953), pp. 462–474.

———, "French Catholicism Confronts Communism," *Thought*, Vol. 28 (Autumn, 1953), pp. 354–374.

Rousseau, Richard, S.J., "Apologetics Today," *Catholic World*, Vol. 187 (Sept., 1958), pp. 440–444.

de Solages, Bruno, "Christianity and Evolution," *Cross Currents*, Vol. 1 (Summer, 1951), pp. 26–37.

Stanley, David M., S.J., "Towards a Biblical Theology of the New Testament," *The McAuley Lectures 1958* (West Hartford, Conn.: St. Joseph's College, 1959), pp. 267–281.

Thils, Gustave, "The Encyclical *Humani Generis*," *American Ecclesiastical Review*, Vol. 124 (March, 1951), pp. 183–189.

Weigel, Gustave, S.J., "Theology," *Catholic Encyclopedia, Supplement II* (New York: Encyclopedia Press, 1950).

———, "The Historical Background of the Encyclical *Humani Generis*," *Theological Studies*, Vol. 12 (June, 1951), pp. 208–230.

WORKS IN FRENCH

Books

Aubert, Roger, *La Théologie catholique au milieu du XXᵉ siècle*. Paris: Casterman, 1954. 101 pp.

Barbier, Emmanuel, *Histoire du catholicisme libéral et du catholicisme social en France (1870–1914)*. Bordeaux: Cadoret, 1924. 6 vols.

Bellamy, J., *La Théologie catholique au XIXᵉ siècle*. Paris: Beauchesne, 1904. 290 pp.

Brugerette, J., *Le Prêtre français et la société contemporaine*. Paris: Lethielleux, 1933–1938. 3 vols.

Congar, Yves, O.P., *Vraie et fausse réforme dans l'église*. Paris: Editions du Cerf, 1950. 648 pp.

Dansette, Adrien, *Destin du catholicisme français, 1926–1956*. Paris: Flammarion, 1957. 493 pp.

Garrigou-Lagrange, Reginald M., O.P., *La Synthèse thomiste*. Paris: Desclée de Brouwer, 1947. 739 pp.

Jarry, E., *L'Eglise contemporaine*. Paris: Bloud & Gay, 1935. 2 vols.

Levie, Jean, S.J., *La Bible: parole humaine et message de Dieu*. Paris, Louvain: Desclée de Brouwer, 1958. 345 pp.

Thils, Gustave, *Orientations de la théologie*. Louvain: Ceuterick, 1958. 188 pp.

Articles

Aubert, Roger, "Discussions récentes autour de la théologie de l'histoire," *Collectanea Mechliniensia*, Vol. 18 (1948), pp. 129–149.

————,"Ouverture au monde moderne," *Nouvelle revue théologique*, Vol. 18 (Sept., 1953), pp. 161–181.

————, "La Théologie catholique au milieu du XXe siècle," *Nouvelle revue théologique*, Vol. 18 (Oct., 1953), pp. 272–292.

Bouyer, Louis, C. Orat., "Le Renouveau des études patristiques," *La Vie Intellectuelle* (Feb., 1947), pp. 6–25.

Caryl, J., "Linéaments d'une spiritualité eschatologique," *La Vie spirituelle*, Vol. 78 (1947), pp. 528–546.

Congar, Yves, O.P., "Tendances actuelles de la pensée religieuse," *Cahiers du monde nouveau*, Vol. 4 (1948), pp. 33–50.

Cristiani, Léon, "L'Eglise de France de 1918 à 1939," *L'Ami du clergé*, Vol. 16 (Feb. 19, 1959), pp. 113–136.

Danielou, Jean, S.J., "Les Orientations présentes de la pensée religieuse," *Etudes*, Vol. 249 (1946), pp. 5–21.

Delhaye, P., "La Théologie morale d'hier et d'aujourd'hui," *Revue des sciences religieuses*, Vol. 27 (1953), pp. 112–130.

Labourdette, M. M., O.P., "La Théologie et ses sources," *Revue thomiste*, Vol. 46 (1946), pp. 353–371.

Rouquette, Robert, S.J., "L'encyclique *Humani Generis*," *Etudes*, Vol. 267 (Oct., 1950), pp. 108–116.

INDEX